3rd Edition

The
QUILTING BIBLE

Creative Publishing international

Copyright © 2010
Creative Publishing international, Inc.
400 First Avenue North Suite 300
Minneapolis, Minnesota 55401
1-800-328-3895
www.creativepub.com

Printed in the United States
10 9 8 7 6 5 4 3 2 1

Library of Congress Cataloging-in-Publication Data

The quilting bible : the complete photo guide to machine quilting
/ by the editors of Creative Publishing International. – 3rd ed.
    p. cm.
  Includes index.
  Summary: "Machine quilting techniques and projects in
step-by-step format"–Provided by publisher.
  ISBN-13: 978-1-58923-512-0 (soft cover)
  ISBN-10: 1-58923-512-6 (soft cover)
  1. Machine quilting. 2. Machine quilting–Patterns.
  I. Creative Publishing International.

  TT835.Q5424 2010
  746.46'041–dc22

2010000692

Photography: Creative Publishing international;
    Corean Komarec, cover, 6, 24, 28, 108 (top), 114-116,
    238, 244-250, 252-259
Photo Coordinator: Joanne Wawra
Page Layout: Trevor Burks
Cover Design: Kim Winscher

Visit www.Craftside.Typepad.com for a behind-the-scenes
peek at our crafty world!

The expanded edition of *The Quilting Bible* draws pages from
individual titles of the Singer® Sewing Reference Library®,
including *Quilting by Machine, Quilt Projects by Machine,
Quilted Projects & Garments,* and *Embellished Quilted
Projects.*

3rd Edition

The Complete Photo Guide to Machine Quilting

THE QUILTING BIBLE

Creative Publishing
international

CONTENTS

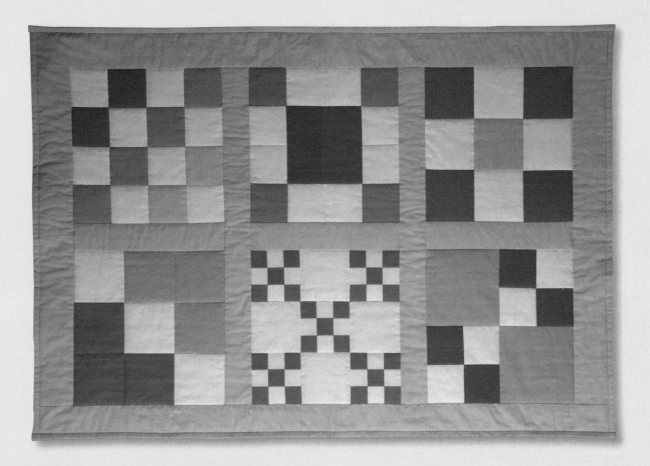

Introduction

We often marvel at the detailed workmanship and painstakingly tiny stitches of vintage quilts, wondering how our foremothers ever found the time to piece and quilt an entire project by hand! After all, they didn't have our modern conveniences to shorten their cooking, cleaning, and child care tasks. Granted, far fewer of them worked outside the home, but with farming chores, gardening, canning foods, sewing and mending clothes, and raising large families, it is hard to imagine a leisurely moment devoted to such self-indulgence as decorative needlework.

Though today's technology has replaced elbow grease on the home front, careers and family and community involvement still leave us with precious little free time. Car pools, volunteer work, and recreational activities gobble up evenings and weekends. Long-term needlework projects are rarely started because we live in a world of instant gratification. We love the stress-relieving, creatively satisfying feeling of making something beautiful with our hands, but we want the finished product right now.

No wonder quilting by machine is so tremendously popular. With rotary cutting and quick-piecing methods, an entire quilt top can be stitched together in an evening. Machine-quilting techniques mimic hand-stitched quilting in a fraction of the time, with amazingly effective results. Short-term small projects, like wall hangings, table runners and placemats, baby quilts and lap quilts, and even mini quilts, provide creative enjoyment with far less time commitment. With machine quilting, even a bed-size quilt is no longer a lofty goal.

The Quilting Bible is designed as a comprehensive guide for machine piecing and quilting. In the quilt basics section, you are introduced to all the tools, terms, and techniques necessary to plan and complete any machine-quilting project. Instructions are photographed step-by-step to give you a clear picture of the quilt-making process, from selecting the fabric to hanging the finished quilt.

The project sections incorporate a wide assortment of block-pieced designs, including many traditional favorites like Log Cabin, Bow Ties, Drunkard's Path, Ocean Waves, and Ohio Star. For added inspiration, we show you different ways of arranging the quilt blocks to achieve interesting variations. There are also many contemporary designs and alternate piecing methods to help you fashion your own original quilt designs. You will find quilts for home decorating, quilts for comfort, and even quilted clothing and accessories. With such concise information and so many inspiring ideas, you will never run out of machine-quilting projects to enhance your leisure hours.

QUILT BASICS

Modern methods for preparing, sewing, and finishing quilts are really very different from the methods used to sew clothes or home décor items. Machine quilting incorporates unique cutting and sewing steps that have been developed for their speed and accuracy. Rotary cutters and rulers make quick work of cutting multiple pieces to exact sizes and tedious handwork is replaced by machine sewing methods. You have more time to enjoy the creative aspects of quilting.

Anatomy of a Quilt

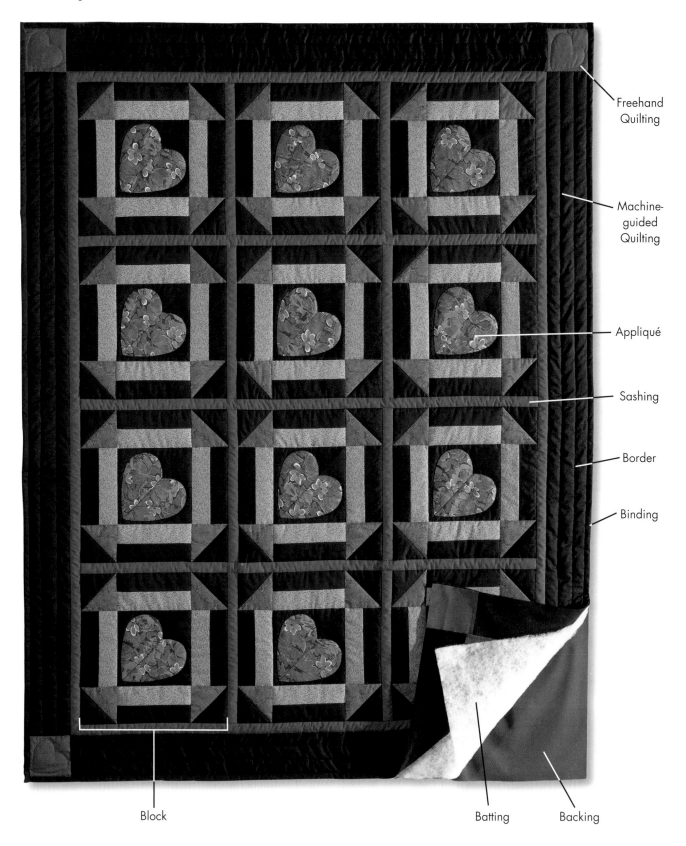

Freehand Quilting

Machine-guided Quilting

Appliqué

Sashing

Border

Binding

Block

Batting

Backing

A Quilter's Vocabulary

Become acquainted with the terms that are used to describe the methods and materials for quilting. You will find these words throughout the book and you will also hear them spoken in your local quilt shop.

Acid-free materials. Paper products, including tissue paper cardboard tubes, and boxes, made especially for the storage of textiles. They do not contain the chemicals, normally found in the wood and paper products, that can weaken and destroy fabric over time.

Appliqué. A cut fabric shape stitched to another piece of fabric.

Backing. Fabric used for the bottom layer of a quilt.

Batting. The middle layer of a quilt, which provides loft and warmth.

Bias. The diagonal of a piece of fabric. A true bias is at a 45-degree angle to both the lengthwise and crosswise grainlines of the fabric. The greatest amount of stretch in a woven fabric is on the true bias.

Binding. The strip of fabric used to enclose the edges of the three layers of a quilt.

Block. A square unit, usually made up of pieces of fabric sewn together in a design. Blocks are combined to make a quilt top.

Borders. Strips of fabric forming a frame around the quilt top. Borders may be plain or pieced.

Chainstitching. Sewing seams of several fabric pieces without breaking the stitching between the pieces. Also called chaining.

Fat quarter. A half-yard (0.5 m) of fabric, cut down the middle to measure 18" x 22" (46 x 56 cm). This is the equivalent of a quarter-yard (0.25 m) of fabric.

Free motion quilting. See freehand quilting.

Freehand quilting. Guiding the quilt through the sewing machine by using your hands, rather than pressure from the feed dogs and presser foot. Also called free motion quilting.

Lattice. See sashing.

Loft. The thickness and springiness of the batting.

Machine-guided quilting. Guiding the quilt through the sewing machine using pressure from the feed dogs and presser foot.

Medallion quilt. Quilt top with a central motif, usually framed by multiple borders.

Miter. To join corners at a 45-degree angle.

Piecing. Stitching together pieces of fabric to create a larger unit.

Quilt. A bedcover or wall hanging made by stitching together a top fabric, batting, and backing fabric.

Quilting. Stitching through a top fabric, a batting layer, and a backing fabric in a design to add texture and to hold layers together.

Sampler quilt. A pieced quilt made up of many different block designs, rather than a single, repeated block design.

Sashing. Strips of fabric, plain or pieced, that divide the blocks in a quilt. Also called lattice.

Set. The way blocks are positioned in a quilt. They may be arranged in a straight or diagonal rows.

Strip-piecing. Creating pieced designs from long strips of fabric by stitching the strips together, cutting them crosswise, and then stitching the pieces together to form a design.

Template. A pattern made of plastic or cardboard, used to trace cutting or stitching lines onto fabric.

Template-free. A method for cutting pieces using a ruler, instead of a template, as a guide.

Tied quilt. A quilt that is held together with ribbon or yarn, rather than with quilting stitches.

Selecting a Quilting Project

Start small and keep choices simple. Before making a full-size quilt, you may want to sew a smaller project that can be completed quickly, such as a pillow, table runner, or doll quilt. Before making a decision, it may be helpful to look through the entire book for more ideas.

You may want to experiment with several piecing techniques, using a different technique for each project. Or you can make a sampler quilt, using a different design for each block. You can also choose one block design for the entire quilt, varying the color and fabric.

Once you have decided on a project, you will need to make several other decisions, such as design, color, whether or not you want sashing or borders, and what type of binding you will use. It is not necessary to make all these decisions before you start your project, but it is helpful to have a basic plan in mind.

Choose template-free patterns. Template-free designs allow you to cut multiple pieces at one time and often allow you to use quick-piecing techniques. Designs that require templates must be traced individually onto fabric. They take more time to cut and are usually more difficult to assemble. Most of the patterns included in this book are template-free. Patterns are arranged in order, from designs that are easy to sew to those that are more difficult.

Table runner

Doll quilt

Pillows

Crib quilt

Wall hanging

SELECTING A DESIGN

Many quilters use a traditional quilt design rather than creating their own. This simplifies the design process. Study designs made by other quilters in order to see the effects of color, fabric, setting, and border variation.

Take your time selecting a design. Look at as many quilts, or photos of quilts, as possible. Quilt shops are a valuable source for design ideas. They generally carry an extensive selection of books and magazines and often have quilts on display.

Or, you may prefer to create your own design, rather than follow instructions from a book or magazine.

Shapes

Most piecing designs for quilt blocks are made up of one or more geometric shapes, such as squares, rectangles, triangles, and diamonds. Designs made up of curved shapes are less common, because they require more time and skill to construct. The more intricate curved shapes are usually appliquéd.

Block Designs

The most common type of quilt top is made up of blocks. A block is a pieced square of fabric. The number of squares that make a block can be four, nine, sixteen, twenty-five, or more. The pieces in a the block may be identical, as in Patience Corner (opposite), which is made up of nine square pieces of fabric. Or they may be varied, as in Ohio Star (page 17), with triangles and squares creating the block, or Churn Dash (page 17), which is made up of squares, rectangles, and triangles. Some block designs, such as Log Cabin (opposite), do not divide into smaller squares.

The possible combinations for making blocks are infinite. Several different block designs can be stitched together to create a sampler quilt. But most quilt tops use a pattern of repeating blocks. The blocks may be arranged in many ways, called settings (pages 20 and 21), which can vary the overall quilt design.

Block Designs with Squares

Autumn Tints: 4-patch

Double Nine-patch: 9-patch

Patience Corner: 9-patch

Nine-patch: 9-patch

Puss in the Corner: 16-patch

Checkerboard: 16-patch

Block Designs with Rectangles

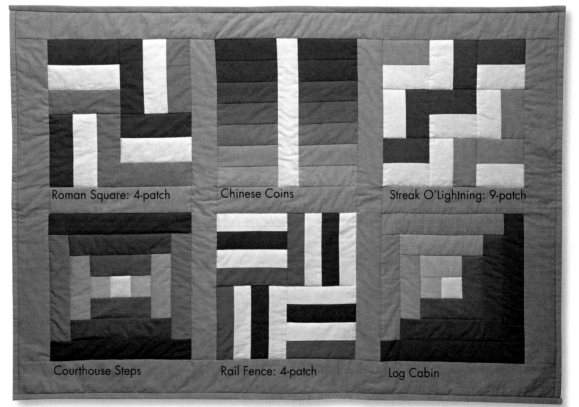

Roman Square: 4-patch

Chinese Coins

Streak O'Lightning: 9-patch

Courthouse Steps

Rail Fence: 4-patch

Log Cabin

Block Designs with Triangles

Yankee Puzzle: 4-patch

Card Trick: 9-patch

Birds in Air: 9-patch

Dutchman's Puzzle: 16-patch

Brown Goose: 16-patch

Lady of the Lake: 25-patch

Block Designs with Curves

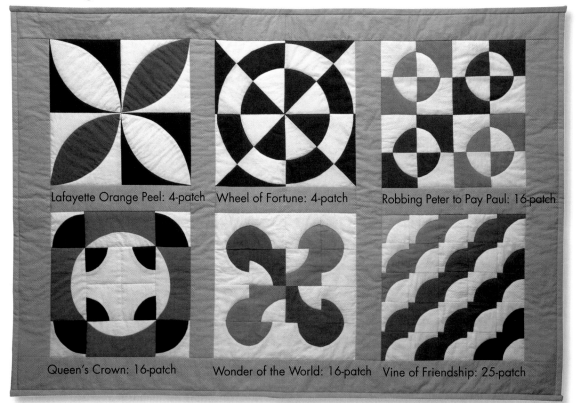

Lafayette Orange Peel: 4-patch

Wheel of Fortune: 4-patch

Robbing Peter to Pay Paul: 16-patch

Queen's Crown: 16-patch

Wonder of the World: 16-patch

Vine of Friendship: 25-patch

Block Designs with a Combination of Shapes

Bright Hopes: 4-patch

Churn Dash: 9-patch

Rolling Stone: 9-patch

Ohio Star: 9-patch

Puzzle Boxes: 9-patch

Maple Leaf: 9-patch

Clay's Choice: 16-patch

Evening Star: 16-patch

Road to Oklahoma: 16-patch

Grandmother's Choice: 25-patch

Cake Stand: 25-patch

Crown of Thorns: 25-patch

COPYING A QUILT DESIGN

To copy a quilt design, isolate one block by finding where the design starts to repeat itself in each direction. Look at the entire quilt to see if all the blocks are the same; some quilts have two or more different block designs. When a quilt includes more than one design, it is necessary to draft each design separately. Quilts with blocks on a diagonal will also have half or quarter blocks to complete the quilt top. Look at each quilt block to see how many squares it is divided into. Draw the block on a plain piece of paper or quilter's graph paper. Divide this block into squares, and then divide it again into smaller shapes. It is easier to copy blocks made up of squares, rectangles, or triangles; most diamonds and curved shapes require templates.

Identifying the Block Design

Examples of quilt designs include those made up of two or more block designs (left), one-block designs set on the diagonal with sashing (middle), or one-block designs set side by side (right). Each block breaks down into squares, rectangles, triangles, or a combination of shapes. Copy each different block design (opposite).

How to Draft a Quilt Block

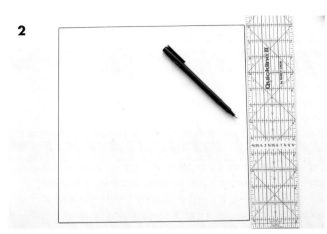

1. Visualize a grid of equal squares on quilt block. The block may be divided into four, nine, sixteen, or more equal squares.

2. Determine desired finished size of the quilt block; choose a size that divides easily, such as 6", 9", or 12" (15, 23, or 30.5 cm) for a 9-patch block, or 8" or 12" (20.5 or 30.5 cm) for a 16-patch block. Draw a square on paper the size of finished block.

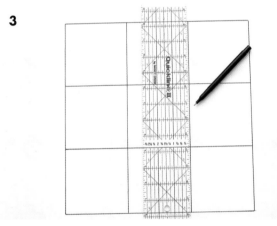

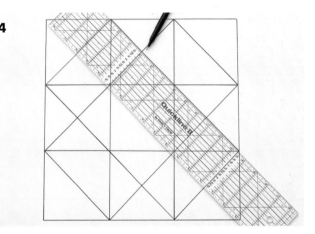

3. Divide each side of the square by the number of squares on each side of quilt block; mark grid.

4. Determine the smaller shapes that make up each square of the quilt block; draw corresponding horizontal, vertical, and diagonal lines.

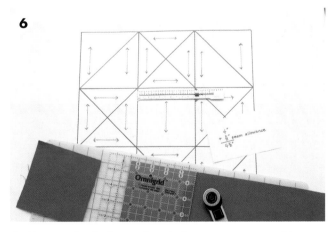

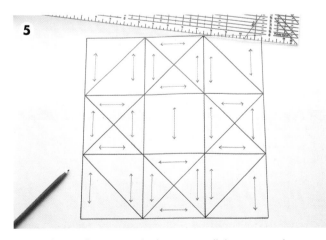

5. Mark grainline on each shape, parallel to outer edges, to use as a reference when cutting.

6. Measure finished size of each shape; cut pieces, adding seam allowances (pages 43 and 51).

SETTINGS FOR QUILTS

Blocks may be arranged in a number of ways, which are called settings, or sets. Changing the setting can make the same block design look different. When pieced blocks are placed side by side, design lines, such as squares or diagonals, may become evident. Placing sashing strips between blocks or alternating plain and pieced blocks can produce two entirely different looks. You can also place the blocks on their points, either with or without sashing. When designing a quilt, you may want to try a variety of settings, using many photocopies of the block design or the actual pieced blocks to determine the setting you like best.

Side-by-side settings are commonly used. Individual blocks are stitched together in rows. This makes the blocks blend together and may reveal an overall pattern.

Diagonal side-by side settings are blocks stitched together in diagonal rows, so that blocks stand on their points. Often, a diagonal setting creates a sense of motion or appears to add curves to a pieced design.

Straight alternating block settings use pieced blocks alternating with plain blocks. The plain blocks reduce the amount of piecing required and provide space for freehand quilting stitches.

Diagonal alternating block settings are the same as straight alternating block settings, except the blocks are turned on their points.

Straight sashing settings have strips of fabric between side-by-side blocks. This defines the individual blocks and provides a framework that unifies different block designs.

Diagonal sashing settings are the same as straight sashing settings, except the blocks are turned on their points.

QUILT DESIGNS WITHOUT BLOCKS

Block designs are the most common designs, but there are many that cannot be broken down into blocks. One-patch quilts are made up of pieces that are all the same shape and size. Any shape can be used for a one-patch quilt. Medallion quilts have a central motif that can be pieced, appliquéd, or quilted. The motif is then surrounded by multiple borders. Many of these quilt designs require a template and specific piecing instructions.

Trip Around the World is a 1-patch quilt made up of squares.

Thousand Pyramids is a 1-patch quilt made up of triangles.

Carpenter's Wheel is a medallion quilt with a central motif surrounded by a larger motif.

Lone Star is a medallion quilt with a single central motif made up of small diamonds.

BORDERS FOR QUILTS

A border is a fabric frame that surrounds a quilt. The color chosen for the border can highlight different designs and fabrics within the quilt. A quilt may have a single border or multiple borders of varied widths. Interrupted or pieced borders add interest and can repeat a design in the quilt or sashing.

Single border is a fabric strip, of any width, stitched to the edges of the pieced design.

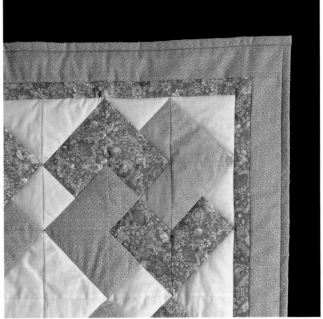

Multiple border is made of two or more borders of varied widths.

A checkerboard unit (page 45) is frequently used.

Pieced border is made of randomly spaced pieces or of pieced strips, such as Flying Geese strips (page 52).

SELECTING FABRICS

Fabric is usually selected after a quilt design and color scheme have been chosen, although a special piece of fabric may help create a design idea or establish color for a quilt. Many kinds of fabric can be used for a quilt, but a primary consideration is fiber content.

Fabric of 100 percent cotton is the best choice for quilts. Cotton fabric is easy to cut, sew, and mark; it is also easy to press, holds a crease well, and is available in a wide range of colors and prints. The quality and weight of cotton fabric is determined by thread count. The thread count is the number of threads per inch (2.5 cm) of fabric. In high-quality cotton fabric, the thread count is equal lengthwise and crosswise; this is called an even weave. Most quilting cottons are either 78-square or 68-square. Fabrics with lower thread counts are too lightweight.

Cotton/polyester blends resist wrinkling and abrasion, making them a suitable choice for frequently washed quilts. The different lengthwise and crosswise thread counts in cotton/polyester blends cause a different amount of stretch along the lengthwise and crosswise grains, which can make it more difficult to piece fabrics accurately. Also, when stitched, cotton/polyester blends tend to pucker more than 100 percent cotton fabrics.

Choose good-quality fabrics that are compatible with the function of your quilt. If you are making a comforter for a child's bed, the quilt will be subject to hard and constant use; select fabrics that can withstand wear and frequent washing. If you are making a wall hanging, the durability of the fabric is less important.

Types of Quilting Fabrics

Quilting fabrics include prints, tone-on-tones, solids, broadcloths, hand-dyed fabrics, flannels, backing fabrics, and muslin.

Prints can include calicos, country prints, novelty prints, and designer-inspired prints. Tone-on-tones are used for backgrounds and transitions in your quilt design.

Solids and broadcloths come in every color including black and white. Kona brand is readily available.

Hand-dyed fabrics are 100% cotton and are available in gradations of color and other designs. Hand-dyed fabrics give your quilt a unique look. These fabrics can be purchased at some quilting stores, quilting shows, and from mail-order sources.

Flannel suitable for quilting is available at some quilt stores. It is especially nice for children's quilts. It also makes a cozy backing for your quilt.

Muslin is a utility fabric used for foundation bases. It is generally a lighter weave and comes in a variety of widths.

Tips for Selecting Backing Fabrics

Solid-colored fabric accentuates the quilting stitches; printed fabric tends to hide the stitches.

SELECTING BACKING FABRICS

Select a backing fabric that has the same care requirements as the fabrics in the quilt top. Fabrics of 100 percent cotton are the best choice for machine quilting, because they do not pucker as much as cotton/polyester blends. Some fabrics are manufactured specifically for quilt backing. They are 100 percent cotton and are available in 90" and 108" (229 and 274.5 cm) widths, so they usually do not require piecing. These fabrics are available in light-colored prints on white backgrounds and a few solid colors. If the quilt will be finished with a mock binding (pages 109 and 110), choose a backing fabric that will coordinate with the quilt top. If you want to showcase the quilting stitches, use a solid. Printed fabrics tend to hide the stitches.

Backing fabric should not show through to the quilt top when the batting has been sandwiched between the layers. If it does show through, change to a lighter-colored backing fabric.

PREPARING THE FABRIC

If you plan to wash the quilt, test dark or vivid-colored fabrics for colorfastness to determine whether the dye bleeds to light-colored fabrics or colors the water. If colors do bleed, repeat the test; if a fabric still bleeds, it is probably not colorfast.

Fabrics can be preshrunk by machine-washing them using a mild soap, such as dishwashing soap. Do not use soap intended for fine woolens; it may yellow cotton fabrics. Machine-dry the fabric, using a warm setting.

Preshrinking fabrics removes excess dyes and chemical finishes used in the manufacturing process. Most cotton fabrics shrink 2 to 3 percent when washed and dried, so if they are not preshrunk, the fabrics may pucker at the stitching lines and the finished size of the quilt may change the first time it is washed. After preshrinking, you may want to press the fabric, using spray starch, to make cutting and stitching easier.

Fabric is not always woven with the threads crossing at 90° angles; however, it is usually not necessary to straighten the grainline. Minor variations in the grainline do not change the overall look of a quilt block and straightening the grainline may waste as much as 4" (10 cm) of a piece of fabric.

How to Test Fabric for Colorfastness

1. Fill jar or glass with warm water and a few drops of mild soap, such as dishwashing soap.

2. Cut 2" to 6" (5 to 15 cm) square of fabric. Place in water. Allow to soak until the water has cooled slightly. Swish fabric.

3. Place wet fabric on sample of light-colored fabric for the quilt; blot dry. If dye transfers to light-colored fabric, repeat the test; if fabric still bleeds, it is probably not colorfast.

SELECTING BATTING

Batting is the middle layer of a quilt. The loft, or thickness, of the batting determines the warmth or springiness of the quilt. Batting is purchased according to the amount of loft desired (opposite). The most widely used fibers for batting are cotton and polyester, or a blend of the two (referred to as 80/20). Cotton batting gives a flat, traditional appearance when quilted. Polyester batting gives a puffy look and is more stable and easier to handle than cotton batting. Cotton/polyester batting combines the flat appearance of cotton with the stability and ease in handling of polyester. New fiber blends are now available including bamboo and silk. Fusible batting eliminates the need for hand basting. It is useful for smaller lap quilts. Your quilt shop can advise you on the benefits of each type of batting.

Two types of batting are frequently used: bonded and needlepunch. Bonded batting is made by layering fibers and then adding a finish to hold the fibers together and make the batting easier to handle. Needlepunch batting is made by layering the fibers and then passing them through a needling machine to give a dense, low-loft batting. It is firm, easy to handle, and warm. Most needlepunch batting is polyester. The minimum distance between quilting stitches varies from one batting type to another and is noted on the batting package.

The fibers in batting may migrate, or move, affecting the appearance of the quilt. Bonded batting is treated to help control fiber migration. There are two forms of fiber migration: bunching and bearding. Bunching is the migration of fibers within a quilt, causing thick and thin areas. Bunching can be controlled by placing the quilting stitches ½" to 1" (1.3 to 2.5 cm) apart. Bearding is the migration of fibers through the surface of the quilt. Polyester batting tends to beard, and these fibers may pill. Cotton batting may beard, but the fibers break off at the surface. To help prevent bearding, use a closely woven fabric for the quilt top and backing. Black batting is the best choice for a dark colored quilt. If bearding does occur, clip the fibers close to the surface of the quilt: do not pull the batting through the fabric. After clipping the fibers, pull the quilt top away from the batting so the fibers return to the inside of the quilt.

Batting is available in a wide range of sizes, although the selection in certain fibers and construction types may be limited. Polyester batting has the widest range of sizes and lofts. Batting should extend 2" to 4" (5 to 10 cm) beyond the edges of the quilt top on all sides to allow for the shrinkage that occurs during quilting. Batting is packaged for standard-size quilts. It is also available by the yard and in smaller packages for clothing and craft projects.

Guidelines for Selecting Batting

Fiber Content	Appearance of Finished Quilt	Characteristics	Spacing of Quilting Stitches
Cotton	Flat	Absorbs moisture, cool in summer and warm in winter	½" to 1" (1.3 to 2.5 cm)
Polyester	Puffy	Warmth and loft without weight, nonallergenic, moth and mildew-resistant	3" to 5" (7.5 to 12.5 cm)
Cotton/polyester blend	Moderately flat	Combines characteristics of cotton and polyester	2" to 4" (5 cm to 10 cm)

Tips for Selecting Batting

Low-loft bonded cotton or cotton/polyester batting is easiest to handle.

Medium-loft adds texture to the finished quilt. The higher the loft, the more difficult to machine-quilt.

High-loft and extra-high-loft battings are best used for tied quilts, because they are difficult to machine-quilt.

Batting Thickness

Low-Loft	⅛" to ⅜" (3 mm to 1cm)
Medium-loft	½" to ¾" (1.3 to 2 cm)
High-loft	1" to 2" (2.5 to 5 cm)
Extra-High-loft	2" to 3" (5 to 7.5 cm)

Packaged Batting Sizes

Crib	45"x 60" (115 x 152.5 cm)
Twin	72"x 90" (183 x 229 cm)
Full	81"x 96" (206 x 244 cm)
Queen	90"x 108" (229 x 274.5 cm)
King	120"x 120" (305 x 305 cm)

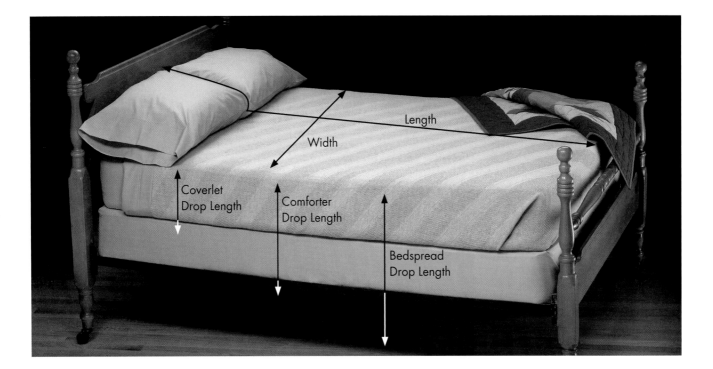

Length

Width

Coverlet
Drop Length

Comforter
Drop Length

Bedspread
Drop Length

DETERMINING THE FINISHED SIZE

The first thing you must know in order to figure yardage requirements is the finished size of the quilt. If you are making the quilt for a bed, the finished size is determined either by the measurements of the bed or by the size of the packaged batting. If you are making the quilt to hang in a particular space, you can measure the space available.

To determine the finished size of a quilt by the bed measurements, measure the bed with the blankets, sheets, and pillows that will be used with the quilt. If you are using a thick batting, place the batting on the bed along with the bedding to ensure that the quilt will be large enough.

Measure the width of the bed from side to side across the top; do not include the pillows. Then measure the length of the bed from the head of the bed to the foot; if the quilt is to include a pillow tuck, include the pillow in the length measurement, tucking the tape around and under the pillow as you plan to tuck the finished quilt. A pillow tuck usually adds an additional 10" to 20" (25.5 to 51 cm) to the length, depending on the size and fullness of the pillows.

For the drop length, measure from the top of the bed to the desired length. For a comforter, measure to just below the mattress, about 9" to 12" (23 to 30.5 cm) down from the top of the bed. For a coverlet, measure to just below the box spring, about 18" (46cm) down from the top of the bed. For a bedspread, measure to the floor, about 20½" (52.3 cm) down from the top of the bed. Add two times the drop length to the width of the bed for the two sides, and a single drop length to the length of the bed for the foot.

Determine the finished quilt size by the packaged batting sizes (page 29). Batting should be 2" to 4" (5 to 10 cm) larger on each side than the finished quilt. Packaged battings are usually sized for coverlets.

Adjust the finished measurements of the quilt according to the thickness of the batting and the amount of quilting you plan to do. For most average-size quilts with low or medium-loft batting, shrinkage due to quilting is about 2 to 3 percent. For high-loft batting, shrinkage may be 5 to 6 percent.

Backing Fabric

Yardage for backing fabric is based on the quilt top measurements and whether or not the backing will be seamed. Backing fabrics should extend 2" to 4" (5 to 10 cm) beyond the edges of the quilt top on all sides to allow for shrinkage during quilting.

Some fabrics are available in 90"and 108" (229 and 274.5 cm) widths, but most are 45" (115 cm) wide and will have to be seamed (page 95). It is helpful to make a sketch of the quilt back, including seams, to calculate yardage. This information below is for 45" (115 cm) fabric with a usable width of about 40" (102 cm).

Crib quilts usually do not require seaming because they can be made from one width of backing fabric cut to the desired length. For crib quilts, allow only 1" to 2" (2.5 to 5 cm) on all sides for shrinkage during quilting.

How to Calculate Yardage for Backing Fabric

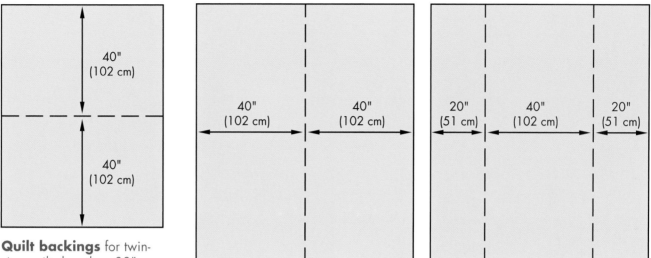

Quilt backings for twin-size quilts less than 80" (203.5 cm) long can be pieced horizontally for the best use of fabric.

Quilt backings 40" to 80" (102 to 203.5 cm) wide require seaming two widths of fabric together. The two widths can be seamed down the center of the quilt, or one of the widths can be cut and seamed to the sides.

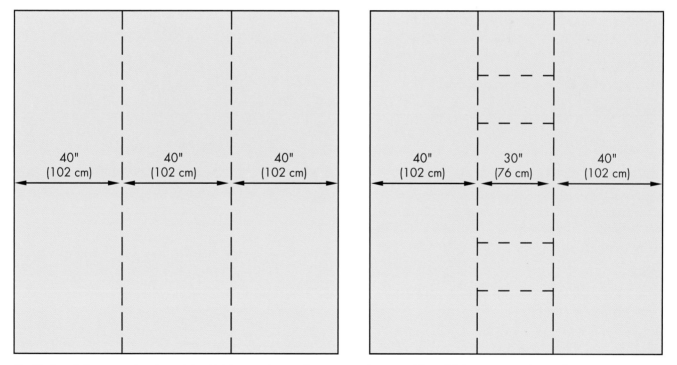

Quilt backings wider than 80" (203.5 cm) usually require three widths of fabric seamed together. Or use two widths of fabric at the sides and piece a center panel from matching or contrasting fabrics.

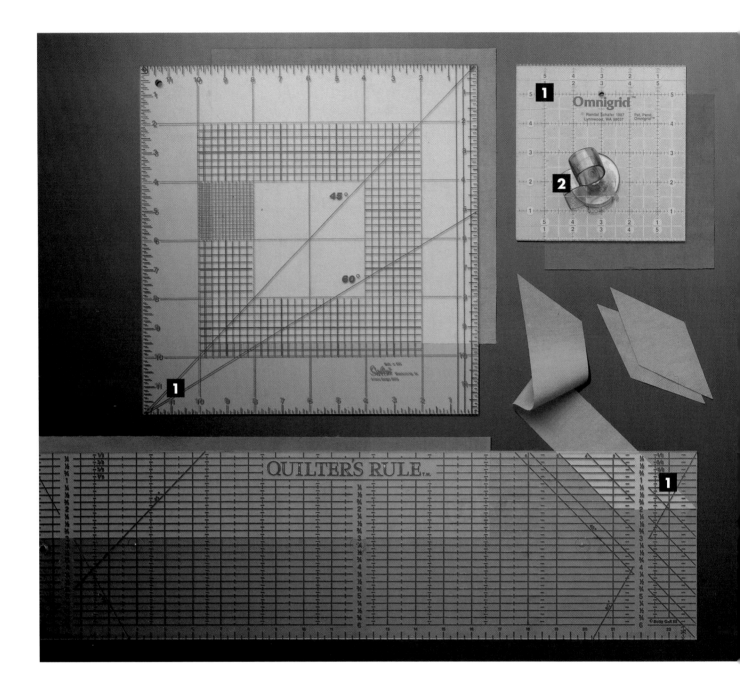

Notions & Equipment

A few carefully selected notions can make quilting easier and help improve your accuracy in cutting, marking, and sewing. Quilting can be done entirely on a straight-stitch conventional sewing machine. Choosing the correct type of sewing machine accessories, such as presser feet and needle plates, can help improve your results.

MEASURING & CUTTING TOOLS

See-through rulers (1) serve as both a measuring tool and a straightedge for cutting with a rotary cutter. Measurements are visible through the ruler, so you can cut without marking. Many sizes and types of see-through rulers are available. A ruler 6"x 24" (15 x 61 cm) is recommended, because it is versatile.

Features of rulers vary widely. Some rulers are printed with measurements in two colors to show clearly on both light and dark fabrics. Some have a lip on one edge to hook onto the

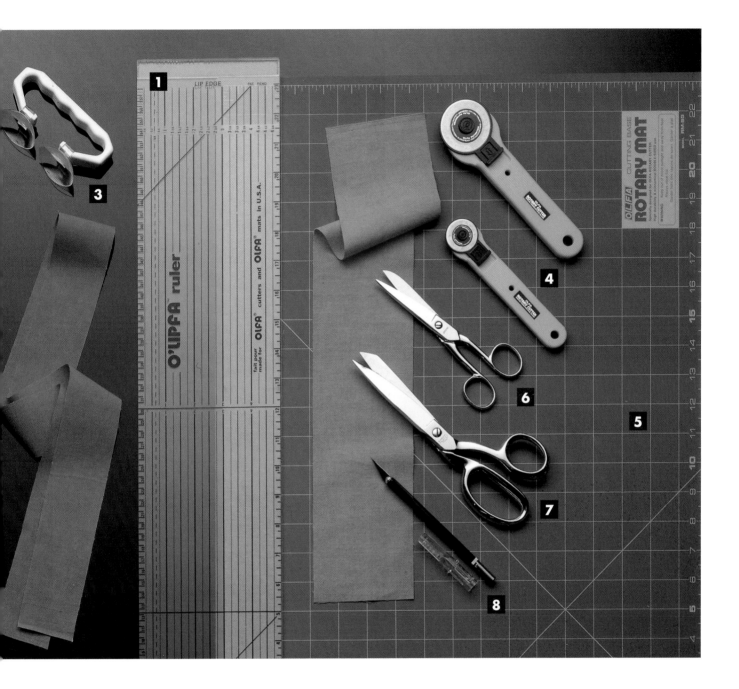

edge of the cutting mat for easier alignment. Some are printed on the underside to prevent distortion and increase accuracy; if the lines and numbers are molded on the underside, it will help prevent slippage. Square rulers, and rulers with 30°, 45°, and 60° angle lines, are available. Choose rulers that have the features most important for the type of quilting you are planning to do.

Suction rings (2) and suction handles (3) are available to help in positioning a ruler.

Rotary cutters (4) allow you to cut smooth edges on multiple layers of fabric quickly and easily. The cutters are available in various sizes: the smaller size works well for cutting curves or a few layers of fabric; the larger sizes work well for cutting long, straight edges or many layers of fabric.

Cutting mats (5), made especially for use with rotary cutters, protect the blades and the table. They may be plain, or printed with a grid and diagonal lines. A mat printed with a grid is helpful for cutting right angles. Mats come in a variety of sizes. Choose a mat at least 22" (56 cm) wide to accommodate a width of fabric folded in half.

Sewing scissors (6) and shears (7) are used for cutting shapes and clipping threads. X-acto knives (8) are used for cutting cardboard, paper, and plastic templates for pieced or appliquéd designs.

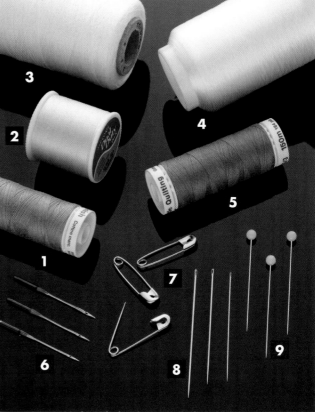

MARKING TOOLS

The markings on a quilt should last only as long as you need them, and you should be able to remove them easily and thoroughly without damaging the quilt. Always test markers on fabrics to see how long the markings last and to be sure they can be removed. Mark lightly; it is more difficult to remove markings that are embedded in the fibers.

A special fabric eraser (1) can be used to remove light lead pencil (2) marks without abrading or leaving marks on the fabric. Oil-free and wax-free colored pencils (3) may also be used for marking. Choose a color close to the fabric color; or choose silver, because it shows on most fabrics. Remove marks before pressing the fabric or washing it in hot water; heat may set pencil marks. White water-soluble pencils (4) are available for marking dark fabrics; remove marks with a damp cloth. Soapstone pencils (5) are made of pressed talc and marks can be rubbed off or wiped off with water.

Chalk wheels (6) are available in a variety of shapes and colors; marking is fine and accurate. Chalk-wheel marks brush off easily, are washable, and will not stain.

A variety of plastic sheets (7) is available for making your own templates. Precut templates (8) are available for marking traditional quilting designs.

SEWING & QUILTING TOOLS

For ease in stitching, thread should be of good quality. For piecing, use 100 percent cotton (1) or all-purpose sewing thread (2); match thread color to the darker fabric or use a neutral color, such as black, cream or gray, to blend. For basting, use a fine, white cotton basting thread (3), or white all-purpose thread; the dye from dark thread could rub off on fabrics.

For quilting, 100 percent cotton thread is usually the best choice. Fine, .004 mm, or size 80 monofilament nylon thread (4), which comes in smoke or clear, is good for quilting and for invisibly stitching appliqués, because it blends with all colors. Cotton quilting thread (5) without a finish may be used for machine quilting; however, quilting thread with a special glacé finish should not be used for machine quilting. Quilting thread may either match or contrast with the fabric.

Insert a new sewing machine needle (6) before beginning a quilting project. For piecing and appliqué, use a size 9/70 or 11/80; for machine quilting, use a size 11/80 or 14/90 needle, depending on the thickness and fiber content of the batting.

Safety pins (7) are essential for pin-basting a quilt; 1" (2.5 cm) rustproof pins work well for most quilting projects. Use milliners needles (8) for thread-basting because they are long and have small, round eyes. Use glass-head quilting pins (9) because they are long, 1¾" (4.5 cm), and strong.

SEWING MACHINE EQUIPMENT

A straight-stitch conventional sewing machine is used for quilting. The stitch length should be easy to adjust, because you start and end lines of stitches by gradually increasing or decreasing the stitch length.

An entire quilt can be made using only the straight stitch, but several additional features, common on most sewing machines, expand your quilting options. A blind-hem stitch can be used for attaching appliqués. Feed dogs that can be covered or dropped allow you to do freehand quilting.

Presser Feet

Special presser feet are not necessary foe machine quilting, but they can improve your results. For machine-guided quilting, an Even Feed foot (1) is recommended for pucker-free stitching. The feed dogs on the Even Feed foot work with the feed dogs of the sewing machine to pull layers of fabric through at the same rate of speed. For freehand quilting, you can either use a darning foot (2) or stitch without a foot, depending on the sewing machine.

Use a general-purpose foot (3), or a special-purpose foot for zigzag and blindstitching. A straight-stitch foot (4) can improve the quality of stitches, particularly when piecing fabrics with the narrow seam allowances that are standard in quilting.

Needle Plates

Use a general-purpose needle plate (5) with the general-purpose or special-purpose foot for zigzag and blindstitching. Use a straight-stitch needle plate (6) with the straight-stitch foot for straight and uniform seams and quilting lines. The small hole in the needle plate keeps the fabric from being pushed down into the sewing machine as you stitch. Also use the straight-stitch needle plate with the Even Feed foot for machine-guided quilting and with the darning foot for freehand quilting.

THE WORK AREA

The most important considerations in arranging a work area for machine quilting are comfort and convenience. Be sure the sewing machine is at a comfortable height, so that your shoulders are relaxed when you are quilting. If possible, choose a cutting surface approximately hip height. The cutting area should be able to accommodate about one yard (0.95 m) of fabric.

Position the sewing, pressing, and cutting areas so they are convenient to each other; be sure you have a good source of light over each area. Set up the iron and ironing board within easy reach, because seam allowances are pressed frequently during piecing.

A flannel board in a neutral color is valuable when you are designing a quilt. You may use felt or batting instead of flannel. When hanging the flannel board on a wall or door, make sure there is room to step back and view the total design. Use the board when determining how fabrics work together before stitching blocks, when judging the effect of different designs, or when evaluating various settings.

To make quilting easier, expand the sewing surface to support the fabric both to the left of and behind the sewing machine. The surface should be continuous and smooth, so the quilt will move freely, without catching. The surface should be at the same height as the bed of the machine, if possible. If you are using a free-arm sewing machine, convert it to a flatbed.

For a portable sewing machine, place the machine 5" to 6" (12.5 or 15 cm) in from the front edge, and allow enough room to the left of the machine to support the quilt.

For a sewing machine in a cabinet, pull the cabinet away from the wall. Place one table behind it, and another under the leaf, to provide support for the quilt and to reduce strain on the hinges of the cabinet.

Hang flannel, felt, or batting on a wall to serve as a flannel board when designing a quilt; fabric pieces will adhere without pins.

Basic Piecing Techniques

The designs in this section are for basic, traditional quilt patterns, and range from simple squares to more complex curves and appliqués. With the exception of curves and appliqués, the pieces are cut using template-free methods.

The techniques for setting up the sewing machine and for cutting, stitching, and pressing the fabrics are the same for most pieced designs.

Accuracy is critical to successful piecing. A small error can multiply itself many times, resulting in a block or quilt that does not fit together properly. Check the accuracy of your cutting and stitching frequently. You may want to practice cutting and stitching techniques on a small project before using them on a large project.

CUTTING TECHNIQUES

The quick-cutting techniques that follow are both timesaving and accurate. Instead of cutting each piece of the quilt individually, stack several layers of fabric and cut them into crosswise strips. The pieces are then cut from these strips, eliminating the need for templates.

Determine the grainline by folding the fabric in half and holding it by the selvages. Then shift one side until the fabric hangs straight. It is not necessary to straighten quilting fabrics that are off-grain or to pull threads or tear fabrics to find the grainline.

Good-quality cutting equipment helps ensure that every piece you cut is exactly the right size and that all the pieces fit together perfectly. Use a rotary cutter with a sharp blade and a cutting mat with a printed grid.

Tape three or four thin strips of fine sandpaper across the width of the bottom of a see-through ruler, using double-stick tape. This prevents the ruler from slipping when you are cutting fabric.

How to Cut Fabric Strips

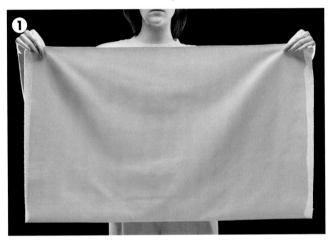

1. Fold fabric in half, selvages together. Hold selvage edges, letting fold hang free. Shift one side of fabric until fold hangs straight. Fold line is straight of grain.

2. Lay fabric on cutting mat, with fold along a grid line. Place ruler on fabric close to raw edge at 90° angle to fold. Trim along edge of ruler, taking care not to move fabric. Hold ruler firmly; apply steady, firm pressure on blade. Stop when rotary cutter gets past hand.

3. Leave blade in position; reposition hand ahead of blade. Hold firmly and continue on cutting. Make sure the fabric and ruler do not shift position.

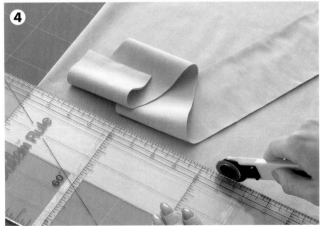

4. Place ruler on fabric, aligning trimmed edge with appropriate measurement on ruler. Hold ruler firmly; cut as in steps 2 and 3. After cutting several strips, check fabric to be sure it is still on-grain, as in step 1.

STITCHING TECHNIQUES

For pieced quilts, seam allowances are traditionally ¼" (6 mm); stitch accurate seam allowances, so all pieces will fit together exactly. If you have a seam guide on your sewing machine, check the placement of the ¼" (6 mm) mark by stitching on a scrap of fabric. If your machine does not have a seam guide, mark one on the bed of the machine with tape.

Use a stitch length of about 15 stitches per inch (2.5 cm). A shorter stitch length may be necessary for stitching curves and is used for securing stitches at the ends of seams. Adjust thread tensions evenly so the fabric does not pucker when stitched.

Chainstitching is a timesaving technique for piecing. Seams are stitched without stopping and cutting the threads between them. After all the pieces are stitched together, the connecting threads are clipped and the seams are finger-pressed.

Although some quilters prefer working on one block at a time for the satisfaction of completing a block quickly, it is more efficient to sew an entire quilt top in units. Chainstitch together all the smallest pieces from all the blocks; then combine them to create larger units.

How to Chain and Assemble Pieces

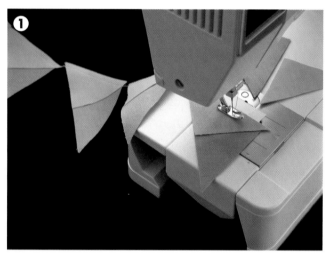

1. Start with smallest pieces; stitch together without backstitching or stopping between pieces to make a chain of two-piece units. Clip threads between units; finger-press seams.

2. Add more pieces to unit if necessary for quilt block design, chainstitching them together. Clip threads and finger-press.

3. Chainstitch units together to create larger units. Clip threads and finger-press.

4. Stitch larger units together to form quilt block. Press with iron.

Finger-press individual seam allowances; pressing with an iron can distort bias seams. Press with iron only after a unit or block has straight grain on all four sides.

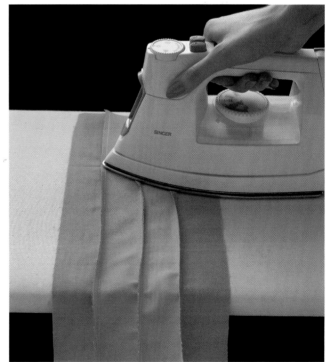

Press long seams with iron by placing strips across, rather than lengthwise on, ironing board, to prevent distorting grainline as you press.

PRESSING TECHNIQUES

Seams are usually pressed to one side in quilts; however, if you are planning to do stipple quilting (page 104) you may prefer to press the seams open to make it easier to quilt. When pressing seams to one side, it is best to press them to the darker fabric to prevent show-through.

Do not press seams with an iron until a unit or block has straight grain on all four sides. Always remove all markings from the fabrics before pressing, because the heat from the iron may set marks permanently. When pressing seams use steam, rather than pressure, to prevent the layers from imprinting on the right side. A heavy pressing motion can distort the shape and size of the pieces. Press the blocks first from the wrong side; then press them again lightly from the right side.

The quilt should not be pressed after it is completed because pressing will flatten the batting.

SEWING DESIGNS WITH SQUARES

Many quilts are made from nine-patch quilt blocks. A Nine-patch block may be made from one-piece squares or pieced squares. A Double Nine-patch block alternates one-piece squares and checkerboard pieced squares. Each of the checkerboard squares is made from nine smaller squares.

There are two ways to assemble a nine-patch quilt block, the traditional method and the strip-piecing method. The traditional method works well when using larger pieces of fabric, such

as 4½" (11.5 cm) squares. The strip-piecing method is used primarily when making quilt blocks with intricate designs, because the piecing can be done quickly without handling small pieces of fabric. A double nine-patch quilt block may be assembled using both the strip-piecing and traditional methods.

The instructions for the Nine-patch quilt block (page 44) and the Double Nine-patch quilt block (page 45) make 12" (30.5 cm) finished blocks.

How to Cut Squares

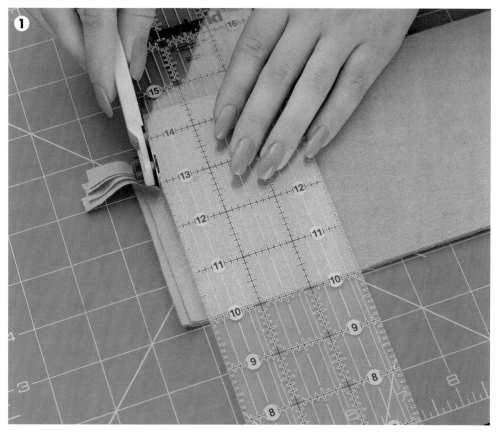

1. Cut strips of fabric (page 39) the width of one side of square plus ½" (1.3 cm) for seam allowances. Stack three or four strips, matching edges exactly; place ruler on fabric near selvages at 90° angle to long edges of strips. Trim off selvages.

2. Place ruler on fabric, aligning short edge of fabric with appropriate measurement on ruler. Cut to same width as strips, holding ruler firmly.

How to Sew a Nine-patch Quilt Block Using Traditional Piecing

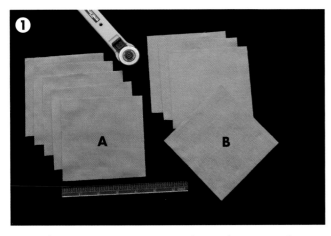

1. Cut five 4½" (11.5 cm) squares from Fabric A. Cut four 4½" (11.5 cm) squares from Fabric B.

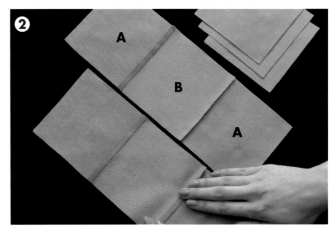

2. Stitch one square of Fabric A and one square of Fabric B, right sides together, using ¼" (6 mm) seam allowances. Stitch another square of Fabric A to other side of Fabric B. Finger-press seam allowances toward darker fabric. Repeat to make two A-B-A units.

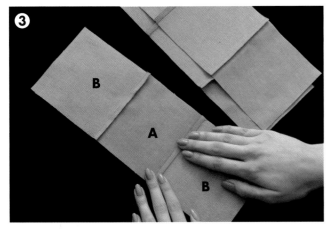

3. Stitch one square of Fabric A and one square of Fabric B, right sides together. Stitch another square of Fabric B to other side of Fabric A. Finger-press seam allowances toward darker fabric.

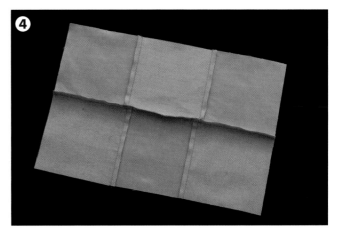

4. Stitch one A-B-A unit to the B-A-B unit, on long edges, right sides together; match seamlines and outside edges, keeping seam allowances toward darker fabric.

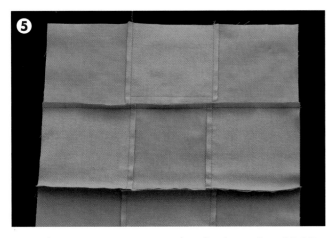

5. Stitch remaining A-B-A unit to the other long edge of B-A-B unit, as in step 4.

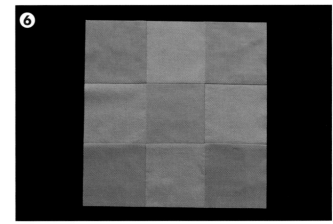

6. Press long seam allowances to one side; then press from right side.

How to Sew a Double Nine-patch Quilt Block Using Strip-Piecing

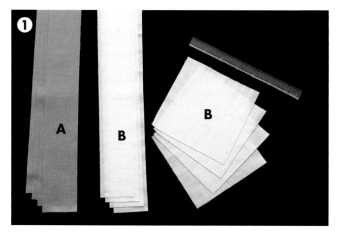

1. Cut two scant 1⅞" (4.7 cm) strips from Fabric A and from Fabric B; cut strips in half to make four 22" (56 cm) strips. Cut four 4½" (11.5 cm) squares from Fabric B.

2. Stitch one B-A-B unit and one A-B-A unit, right sides together, using ¼" (6mm) seam allowances. Press seam allowances toward darker fabric.

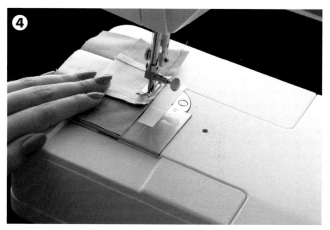

3. Trim short edge of each pieced unit at 90° angle. Cut ten scant 1⅞" (4.7 cm) strips from A-B-A unit. Cut five scant 1⅞" (4.7 cm) strips from B-A-B unit.

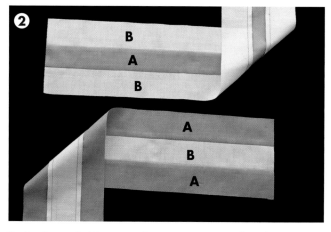

4. Stitch one A-B-A unit to one B-A-B unit on long edges, right sides together. Then stitch A-B-A unit to other long edge of B-A-B unit, right sides together, to form checkerboard.

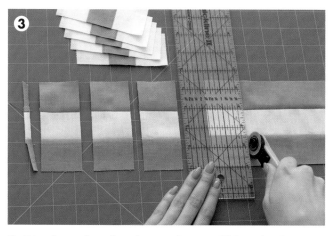

5. Repeat step four for remaining checkerboard units. Press each seam toward side with two darker squares.

6. Stitch checkerboard units and plain units to form a nine-patch quilt block, as in steps 2 to 6 (opposite).

SEWING DESIGNS WITH RECTANGLES

Rectangles are used in many block designs. Strip-piecing methods are frequently used to piece designs created from rectangles. Streak O' Lightning is one of the easiest of all quilt blocks to strip-piece. Rail Fence uses the same piecing methods, but the strips are narrower.

Log Cabin is one of the most popular and variable traditional designs. Quick-cutting and quick-piecing methods can be used for the Log Cabin block.

Choose fabrics carefully for all three designs, as they define the overall pattern in the quilt top. For example, in the Streak O' Lightning design, choose a light color and a dark color. In the Rail Fence design, where two of the fabrics will define the zigzag pattern on the quilt top, light-to-dark color progressions can be effective. For the Log Cabin design, three fabrics can be a light color and three a dark color; the center square should be a solid, contrasting, complementary color.

The instructions for Streak O' Lightning and Rail Fence quilt blocks are used when only one quilt block is needed, such as in a sampler quilt or a pillow top. However, when making a quilt top from these designs, it is easier to sew an entire row of squares in a horizontal-vertical-horizontal arrangement the width of the quilt top and then join the rows together.

The instructions for the Streak O' Lightning quilt block (opposite), the Rail Fence quilt block (page 48), and the Log Cabin quilt block (page 49) make a 12" (30.5cm) finished blocks.

How to Make a Streak O' Lightning Quilt Block

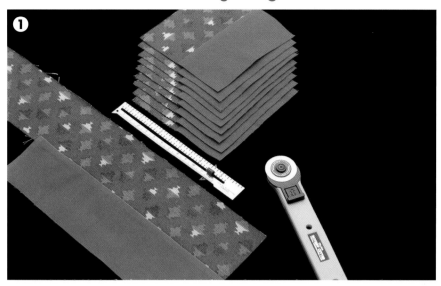

1. Cut one 2½" (6.5cm) strip (page 39) from each of two different fabrics. Stitch strips, right sides together, on long edge. Press seams to one side. Cut nine 4½" (11.5 cm) squares from unit at 90° angle to seams.

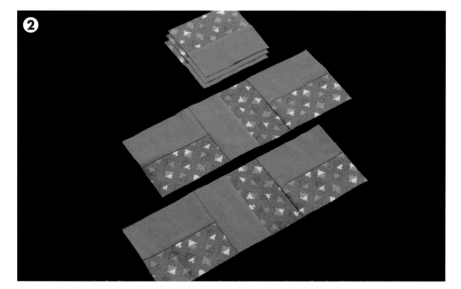

2. Stitch three squares together in a horizontal-vertical-horizontal sequence, as shown. Repeat with three more squares. Keep fabrics in same sequence, from left to right and from top to bottom, throughout quilt. Press seams to same side.

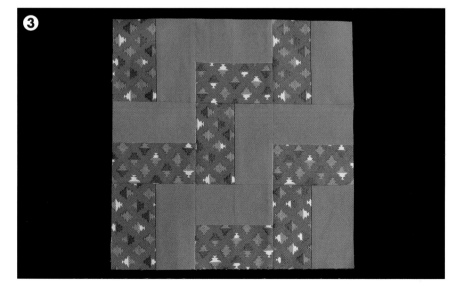

3. Stitch remaining three squares in a vertical-horizontal-vertical sequence. Press seams in opposite direction from other rows. Stitch rows together, with the vertical-horizontal-vertical row in middle. Press seams to one side.

How to Make a Rail Fence Quilt Block

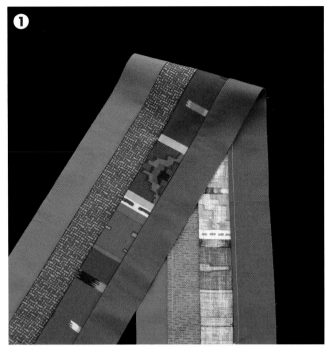

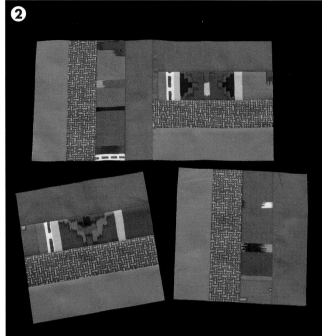

1. Cut one 2" (5 cm) strip (page 39) from each of four different fabrics. When strips are stitched together, outside strips define zigzag pattern. Stitch strips, in sequence, right sides together, along length. Press seam allowances to one side.

2. Cut four 6½" (16.3 cm) squares from unit, at 90° angle to seams. Stitch two squares together, in vertical-horizontal arrangement, as shown. Press seam allowances to one side.

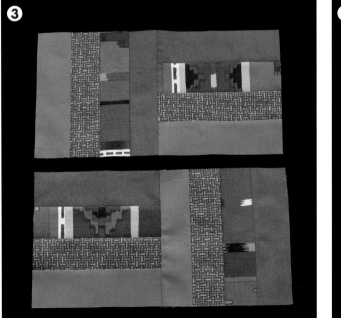

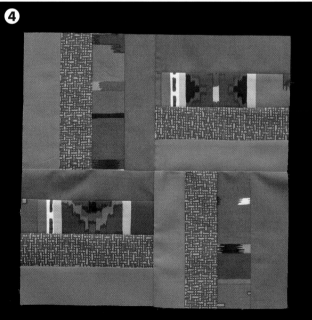

3. Stitch remaining two squares together in horizontal-vertical arrangement, as shown; keep fabrics in same sequence from left to right and from top to bottom throughout quilt. Press seam allowances in opposite direction from first row.

4. Stitch the two rows together, matching seamlines. Press seam allowances to one side.

How to Make a Log Cabin Quilt Block

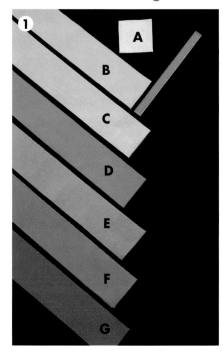

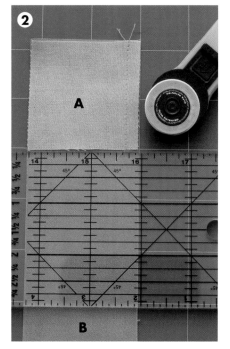

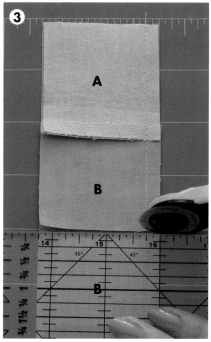

1. Cut one scant 2¼" (6 cm) square from Fabric A. Cut one scant 2¼" (6 cm) strip (page 39) from each of six different fabrics. Label strips from B to G, as shown.

2. Place solid square on Strip B, right sides together. Stitch along one side. Trim stitch even with square. Press seam allowances away from center square.

3. Place pieced unit on remaining length of Strip B, as shown. Stitch on long side. Trim strip even with bottom of pieced unit. Press seam allowance away from center square.

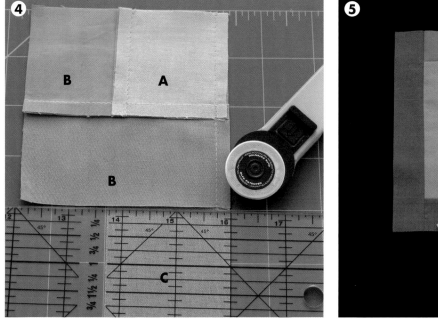

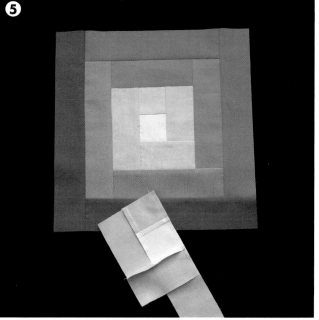

4. Place three-piece unit on Strip C at 90° angle to most recent seam. Stitch on long side. Trim strip even with bottom of pieced unit. Press seam allowance away from center square.

5. Place four-piece unit on remaining length of Strip C at 90° angle to most recent seam. Continue in this manner, stitching two strips of each color to pieced unit in sequence. Press seam allowances away from center square.

SEWING DESIGNS WITH TRIANGLES

Triangles are frequently used for quilt blocks. There are two methods for cutting and sewing triangles: the quick-cutting method with traditional piecing and the grid-piecing method.

The quick-cutting method allows you to cut several layers of fabric at one time. Some right triangles are cut with the grainline on the long side and some with the grainline on the short side. The grainline should be on the outside edges of each unit so the edges are stable and will not stretch when units are stitched together. The triangles are then assembled using a traditional piecing method.

The quick-cutting method is used to cut the right triangles for the Flying Geese quilt block (pages 52 and 53); avoid using a fabric with a one-way design. Flying Geese strips may be used for sashing or borders, or sewn together to make an entire quilt, as in the crib quilt (below).

The grid-piecing method (page 54) allows you to cut and piece the triangles in one operation. It is used whenever two triangles are stitched together to make a square, commonly referred to as a triangle-square, as in the Pinwheel quilt block (page 55). The grid-piecing method is especially useful when piecing small triangles.

The following instructions for the Flying Geese quilt block (pages 52 and 53) and the Pinwheel quilt block (page 55) make 12" (30.5 cm) finished blocks.

How to Cut Right Triangles Using the Quick-cutting Method

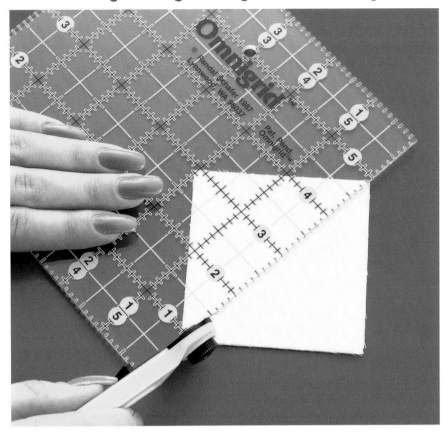

Triangles with short sides on grainline. Cut squares (page 43) with sides the length of finished short side of triangle plus ⅞" (2.2 cm). Cut half as many squares as number of triangles needed. Stack three or four squares, matching edges exactly. Place ruler diagonally across stack, holding ruler firmly; cut.

Triangles with long side on grainline. Cut squares (page 43) with sides the length of finished long side of triangle plus 1¼" (3.2 cm). Cut one-fourth as many squares as number of triangles needed. Place ruler diagonally across stack, holding ruler firmly; cut. Place ruler diagonally across stack in other direction; cut.

How to Make a Flying Geese Quilt Block

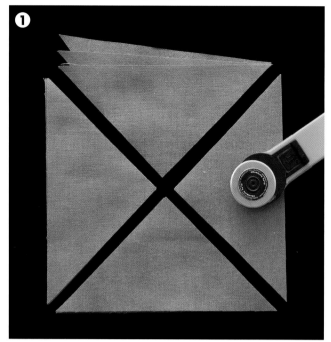

1. Cut three 5¼" (13.1cm) squares of one fabric. Cut through squares diagonally in both directions so long side of each large triangle is on grainline.

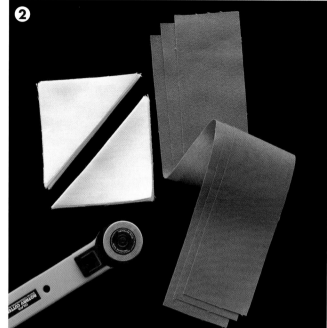

2. Cut twelve 2⅞" (7.2 cm) squares of second fabric. Cut through squares diagonally in one direction so short sides of each small triangle are on grainline. Cut three 1⅞" x 12½" (4.7 x 31.8 cm) strips of third fabric.

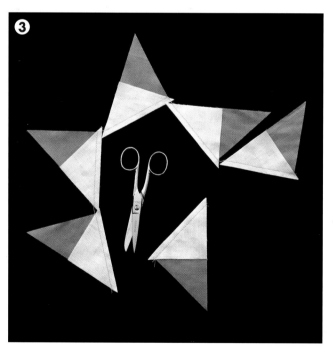

3. Stitch long side of one small triangle to short side of one large triangle, right sides together, using ¼" (6mm) seam allowances and matching corners at base of large triangle; take care not to stretch bias edges. Repeat, using chainstitching, for remaining units; clip apart.

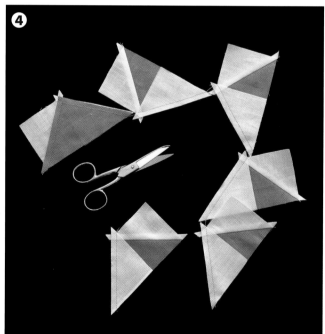

4. Finger-press seam allowances toward small triangle. Stitch a small triangle to other short side of large triangle, right sides together, matching corners at base of large triangle. Take care not to stitch a tuck in first seam. Repeat, using chainstitching, for remaining units; clip apart.

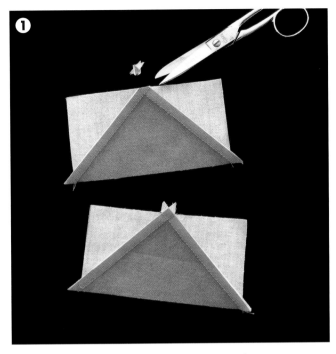

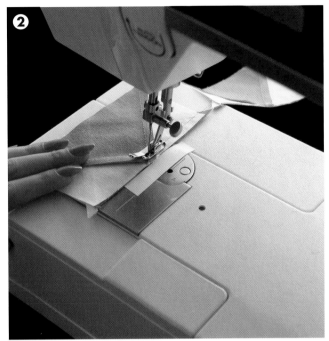

5. Press seam allowances toward small triangles. Trim points

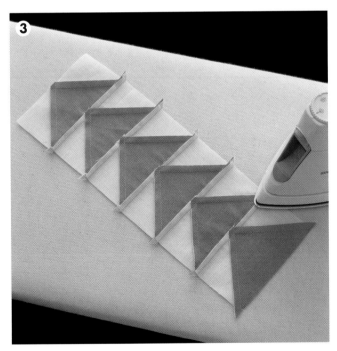

6. Place two units right sides together, matching top of one unit to bottom of other, so large triangles are pointing in same direction. Stitch, with point of large triangle on top, to make sure stitching goes through point. Repeat, using chainstitching, for remaining units; clip apart.

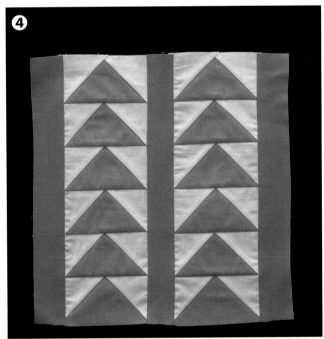

7. Stitch three units together to make a pieced strip of six units. Repeat for a second pieced strip. Press seam allowances toward bases of large triangles.

8. Stitch one long strip between two pieced strips; stitch remaining long strips at sides of block. Press seam allowances toward long strips.

How to Make Triangle-squares Using the Grid-piecing Method

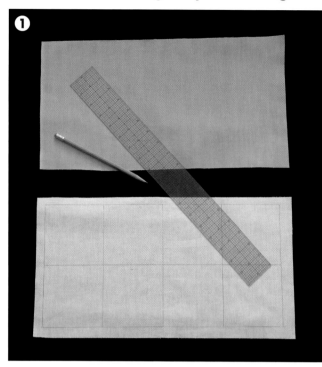

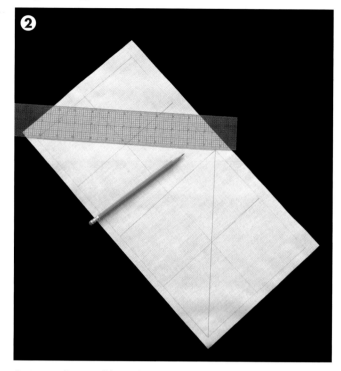

1. Cut one rectangle from each of two different fabrics. Draw grid of squares on wrong side of lighter-colored fabric, making grid squares ⅞" (2.2 cm) larger than finished triangle-square; each square of grid makes two triangle-squares.

2. Draw diagonal lines through the grid, as shown.

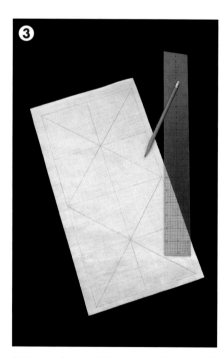

3. Draw diagonal lines through the grid in opposite direction.

4. Mark dotted stitching lines ¼" (6 mm) on both sides of all diagonal lines. Pin the fabrics, right sides together.

5. Stitch on dotted lines. Cut on all solid lines to make triangle-squares. Press seam allowances toward darker fabric. Trim points.

How to Make a Pinwheel Quilt Block

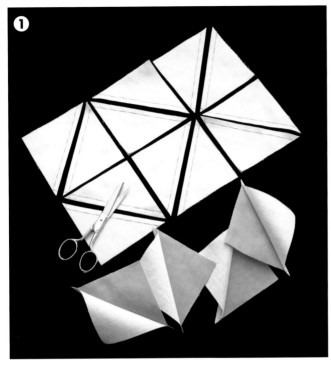

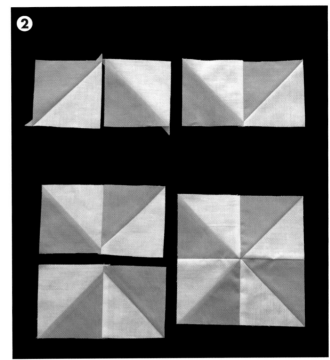

1. Cut one 7¾" x 15½" (20 x 40 cm) rectangle from each of two different fabrics. Draw 3⅞" (9.7 cm) grid, as in step 1, opposite. Draw the diagonal lines, stitch, and cut as in steps 2 to 5, opposite, to make 16 triangle-squares.

2. Stitch two triangle-squares, right sides together, as shown. Repeat with two more triangle-squares. Press seam allowances toward lighter fabric. Stitch two units together to form pinwheel, matching points. Keep seam allowances in alternating directions to eliminate bulk at points. Repeat for three more pinwheels.

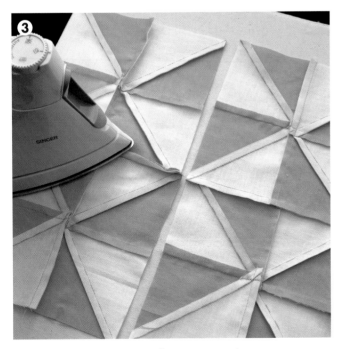

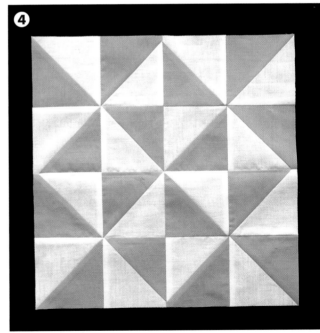

3. Stitch two pinwheels together. Repeat with two remaining pinwheels. Press seam allowances in alternating directions.

4. Stitch remaining seam to form block. Press seam allowances to one side. Release stitching at centers of pinwheels to make seam allowances lie flat, if necessary, as on page 59, step 10. (continued)

SEWING DESIGNS WITH DIAMONDS

Diamonds are frequently used to make star designs. Select fabric that has an all-over print or is a solid color rather than fabric with a one-way design or stripes, so you do not have to be concerned about the direction of the design when stitching the pieces together.

Cut diamonds carefully to ensure that the angles are accurate. The cutting directions, opposite, are for diamonds that have 45° angles. Other diamond shapes used in quilting require templates for accurate cutting. Because diamonds are cut on the bias, take care not to stretch the edges when stitching.

The instructions for the Eight-pointed Star quilt block (opposite) make a 12" (30.5 cm) finished block.

How to Cut Diamonds

1. Cut strips (page 39) the width of finished diamond plus ½" (1.3 cm). Stack three or four strips, matching edges exactly. Place on cutting mat, along grid line.

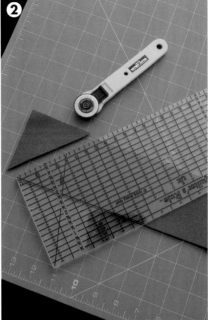

2. Place ruler at 45° angle to long edge of fabric; hold ruler firmly, and cut.

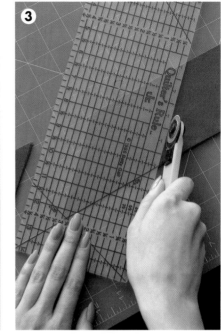

3. Shift ruler on fabric, aligning fabric edge with measurement mark that is equal to width of strip; hold firmly, and cut. Check accuracy of angle frequently.

How to Make an Eight-pointed Star Quilt Block

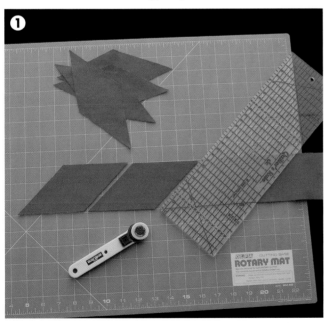

1. Cut eight 3" (7.5 cm) diamonds from one 3" (7.5 cm) strip of fabric, above, for star.

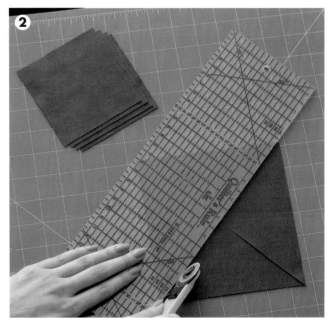

2. Cut four 4" (10 cm) squares and one 6¼" (15.7 cm) square of background fabric. Cut large square in half diagonally; then cut diagonally in other direction, to make four right triangles. (continued)

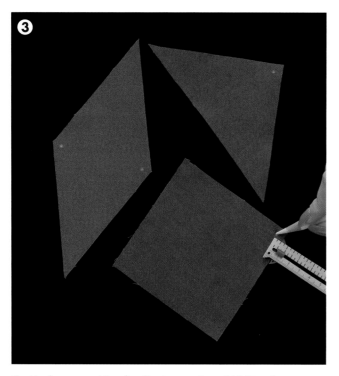

3. Mark wrong side of quilt pieces where ¼" (6mm) seams will intersect, placing dots at right-angle corner of each triangle, both wide-angle corners of each diamond, and one corner of each square.

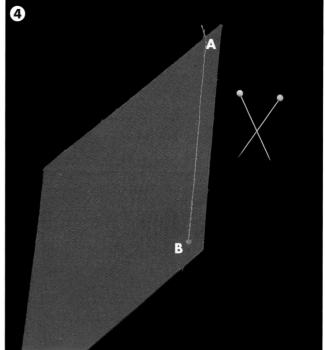

4. Align two diamonds along one side, right sides together, matching inner points (A) and dots (B). Stitch from inner point exactly to dot; backstitch. Repeat for remaining diamonds.

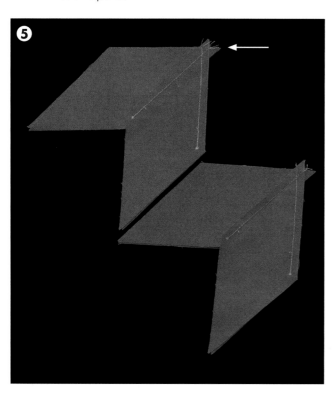

5. Stitch two 2-diamond units, right sides together, as in step 4, folding seam allowances in opposite directions (arrow). Repeat for remaining units.

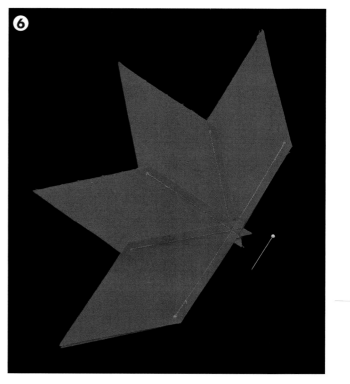

6. Place two 4-diamond units right sides together. Pin, matching inner points at center. Fold seam allowances of each four-diamond unit in opposite directions to minimize bulk; stitch between dots, securing seams at ends. Do not press.

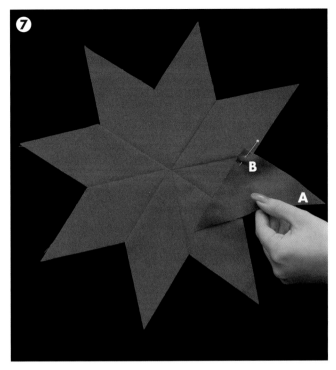

7. Align short side of triangle to a diamond, right sides together, matching edges at outer point (A) and dots at inner point (B). Stitch from outer edge exactly to dot, with diamond side up; backstitch.

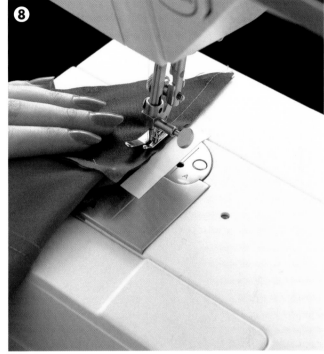

8. Align remaining side of triangle to adjoining diamond, and stitch seam as in step 7, with triangle side up. Repeat for remaining triangles, stitching them between every other set of points on the star.

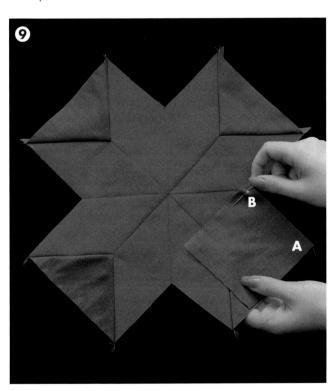

9. Align squares to diamonds between remaining points of star, matching edges at outer point (A) and dots at inner point (B) stitch with diamond side up, as in step 7. Align the remaining sides of squares and diamonds, stitching with square side up.

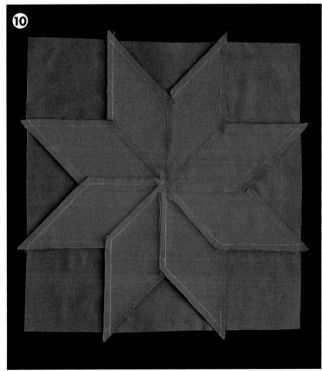

10. Release stitching within seam allowances at center of star, so seam allowances will lie flat. Press from wrong side, working from center out.

SEWING DESIGNS WITH CURVES

Some traditional quilt designs are based on curved pieces. Curves are the most difficult shapes to piece, but the more gradual the curve, the easier it is to piece. More intricate curved designs are usually done with appliqué.

Templates are required for cutting curved designs. They are available at quilting stores and by mail order, or you can make your own templates by cutting them from heavy cardboard or plastic template materials. Templates for machine-pieced designs include ¼" (6 mm) seam allowances.

Make sure, when tracing and cutting templates, that the edges are smooth and the sizes are exact.

The Drunkard's Path is an easy curved pattern to piece. The pieced squares of the Drunkard's Path can be arranged in many different ways. Three different arrangements are shown (opposite). The method for cutting the templates and fabric for the Drunkard's Path can be use for cutting any machine-pieced curved designs.

The instructions for the Drunkard's Path quilt block (pages 62 and 63) make a 12" (30.5 cm) finished block.

Pattern for Drunkard's Path Template

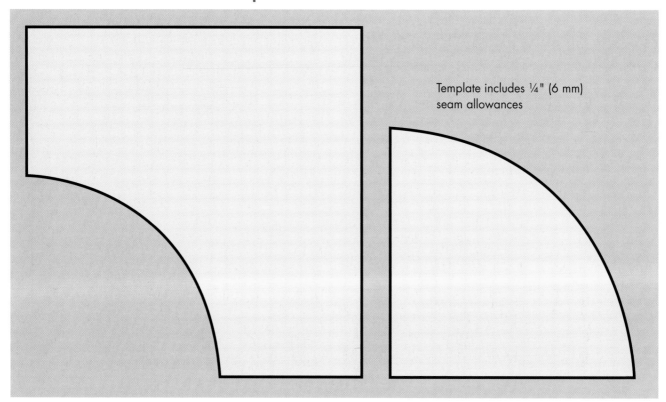

Template includes ¼" (6 mm) seam allowances

Trace pattern actual size onto tracing paper to make and cut template (page 62).

How to Cut Templates and Fabric for a Drunkard's Path Quilt Block

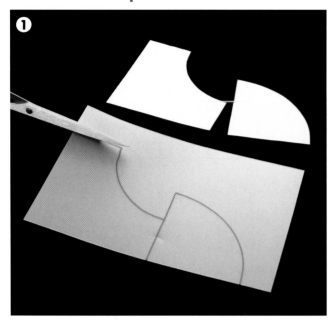

1. Trace template pattern (page 60) accurately onto tracing paper; cut. Place on cardboard or template plastic; trace. Cut accurately.

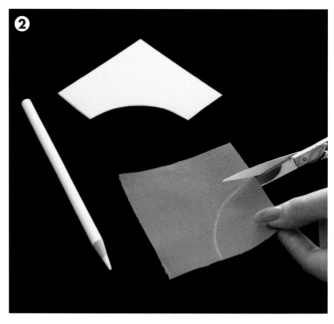

2. Place template on fabric; trace. Cut fabric on marked line, using scissors or rotary cutter.

How to Make a Drunkard's Path Quilt Block

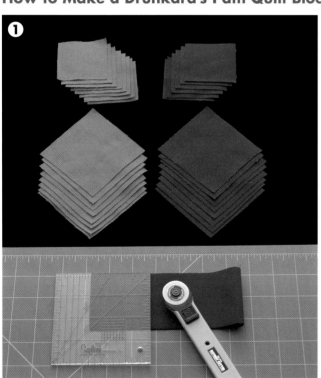

1. Cut eight 3½" (9 cm) squares and eight 2½" (6.5 cm) squares from each of two fabrics.

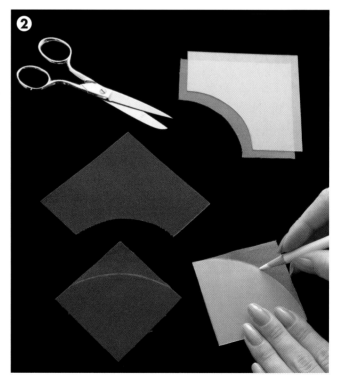

2. Place large template on one large square, matching edges exactly; trace curve. Repeat for remaining large squares. Cut on marked lines. Discard scraps. Repeat for small squares, using small template.

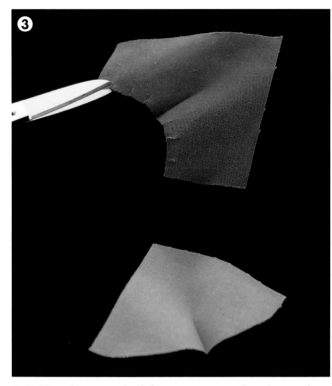

3. Fold each piece in half; finger-press to mark midpoint of curved edge. Clip seam allowances along curves of large pieces ⅜" (1 cm) apart, and a scant ¼" (6 mm) deep.

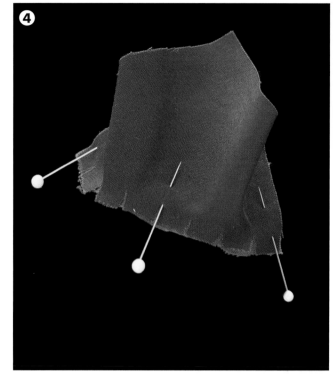

4. Pin one large and one small piece of different fabrics, right sides together, matching center creases. Pin at each corner, aligning edges.

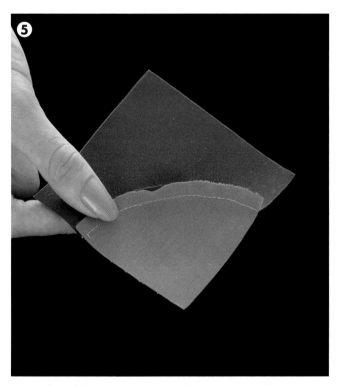

5. Stitch, with large piece on top, lining up raw edges as you sew. Finger-press seam allowance toward large piece. Repeat for remaining pieces.

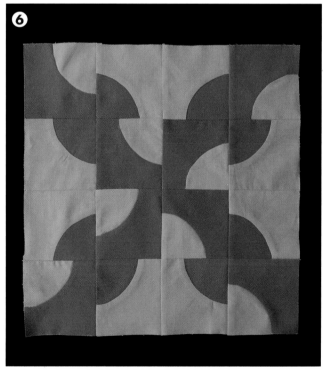

6. Arrange pieced squares in block, four across by four down. First, stitch squares into rows of four; then stitch rows together to complete block. Press.

Sashing & Borders

Sashing separates the blocks in a quilt design, and borders frame the quilt. Both should be chosen carefully.

The sashing strips may be placed horizontally and vertically, or they may be placed diagonally. Once the blocks are completed, you may want to experiment with various widths of sashing. Sashing may be made from contrasting or background fabric and may be solid or pieced.

Make the final decision on a border design after the blocks and sashing are stitched together. A simple design that works well is a narrow, dark border next to the blocks, with a wide, lighter border around the outside. This sets off the piecing and unifies the quilt top.

SASHING

Sashing strips separate and frame individual quilt blocks, while they unify a quilt and change its finished size. A quilt top can be made larger by using sashing strips.

The sashing strips are cut after the quilt blocks are pieced and measured; this allows for any variance in size that may have occurred in seaming. Sashing strips are usually cut on the crosswise grain. If it is necessary to piece long sashing strips, the seam placement is usually planned so the seams are at the center of each strip.

To determine the number of sashing strips required, draw a sketch of the quilt top or arrange the quilt blocks on a large, flat surface. When estimating the yardage for sashing, do not include the selvages. Allow for some shrinkage if the fabric will be prewashed. On the cutting layouts, plan for about 40" (102 cm) of usable width for 45" (115 cm) fabric.

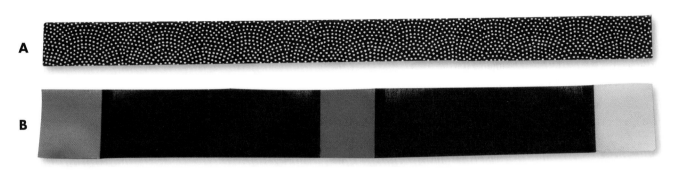

A

B

Plain sashing (A) is a good choice for a quilt with complex block design and may be used with a matching border. Short, vertical sashing strips join the blocks into rows, and long, horizontal sashing strips join the rows. Sashing with connecting squares (B) adds more interest to a quilt. When this method is used, an outer sashing frames the blocks.

How to Estimate Yardage for Sashing

1

1. Draw a sketch of the quilt top, labeled with the measurements of blocks, borders, and sashing strips; draw seams for sashing on sketch.

2

2. Draw cutting layout for sashing strips, labeling usable width of fabric. Sketch sashing strips, including seam allowances, on crosswise or lengthwise grainline, labeling measurements. Add the measurements to estimate yardage.

How to Make and Apply Plain Sashing

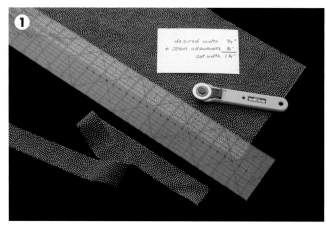

1. Cut sashing strips to the desired width of sashing plus ½" (1.3 cm) for seam allowances.

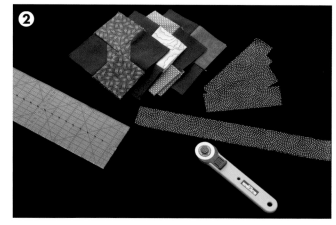

2. Measure sides of several quilt blocks to determine the shortest measurement; cut short sashing strips to this length.

3. Stitch short sashing strips between blocks, right sides together, to form rows; do not stitch strips to ends of rows. Press seam allowances toward sashing.

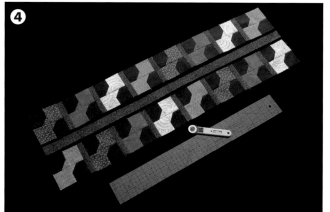

4. Measure length of rows to determine the shortest measurement. Cut the long sashing strips to this length, piecing as necessary.

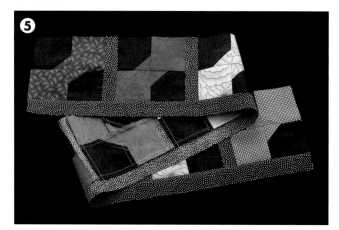

5. Mark centers of sashing strips and rows. Place one long sashing strip along bottom of one row, right sides together; match and pin centers and ends. Pin along length, easing in any excess fullness; stitch. Repeat for remaining rows, except for bottom row. Press seam allowances toward sashing strips.

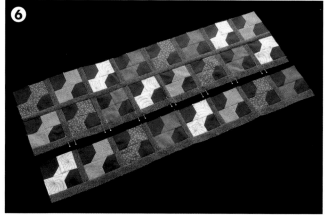

6. Align rows of blocks and mark sashing strips, as shown. Pin bottom of sashing strip to top of next row, right sides together; align marks to seamlines. Stitch as in step 5. Press seam allowances toward sashing. Continue until all rows are joined.

How to Make and Apply Sashing with Connecting Squares

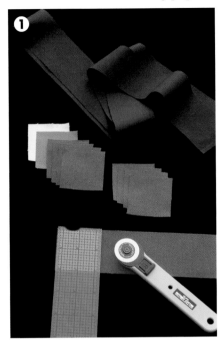

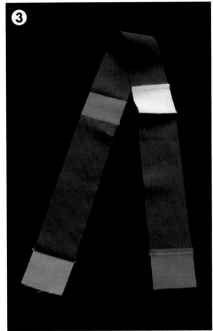

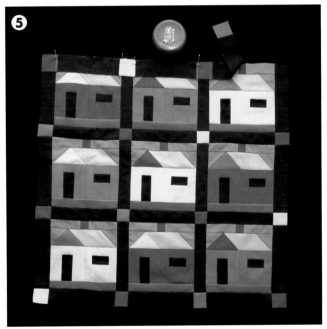

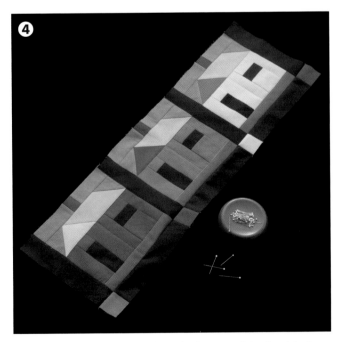

1. Cut strips to desired width of the sashing plus ½" (1.3 cm) for seam allowances. From contrasting fabric, cut connecting squares for corners, with sides of squares equal to cut width of sashing strips.

2. Measure sides of several blocks to determine shortest measurements; cut sashing strips to this length. Stitch strips between blocks, right sides together, to form rows; ease in fullness. Stitch strips to ends of rows. Press seam allowances toward strips.

3. Stitch the remaining sashing strips alternately to connecting squares, to equal the length of the block-and-sashing row; there will be a connecting square at each end. Press seam allowances toward sashing strips.

4. Place one sashing unit along the bottom of the first block-and-sashing row, right sides together, matching seams. Pin along length, easing in any fullness; stitch. Repeat for remaining rows.

5. Pin bottom of one sashing unit to top of next row, matching seams, as in step 4; stitch. Press seam allowances toward sashing strip. Continue until all rows are joined. Stitch sashing unit to upper edge.

FRAME SASHING

Frame sashing is pieced to form a unique design of parallelograms and triangles. For easy construction, the sashing pieces are stitched to each quilt block. When the framed blocks are stitched together, the sashing forms an eight-pointed star where the corners of four blocks meet, and the pieced triangles form squares in the design.

The unpieced quilt blocks, cut from a single fabric, may be embellished with quilting or appliqués. The sashing is constructed from gradations of a color. The choice of color in the sashing can create either a subtle frame around each block or a bold design.

The instructions that follow are for a bed quilt. For a twin-size, which measures about 68" x 86" (173 x 218.5 cm), three rows of two blocks are pieced. For a full/queen-size, which measures about 86" (218.5 cm) square, three rows of three blocks are pieced. The sashing is constructed around

12" (30.5 cm) quilt blocks. Each block framed with 3" (7.5 cm) sashing measures 18" (46 cm) square. Wide 16" (40.5 cm) borders complete the quilt and provide a background for decorative quilting. To eliminate the need for piecing, the border strips are cut on the lengthwise grain.

Cut two 3½" (9 cm) strips of each of the eight solid-colored fabrics for sashing; these will be cut into parallelograms (page 72).

Cut the four fabrics for sashing triangles into 7¼" (18.7 cm) squares; for a twin-size quilt, cut two squares of each fabric, and for a full/queen-size quilt, cut three squares of each fabric. Cut all squares diagonally in both directions (page 187, step 2), making four triangles from each square.

For the quilt blocks, cut 12½" (31.8 cm) fabric strips; cut the strips into squares, cutting six for a twin-size quilt and nine for a full/queen-size.

YOU WILL NEED

For twin-size:

- ¾ yd. (0.7 m) fabric, to be used for quilt blocks.
- ¼ yd. (0.25 m) each of eight solid-colored fabrics for sashing parallelograms; choose eight shades of one color.
- Scraps or ¼ yd. (0.25 m) each of four fabrics for sashing triangles.
- 3¾ yd. (3.45 m) fabric, to be used for continuous-length 16" (40.5 cm) borders.
- 2¾ yd. (2.55 m) fabric in 90" (229 cm) width, or 5¼ yd. (4.8 m) in 45" (115 cm) width, for backing.
- ¾ yd. (0.7 m) fabric for binding.
- Batting, sized for twin-size quilt.

For full/queen-size:

- 1⅛ yd. (1.05 m) fabric, to be used for quilt blocks.
- ¼ yd. (0.25 m) each of eight solid-colored fabrics for sashing parallelograms; choose eight shades of one color.
- Scraps or ¼ yd. (0.25 m) each of four fabrics for sashing triangles.
- 4¼ yd. (3.9 m) fabric, to be used for continuous length 16" (40.5 cm) borders.
- 2¾ yd. (2.55 m) fabric in 108" (274.5 cm) width, or 7¾ yd. (7.1 m) in 45" (115 cm) width, for backing.
- ¾ yd. (0.7 m) fabric for binding.
- Batting, sized for full/queen-size quilt.

How to Make a Quilt with Frame Sashing

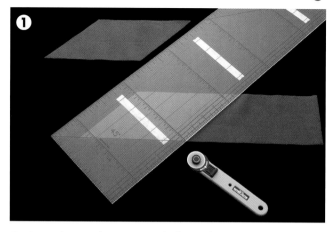

1. Cut a 45° angle in one end of strip for sashing. Place 4¾" (12 cm) mark of ruler along angled cut; cut strip to make parallelogram.

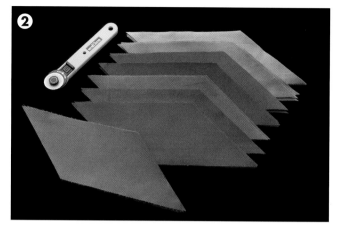

2. Continue cutting parallelograms from fabric strips, cutting six of each fabric for twin-size or nine of each fabric for full/queen-size.

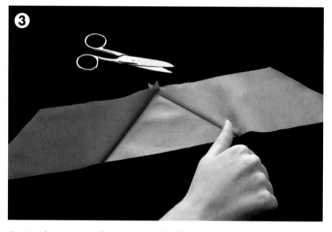

3. Stitch two parallelograms of different colors to short sides of one triangle, as shown; finger-press seam allowances toward parallelograms. Trim points that extend beyond sashing.

4. Repeat step 3 to make four pieced sashing strips for each quilt block; randomly use each parallelogram and triangle fabric once in each set.

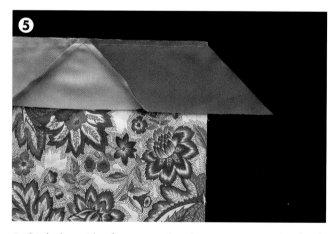

5. Stitch short side of one pieced sashing strip to one side of quilt block; begin and end stitching ¼" (6 mm) from edges of block, backstitching at ends. Repeat for remaining sides of blocks.

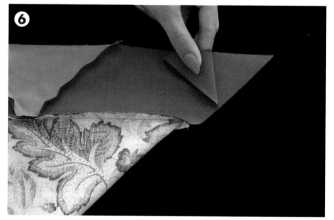

6. Fold quilt block diagonally, right sides together, matching seamlines and edges of parallelograms.

7. Stitch corner seam, backstitching at inside corner; do not catch seam allowances in stitching. Repeat for remaining corners.

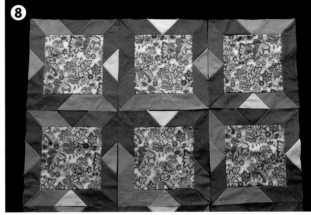

8. Repeat steps 5 to 7 for remaining blocks, varying color arrangement. Arrange blocks in rows.

9. Stitch blocks into rows, matching points; stitch rows together, finger-pressing seam allowances at corners in opposite directions. Press the quilt top, pressing seam allowances toward blocks.

10. Cut and attach border strips (pages 84 to 89), cutting strips on lengthwise grain; cut width of border strips is 16½" (41.8 cm). Mark quilting design on border and blocks (page 100).

11. Cut backing and batting about 4" (10 cm) larger than quilt top. Layer and baste quilt top, batting, and backing (pages 92 to 97).

12. Quilt (102 to 107). Cut and apply binding (pages 111 and 116); cut width of binding is 2½" (6.5 cm).

STAR SASHING

Sashing strips with connecting stars create a sashing design bold enough to be used with plain quilt blocks. Quick methods for cutting and piecing are used to construct the stars, making this an easy quilt project.

The instructions that follow are for a quilt made from thirty 5½" (14 cm) quilt blocks and 2¼" (6 cm) sashing. The finished quilt with a double lapped border measures about 45" x 53" (115 x 134.5 cm).

YOU WILL NEED

- 1 yd. (0.95 m) fabric for quilt blocks.
- ⅞ yd. (0.8 m) fabric for sashing strips.
- ⅔ yd. (0.63m) fabric for stars and ½" (1.3 cm) inner border.
- ¾ yd. (0.7 m) fabric for 3½" (9 cm) outer border.
- ½ yd. (0.5 m) fabric for binding.
- 2¾ yd. (2.55 m) fabric for backing.
- Batting, about 49" x 57" (125 x 144.5 cm).

CUTTING DIRECTIONS ✂

- Cut eight 2¾" (7 cm) strips from the fabric for the sashing strips, and cut the strips into forty-nine 6" (15 cm) rectangles.
- Cut two 2¾" (7 cm) strips from the fabric for the stars; cut into twenty 2¾" (7 cm) squares.
- Cut seven 1⅝" (4 cm) strips from the fabric for the stars; cut into 160 squares to be used for the points of the stars.
- For the quilt blocks, cut five 6" (15 cm) fabric strips; cut into 30 squares.

How to Make a Quilt with Star Sashing

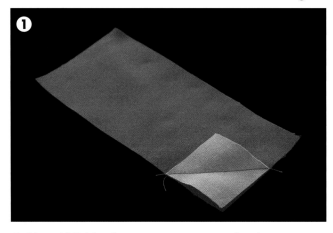

1. Place 1⅝" (4 cm) square in one corner of sashing strip, with right sides together and raw edges even. Stitch diagonally as shown.

2. Press square in half along stitched line, matching outer edges to sashing strip. Trim fabric at stitched corner, leaving ¼" (6 mm) seam allowance.

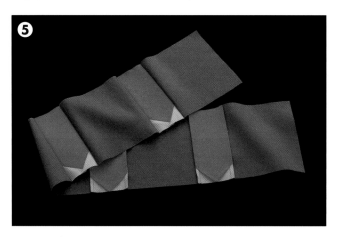

3. Repeat steps 1 and 2 at opposite corner. Continue piecing squares at one end of rectangles for a total of 18 pieced strips; these will be used as end strips.

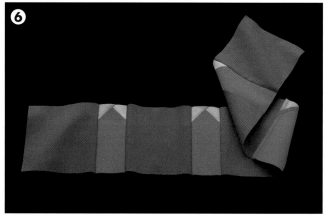

4. Stitch squares to all four corners of remaining sashing strips; these will be used as inner strips.

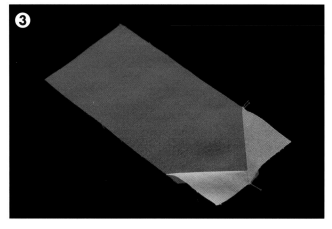

5. Stitch four end strips between five quilt blocks, placing plain ends at upper edge; this will be top row of quilt. Press seam allowances toward blocks.

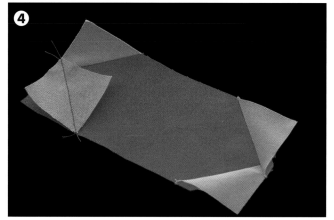

6. Repeat step 5 to make a second row, placing plain ends at lower edge; this will be bottom row of quilt.

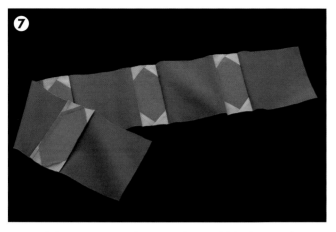

7. Stitch four inner strips between five quilt blocks to make one of the middle rows. Press seam allowances toward blocks. Repeat for three more rows.

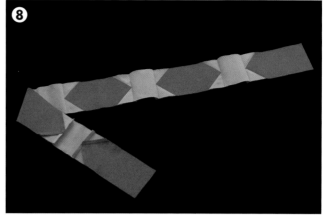

8. Stitch five sashing strips alternately to the sashing squares, using an end strip at each end. Press seam allowances toward squares. Repeat for four more rows.

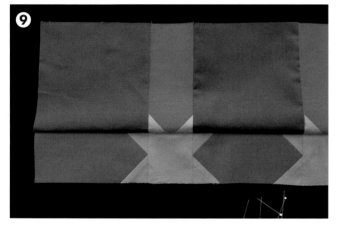

9. Pin one sashing unit along bottom of top row, right sides together, matching seams; stitch. Repeat for remaining rows, except for bottom row.

10. Pin bottom of one sashing unit to top of next row, matching seams; stitch. Continue until all rows are joined. Press seam allowances toward sashing.

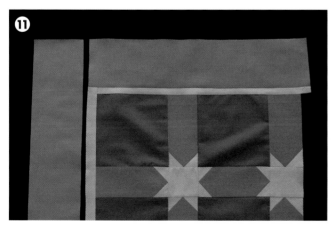

11. Cut and attach border strips (page 84); cut width of border strips is 1" (2.5 cm) for inner border and 4" (10 cm) for outer border. Cut backing 4" (10 cm) larger than quilt top. Layer and baste quilt top, batting, and backing (page 92-97).

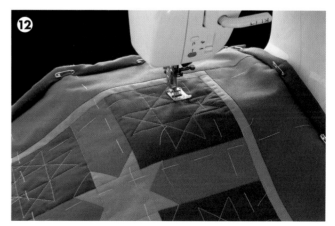

12. Quilt (pages 102 to 107). Cut and apply binding (pages 111 to 116); cut width of binding is 2½" (6.5 cm). For wall hanging, apply fabric sleeve (page 171).

MORE STAR SASHING DESIGNS

Add variety to star sashing by piecing each star in a different color or by using a gradation of colors for the sashing strips. Or for a more intricate design, use strip-pieced sashing. When using a variety of fabrics, make a sketch of the quilt for easier cutting and assembly.

Graduated colors are used for the sashing strips in the quilt at right to add subtle interest to the design.

Bright stars in a rainbow of colors are used for this child's quilt. The multicolored printed fabric in the quilt blocks adds interest to the quilt. A brightly colored stripe is used for one of the fabrics in the triple border.

Calicos and plaids create a traditional look, with template-quilted blocks complementing the style. The sashing had been strip-pieced for a more intricate design.

Dark and jewel-tone fabrics create an Amish-style quilt. Strip-pieced sashing adds more interest.

How to Make Strip-pieced Star Sashing

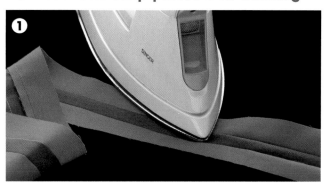

1. Cut fabric strips on crosswise grain 1¼" (3.2 cm) wide, cutting three for each row of sashing. Stitch strips together lengthwise in desired sequence, right sides together. Press.

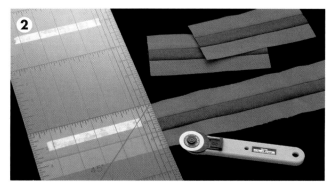

2. Cut pieced fabric into 6" (15 cm) rectangles for sashing strips. Make quilt as on pages 74 to 77.

STRIP-PIECED SASHING

Sashing with connecting squares gives a quilt an updated look when strip-pieced from graduated fabric. Connecting squares in a bold contrasting color add another design element.

You may want to select a printed fabric for the quilt blocks and choose colors from that fabric to use for gradation and connecting squares; the sharper the contrast, the bolder the design will be.

The instructions that follow are for a wall hanging made from nine 8" (20.5 cm) quilt blocks and 2" (5 cm) sashing. Random quilting lines complement the style of the quilt and create interest in the center of the quilt where the lines intersect. Instead of the narrow binding that is usually used on small wall hangings, the traditional binding acts as a small border. The finished project measures about 32" (81.5 cm) square.

Cut 1½" (3.8 cm) strips each graduated color for sashing strips; cut four strips from 45" (115 cm) yardage. Cut one 2½" (6.5 cm) squares. For the quilt blocks, cut two 8½" (21.8 cm) fabric strips; cut into nine 8½" (21.8 cm) squares.

YOU WILL NEED

- ⅛ yd. (0.15 m) each of eight fabrics, or one packet of hand-dyed fabrics in fat quarters, for sashing.

- ⅛ yd. (0.15 m) fabric for connecting squares.

- ¾ yd. (0.7 m) printed fabric for quilt blocks.

- ⅓ yd. (0.32 m) fabric for binding.

- 1 yd. (0.95m) fabric for backing.

- Batting, about 36" (92.5 cm) square.

How to Make a Quilt with Graduated Sashing

1. Stitch one strip of each color together lengthwise, with right sides together and in graduated sequence; repeat for remaining strips. Press seam allowances in one direction.

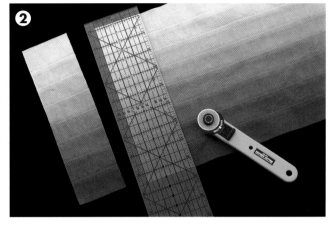

2. Cut the pieced fabric crosswise into 2½" (6.5 cm) trips, using rotary cutter.

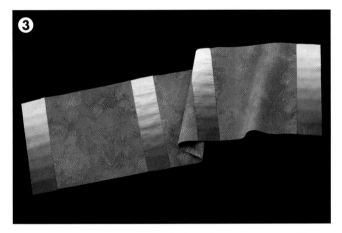

3. Stitch pieced strips between blocks to form three rows of three blocks, with darkest color at bottom of quilt blocks; stitch pieced strips to ends of rows. Press seam allowances toward blocks.

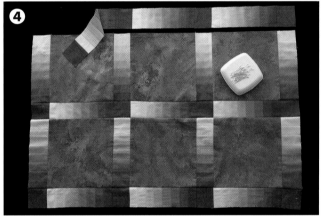

4. Complete sashing, as on page 69, steps 3 to 5; arrange strips as shown.

5. Mark quilting lines (page 100); draw lines randomly across quilt top, drawing about four lines from each side. Layer and baste quilt top, batting, and backing fabric (pages 92 to 97). (Markings were exaggerated for clarity.)

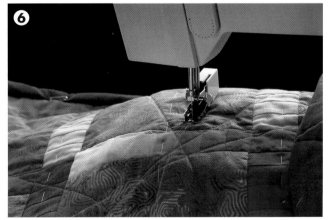

6. Quilt along sashing as on page 103, stitch-in-the-ditch method; then quilt on marked lines. Cut and apply binding (pages 111 to 116); cut width of binding is 2½" (6.5 cm). For wall hangings, attach fabric sleeve (page 171).

MORE STRIP-PIECED SASHING DESIGNS

For more colorful designs, piece fabric strips from graduated blends of two or more colors. Or cut the connecting squares from several colors. To create more motion in the quilt design, vary the arrangement of the sashing strips.

Rainbow colors in the sashing are used with solid-colored blocks to make the quilt shown above. The blocks are embellished with template quilting.

Graduated strips are arranged in the quilt above so the dark and light colors alternately radiate from connecting squares.

Printed fabrics in blended colors are used for the pieced sashing in the quilt above. The blocks have been quilted, using free-motion quilting, to enhance the design of the mottled fabric.

BORDERS

A border frames the quilt and visually finishes the edges. The three basic styles of borders are lapped borders, borders with interrupted corners, and mitered borders. In general, a lapped border is used with solid fabrics or all-over prints, and a mitered border is used with striped or border-print fabrics. A border with interrupted corners is suitable with all types of fabrics.

Any of these basic styles can be used as a single or double border. A single border provides a simple frame for the quilt design. A double border can be used to enhance and unify a design by repeating two or more of the colors in the quilt top.

The border strips are cut after the quilt top is pieced and measured, because even the slightest variance in seam allowances can affect the finished size of the quilt top. The cut length of the border strips

is determined by measuring through the middle of the quilt; this maintains the overall dimensions of the quilt.

Border strips are usually cut on the crosswise grain and pieced together for the necessary length. If seaming is required, the seam placement may be random; however, the seams should generally not be closer than 12" (30.5 cm) to a corner. For less noticeable seams, piece the strips diagonally. Borders cut from striped fabrics or border prints will usually have to be cut on the lengthwise grainline.

When estimating yardage, do not include selvages. Allow for shrinkage if the fabric will be prewashed; plan for about 40" (102 cm) of usable width on the cutting layouts for 45" (115 cm) fabric.

How to Estimate Yardage for Borders

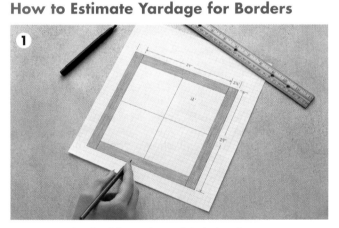

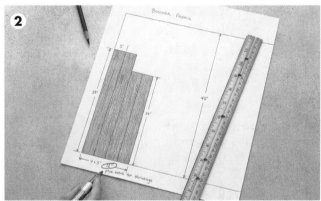

1. Draw a sketch of the quilt top, labeled with measurements of blocks, borders, and sashing strips. Plan placement of border seams, if desired; draw seams on sketch.

2. Draw cutting layout for borders, labeling usable width of fabric. Sketch crosswise or lengthwise border strips, including the seam allowances; label the measurements. Add lengthwise measurements to estimate yardage.

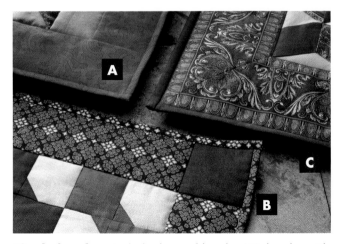

Single borders include: lapped border (A), border with interrupted corners (B), and mitered border (C).

Double borders may be lapped or mitered or have interrupted corners. The inner border is generally narrower than the outer border.

How to Make and Apply a Lapped Border

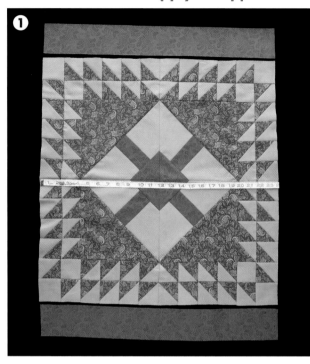

1. (Single border) Measure the quilt top across the middle. Cut two strips equal to this measurement, piecing as necessary; width of strips is equal to finished width of border plus ½" (1.3 cm).

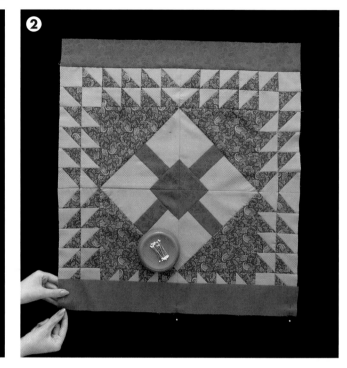

2. Pin strip to upper edge of quilt top at center and ends, right sides together; pin along length, easing in any fullness. Stitch; press seam allowances toward border. Repeat at lower edge.

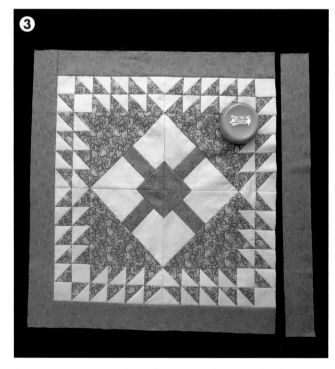

3. Measure quilt top down the middle, including border strips. Cut two strips as in step 1. Pin and stitch strips to sides of quilt top as in step 2. Press seam allowances toward border.

(Double border) Apply inner border, following steps 1 to 3, above. Measure the quilt top across and down the middle, including the inner border; cut and apply the outer border as for inner border.

How to Make and Apply a Border with Interrupted Corners

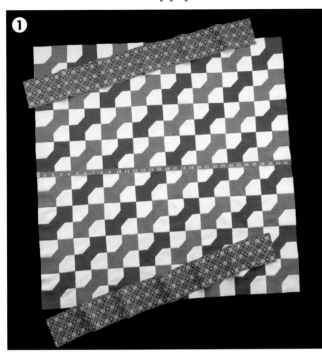

1. (Single border) Measure the quilt top across the middle. Cut two strips equal to this measurement; width of strips is equal to finished width of border plus ½" (1.3 cm). Repeat, measuring the quilt top down the middle from top to bottom.

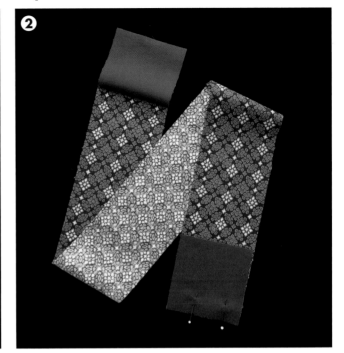

2. Cut four squares from contrasting fabric, with sides of squares equal to cut width of border strips. Stitch squares, right sides together, to ends of side border strips.

3. Pin upper border strip to upper edge of quilt top at center and ends, right sides together; pin along length, easing in any fullness. Stitch; press seam allowances toward border. Repeat at lower edge.

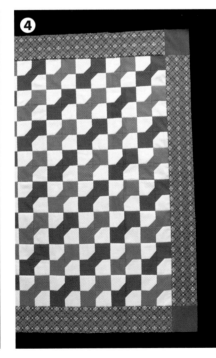

4. Pin and stitch pieced border strips to sides of quilt top as in step 3, matching seamlines at corners. Press seam allowances toward border.

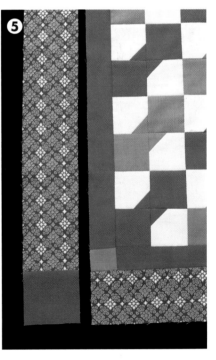

5. (Double border) Apply the inner border, following steps 1 to 4. Measure the quilt top across and down the middle, including the inner border; cut and apply outer border as for inner border.

How to Make and Apply a Mitered Border

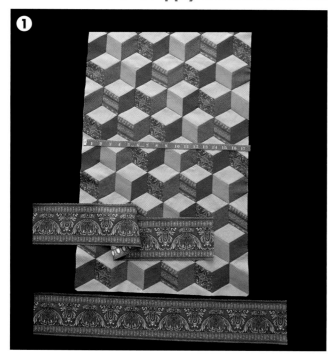

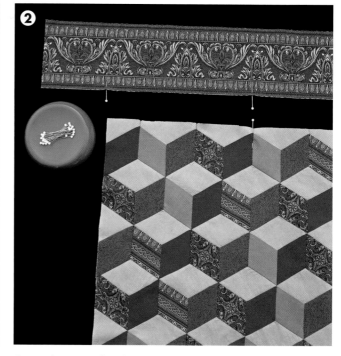

1. (Single border) Measure quilt top across the middle. Cut two strips, with length equal to this measurement plus 2 times finished width of border plus 1" (2.5 cm); cut width is equal to finished width of border plus ½" (1.3 cm). Repeat for side strips, measuring quilt top down the middle from top to bottom.

2. Mark center of quilt top at upper and lower edges; mark center of upper and lower border strips. From each end of border strips, mark the finished width of the border plus ½" (1.3 cm). Place upper border strip on quilt top, right sides together, matching pin marks at center.

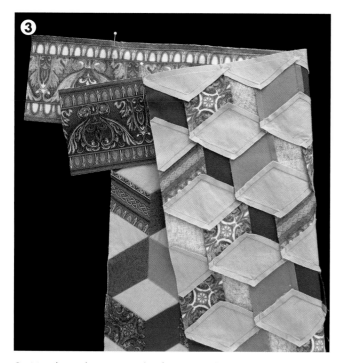

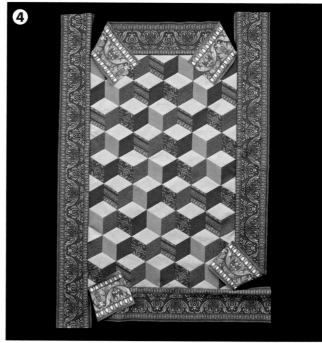

3. Match markings at ends of strip to edges of quilt top; pin. Pin along length, easing in any fullness. Stitch, beginning and ending ¼" (6 mm) from edges of quilt top; backstitch at ends. Repeat at lower edge.

4. Repeat steps 2 and 3 for sides of quilt top.

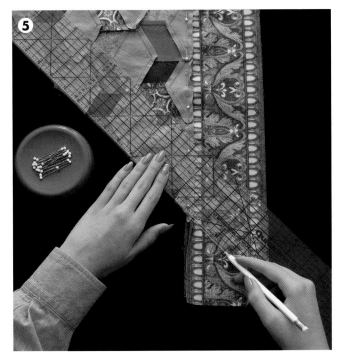

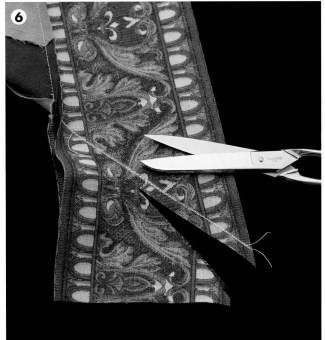

5. Fold quilt top at corner diagonally, right sides together, matching border seamlines; pin securely. Draw diagonal line on border strip, extending line formed by fold of quilt top.

6. Stitch on the marked line; do not catch the seam allowances in stitching. Trim ends of border strips to ¼" (6 mm) seam allowances.

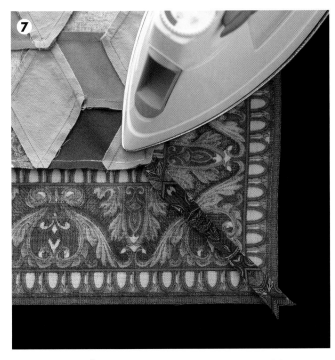

7. Press seam allowances open at corner; press remaining seam allowances toward border strip. Repeat for remaining corners.

(Double border) Apply inner border as in steps 1 to 7. Measure the quilt top across and down the middle, including the inner border; cut and apply outer border as for inner border.

CREATIVE BORDERS

Borders, such as the appliquéd border shown here, can become an integral and important part of the quilt design instead of merely a frame for the quilt. Or borders can add an unexpected finishing touch, as shown on the quilts on pages 90 and 91.

Appliquéd Borders

An asymmetrical border, applied as an overlay, adds interest to a quilt. The edges of the border are appliquéd to the quilt top, following the design of the fabric. The border can provide a strong contrast to the pieced top or can blend subtly.

An appliquéd border may be added to as many sides of the quilt as desired. When planning the border, you may want to make a sketch of the quilt, or lay strips of the border fabric on the pieced quilt top to determine the desired size of the border pieces.

For the border, choose a printed fabric that can be cut and pressed along a design line. The yardage requirements will vary, depending on the size of the quilt and the width of the border strips. Estimate the yardage for the border as on page 83; for best results, plan for continuous border strips. When cutting the strips, you may want to allow extra width on the appliquéd borders to allow for adjusting the placement of the design line.

How to Apply an Appliquéd Border

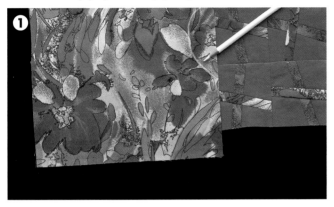

1. Press quilt top. Determine side, or portion of side, to be covered by first border strip. Cut the length of border strip to this measurement; cut width is equal to desired depth at widest point plus ½" (1.3 cm). Mark inner edge of border strip along design line.

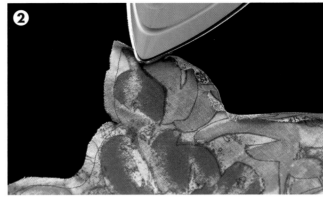

2. Stitch on the marked lines; trim ¼" (6 mm) from the stitching. Press under edge of fabric just beyond stitching line; clip as necessary.

3. Pin border strip to quilt top, making sure the edges overlap and the sides are parallel with the quilt. Blind-stitch along pressed edges as on page 180, step 5. Trim excess fabric from wrong side, allowing ¼" (6 mm) seam allowances.

4. Measure adjacent side, or portion of that side, to be covered by second border strip. Cut the length of second strip to this measurement plus extra to overlap first strip; cut width is equal to desired depth at widest point plus ½" (1.3 cm). Mark inner edge of strip.

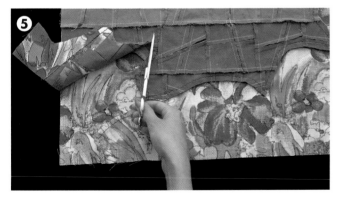

5. Stitch and press inner edge of second border strip as in step 2. Pin and blindstitch border as in step 3; trim excess fabric from wrong side; allowing ¼" (6 mm) seam allowance. Apply any remaining border strips as for second strip.

6. Cut and attach outer border, if desired (pages 83 to 87). Cut backing about 4" (10 cm) larger than quilt top. Layer and baste quilt top, batting, and backing (pages 92 to 97). Quilt (pages 102 to 107). Cut and apply binding (pages 111 to 116). For wall hanging, attach fabric sleeve (page 171).

More Creative Border Designs

A creative border adds a new area of interest to a quilt, instead of a simple, complementary frame. The border can emphasize the colors used in piecing and can change the balance of the quilt.

Randomly pieced borders can incorporate fabrics that are too overpowering to use as continuous strips. Piece scraps together for the necessary yardage for the border strips.

Another way to incorporate several fabrics is by applying multiple borders. Instead of the usual single or double borders, several borders may be used on one quilt.

Unbalanced borders are especially pleasing on wall hangings. An unbalanced border creates motion in the quilt design, making the quilt more interesting when viewed from a distance.

Mitered border is applied to two sides only. The Pine Trees quilt (page 124) is displayed on point, with the top hanging free to reveal the quilt's patterned backing.

Randomly pieced border adds a creative frame to this table runner with satin-stitched appliqués.

Contrasting insert strips make a contemporary frame for a landscape wall hanging; add the strips to the border. Start by applying the border strip on the left side of the quilt; then work counterclockwise, and miter the upper left corner.

Bias tape is gently curved along the border of the contemporary crazy quilt (page 148) shown at right. Use the machine blindstitch to apply the bias tape (page 180, step 5).

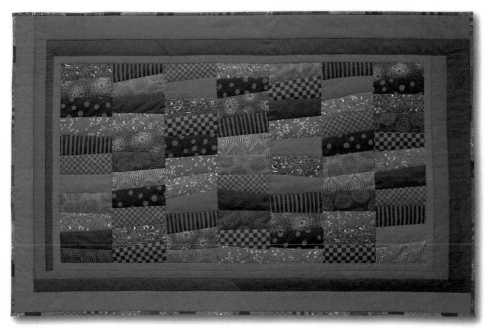

Multiple borders of various colors and widths, shown at left on a string-pieced quilt, were applied using the method for lapped borders (page 84). The inner, or first, border is entirely red. The second and third borders are each half blue and half purple. The fourth partial border, applied only to the top and left side, repeats the red.

Batting & Backing

Although batting is available in different sizes, it may need to be pieced for larger projects. Battings differ in loft and fiber content (pages 28 and 29). Loft is the thickness and springiness of a batting. It determines the degree of texture in a quilt.

The batting and backing should extend 2" to 4" (5 to 10 cm) beyond the edges of the quilt top on all sides, to allow for the shrinkage that occurs during quilting. It may be necessary to piece the batting and backing.

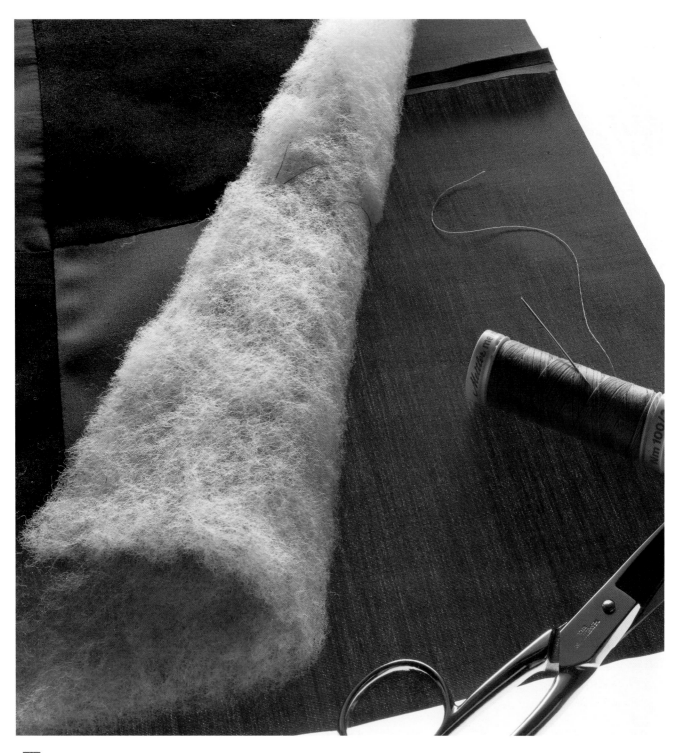

How to Piece Batting and Backing Fabric

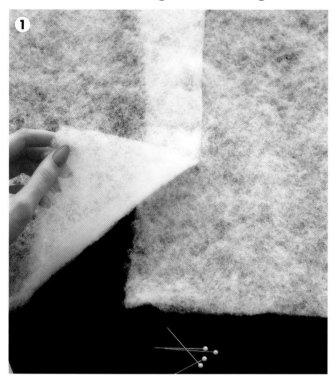

1. (Batting) Overlap two pieces of batting, 1" to 2" (2.5 to 5 cm).

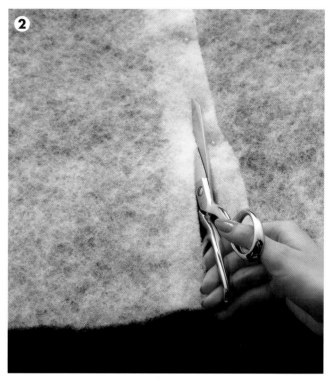

2. Cut with shears through both layers, down the center of overlapped section.

3. Remove trimmed edges. Butt batting edges, and whipstitch by hand to secure.

(Backing) Cut selvages from fabric. Piece fabric as necessary, positioning seams as on page 31. Stitch, using a stitch length of 12 to 15 stitches per inch (2.5 cm) and ¼" (6 mm) seam allowances. Press seam allowances to one side or open.

BASTING THE LAYERS FOR QUILTING

Basting keeps the three layers of the quilt from shifting during the quilting process. Traditionally, quilts were basted using needle and thread; however, safety-pin basting may be used instead. Lay the quilt out flat on a hard surface, such as the floor or a large table and baste the entire quilt. Or baste the quilt in sections on a table at least one-fourth the size of the quilt.

Press the quilt top and backing fabric flat before layering and basting. If basting with safety pins, use 1" (2.5 cm)

rustproof steel pins. Steel pins glide through fabrics more easily than brass pins, and the 1" (2.5 cm) size is easier to handle.

If basting with thread, use white cotton thread and a large milliners or darning needle. Use a large running stitch, about 1" (2.5 cm) long. Pull the stitches snug so the layers will not shift. Backstitch at the ends to secure the stitching.

How to Baste a Quilt on a Surface Larger Than the Quilt

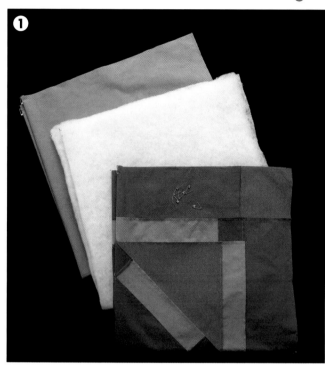

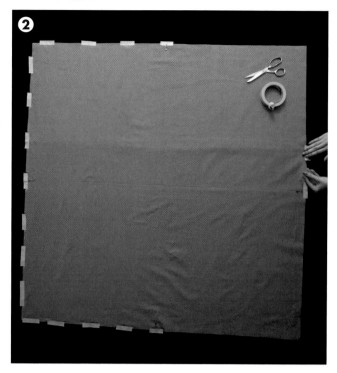

1. Fold quilt top, right sides together, into quarters, without creasing. Mark center of each side at raw edges with safety pins. Repeat for batting and backing, folding backing wrong sides together.

2. Unfold backing on work surface, wrong side up. Tape securely, beginning at center of each side and working toward corners, stretching fabric slightly. Backing should be taut, but not overly stretched.

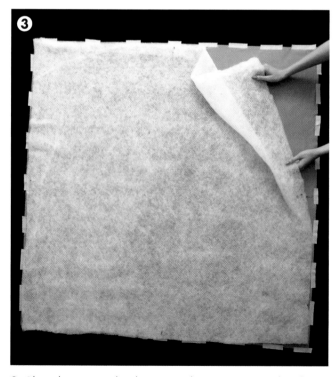

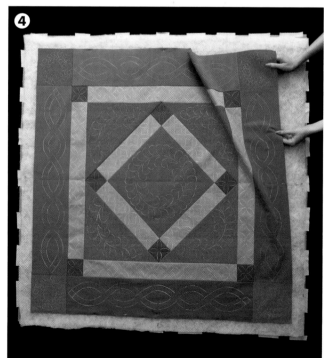

3. Place batting on backing, matching pins on each side. Smooth, but do not stretch, working from center of quilt out to sides.

4. Place quilt top, right side up, on batting, matching pins on each side; smooth, but do not stretch.

(continued)

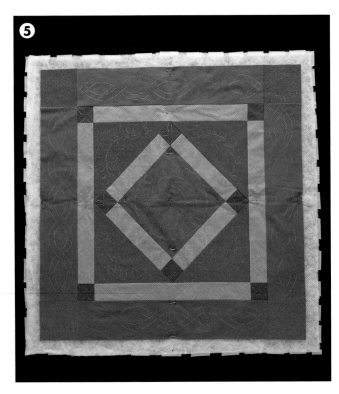

5. Baste with pins or thread from center of quilt to pins on sides; if thread-basting, pull stitches snug so layers will not shift. Avoid basting on marked quilting lines or through seams.

6. Baste one quarter-section in parallel rows about 6" (15 cm) apart, working toward raw edges. If thread-basting, also baste quarter-section in parallel rows in opposite direction, as shown in step 2 (opposite).

7. Repeat step 6 for remaining quarter-sections. Remove tape from backing.

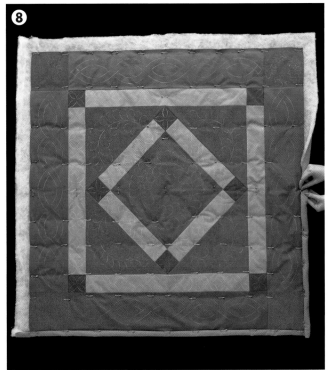

8. Fold edges of backing over batting and edges of quilt top to prevent raw edges of fabric from raveling and batting from catching on needle and feed dogs during quilting. Pin-baste.

How to Baste a Quilt on a Surface Smaller Than the Quilt

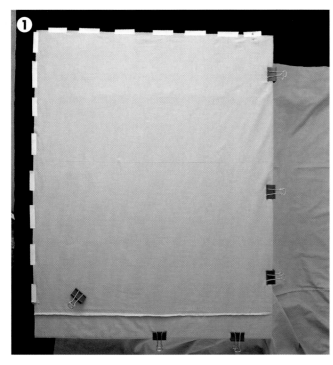

1. Fold and mark quilt as in step 1, page 95. Lay backing on table, wrong side up; let sides hang over edge of table. Tape raw edges of backing to tabletop. Clamp backing securely to table, stretching slightly, beginning at center of each side and working toward corners; place clamps about 12" (30.5 cm) apart.

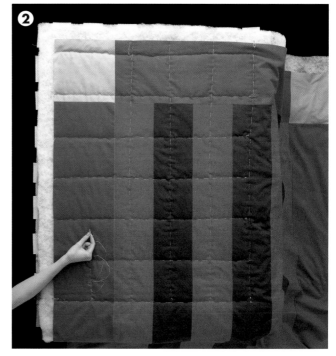

2. Place batting on backing, matching pins on each side. Place quilt top right side up on batting, matching pins on each side; smooth, but do not stretch. Baste one quarter-section of quilt as in steps 5 and 6, opposite. Remove tape and clamps.

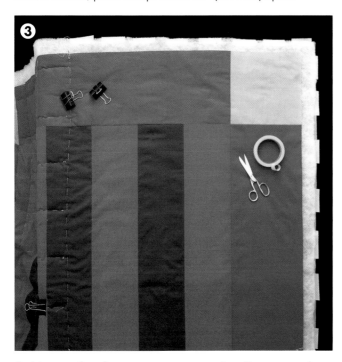

3. Move quilt to baste next quarter-section. Tape raw edges of backing to tabletop, stretching slightly; clamp all layers of quilt to edges of table. Baste quarter-section as in steps 5 and 6 (opposite).

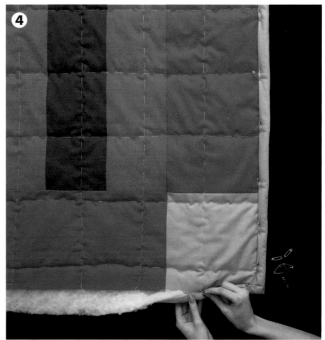

4. Repeat for remaining quarter-sections. Check for any tucks on backing; rebaste as necessary. Fold and pin-baste edges as in step 8 (opposite).

Channel Quilting   Stipple Quilting   Motif Quilting

Quilting Basics

Machine quilting is used to hold the layers of the quilt together, but it also adds surface texture and depth to the quilt. A large variety of quilting designs can be created using either machine-guided or free-motion quilting or a combination of both. Plan quilting designs to cover the quilt uniformly, because heavily quilted areas tend to shrink the fabric more than lightly quilted areas.

Machine-guided Quilting

In machine-guided quilting, the feed dogs and the presser foot guide the fabric. This method of quilting is used for stitching long, straight lines or slight curves, and includes stitch-in-the-ditch quilting and channel quilting. Stitch-in-the-ditch quilting is used to give definition to the blocks, borders, and sashing. It is the easiest method of quilting, and is often the only type of quilting needed to complete a project.

Channel quilting is the stitching of parallel lines. The quilting lines may be either diagonal, vertical, or horizontal and are usually evenly spaced. Mark the quilting lines with a straightedge.

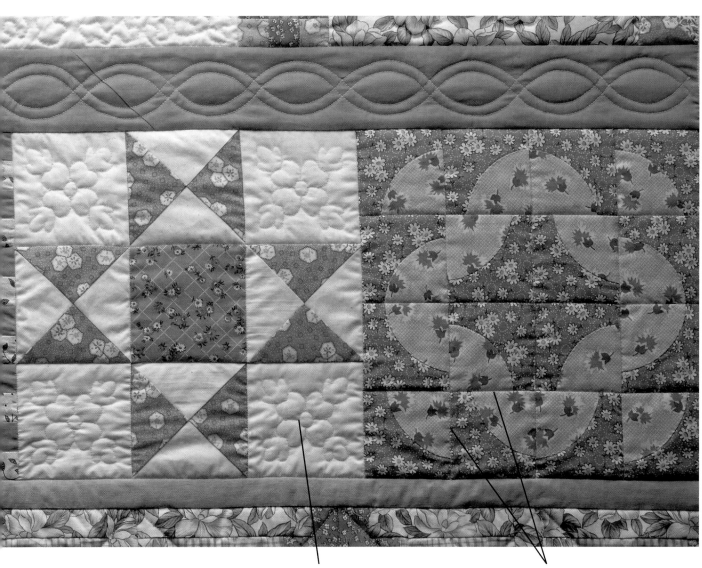

Template Quilting   Stitch-in-the-ditch Quilting

Free-motion Quilting

In free-motion quilting, the quilt top is guided by hand, allowing you to stitch in any direction without repositioning the quilt. The feed dogs are covered or dropped for this method of quilting. Free-motion quilting is used to quilt designs with sharp turns and intricate curves, and includes template quilting, motif quilting, and stipple quilting.

Template quilting is used to add designs, such as motifs and continuous border designs, to a quilt. Template quilting can be done using plastic stencils or tear-away stencils. For plastic stencils, designs are transferred to the quilt top (page 100). Tear-away stencils allow you to stitch the motifs without marking the quilt top. A design, printed on translucent paper, is pinned to the basted quilt top and torn away after quilting.

Free-motion stitching is generally used for template quilting (page 104); however, some designs, such as cables with gentle curves, may be quilted using machine-guided stitching.

Motif quilting is used to emphasize the printed design of a fabric and is accomplished by outlining the desired motifs. Continue stitching from one motif to the next without stopping. Although free-motion is frequently used for this type of quilting, machine-guided quilting can be used if the motifs consist of subtle curves or if the quilted project is small and can be manipulated easily under the presser foot.

Stipple quilting is used to fill in the background. It can be used to create areas of textured fabric. For uniformity throughout a project, it is best to use loose stipple quilting when combining this method with other types of quilting.

MARKING THE QUILTING DESIGN

With some methods of quilting, it is necessary to mark the quilt before you begin. For channel quilting or template quilting with plastic stencils, mark the design on the quilt top before layering and basting, using a pencil or marking pencil intended for quilting. For stitch-in-the-ditch quilting, motif quilting, and stipple quilting, it is not necessary to mark the quilt top. For template quilting with tear-away stencils, the paper stencil is pinned to the quilt top after the quilt layers are basted together, eliminating the need for any additional marking.

If marking designs with pencils, test the pencils on a fabric scrap before using them on the quilt to be sure that the markings do not rub off too easily, but that they can be thoroughly brushed or erased away with a fabric eraser after quilting. Avoid using water-soluble marking pens, because the entire quilt must be rinsed thoroughly to completely remove the markings.

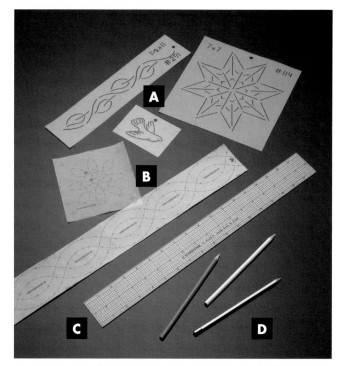

Marking tools and materials are helpful for marking intricate design lines. Marking tools and materials include plastic stencils (A), tear-away stencils (B), clear see-through ruler (C), and marking pencils (D).

How to Mark a Quilting Design

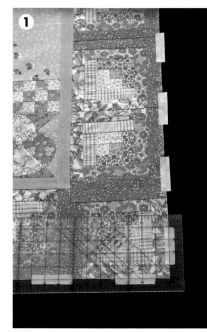

1. (Marking pencil) Press quilt top; place on hard surface, with corners squared and sides parallel. Tape securely, keeping quilt top smooth and taut.

2. Mark the quilting design, using straightedge or template as a guide, beginning at corners of quilt. Mark thin lines, using light pressure. For continuous designs, adjust length of several motifs slightly to achieve correct length.

(Tear-away stencils) Press quilt top. Layer and baste quilt (pages 92 to 97). Cut stencil design and place on quilt; secure with straight pins about 3" to 4" (7.5 to 10 cm) apart.

Quilt large projects by rolling one side of the quilt, allowing it to fit on the sewing machine bed. For even stitching, support the quilt to the left of and behind the machine.

STITCHING & HANDLING

Cotton thread is traditionally used for quilting. Select the thread color according to how much you want the stitching to show. To avoid changing thread colors often, select one thread color that blends with all the fabrics in the quilt top. Or, to emphasize the quilting stitches and to add interest, select a contrasting or metallic thread for the quilting. Thread the machine, and loosen the needle thread tension, if necessary, so the bobbin thread does not show on the right side.

To maintain an even stitch length and to help the quilt feed through the machine evenly, do not allow the quilt to hang over the back or side of the sewing table. Set up the sewing area so the quilt will be supported both to the left of and behind the sewing machine.

Small projects are easily maneuvered as you machine-quilt. Before quilting larger projects, roll up one side of the quilt to allow it to

fit on the sewing machine bed. If the sewing surface is not large enough to hold the remaining width, roll up both sides of the quilt.

Plan the sequence of the quilting before you begin to stitch. Begin by anchoring the quilt horizontally and vertically by stitching in the ditch of a seamline near the center and then stitching along any borders; this prevents the layers from shifting. Next, stitch along any sashing strips or between blocks. Once the quilt has been anchored into sections, quilt the areas within the blocks and borders.

Stitch continuously, with as few starts and stops as possible. Prevent tucks from being stitched in the backing fabric by feeling through the layers of the quilt ahead of the sewing machine needle and continuously easing in any excess fabric before it reaches the needle. If a tuck does occur, release the stitches for 3" (7.5 cm) or more and restitch, easing in excess fabric.

QUILTING TECHNIQUES

For machine-guided quilting, such as stitch-in-the-ditch and channel quilting, it is helpful to stitch with an Even Feed foot, or walking foot, if one is available; this type of presser foot helps to prevent puckering. Position your hands on either side of the presser foot and hold the fabric taut to prevent the layers from shifting. Stitch, using a stitch length of 10 to 12 stitches per inch (2.5 cm), and ease any excess fabric under the foot as you stitch. The presser foot and feed dogs guide the quilt through the machine.

For free-motion quilting, such as template, motif, and stipple quilting, remove the regular presser foot and attach a darning foot. Set the machine for a straight stitch, and use a straight-stitch needle plate; cover the feed dogs, or lower them. It is not necessary to adjust the stitch length setting on the machine, because the stitch length is determined by a combination of the movement of the quilt and the speed of the needle. Use your hands to guide the fabric as you stitch, applying gentle tension. With the presser foot lifter in the lowered position, stitch, moving the fabric with wrist and hand movements. Maintain a steady rhythm and speed as you stitch, to keep the stitch length uniform. When changing your hand positions, stop stitching, with the needle down in the fabric.

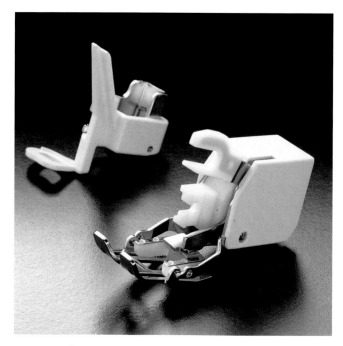

Presser feet recommended for quilting include the darning foot (left) and the Even Feed or walking foot (right). An Even Feed foot is used for machine-guided quilting. A darning foot is used for free-motion quilting.

Quilting techniques, including both free-motion and machine-guided, are used to add dimension to a quilt.

How to Secure the Thread Tails

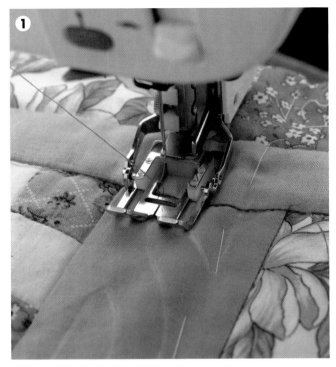

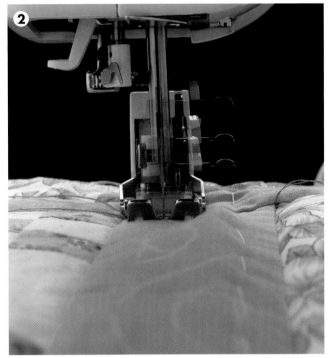

1. Draw up the bobbin thread to the quilt top by turning flywheel by hand and stopping with needle at highest position. Pull on needle thread to bring the bobbin thread up through the fabric.

2. Stitch several short stitches to secure threads at the beginning of stitching line, gradually increasing stitch length for about ½" (1.3 cm), until it is desired length. Reverse procedure at end of stitching.

How to Quilt Using Machine-guided and Free-motion Techniques

Stitch-in-the-ditch quilting. Stitch over the seamline, stitching in the well of the seam.

Channel quilting. Stitch parallel quilting lines, starting with inner marked line and working outward.

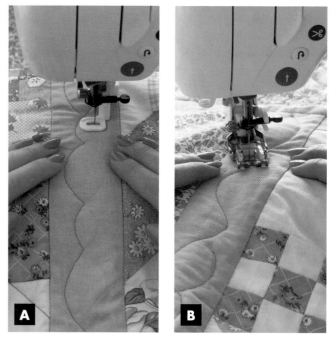

Single-motif template quilting with plastic stencils. Mark design, using marking pencil and plastic stencil (page 100). Stitch as much of design as possible in long, continuous lines, without stopping.

Continuous-motif template quilting with plastic stencils. Mark design, using marking pencil and stencil (page 100). Stitch motifs along one side to points where motifs connect (A). Or stitch one side of first motif, then opposite side of second motif, and repeat (B). Return to starting point; stitch motifs on opposite side.

Template quilting with tear-away stencils. Stitch either single motif or continuous motif, following the directional arrows on paper stencil. Tear away the paper stencil.

Stipple quilting. Stitch random, curving lines, beginning and ending at an edge and covering background evenly. Work in small sections; keep spaces between quilting lines close. Do not cross over lines.

Motif quilting. Determine longest continuous stitching line possible around desired motif. Stitch around motif without stopping; continue to next motif. Stitch any additional design lines as necessary.

How to Grid-quilt on the Diagonal

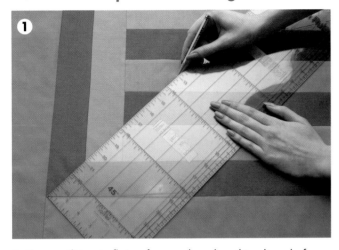

1. Tape quilt top to flat surface and mark quilting lines before basting quilt. Mark first line at an exact 45° angle to edge of design, starting at one corner; continue line to edge of design on opposite side.

2. Mark a line from end of previous line to opposite edge, keeping marked lines at 90° angles to each other and 45° angle to edge of design; continue marking lines in this manner until a line ends at a corner.

3. Mark a line, starting from another corner, if lines do not yet complete the grid design; continue marking lines to form a grid.

4. Mark additional quilting lines halfway between grid marks and parallel to previous lines, if smaller grid is desired.

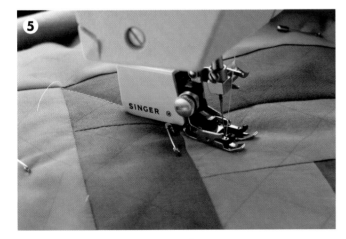

5. Place quilt layers together and baste (pages 92 to 97). Stitch on marked lines, starting in one corner.

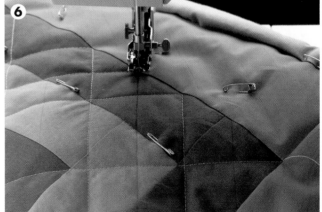

6. Stitch lines in same sequence as marked; Turn fabric 90° at edge of design, pivoting with needle down.

How to Prepare a Large Quilt for Machine Quilting

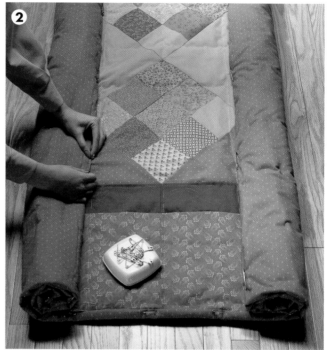

1. Lay the quilt flat, right side up. For quilts with polyester batting, roll one side to within 2" or 3" (5 or 7.5 cm) of center basting line. If necessary, secure roll with larger safety pins or plastic headband. For quilts with cotton batting, loosely fold one side into accordion folds; it will stay without pins.

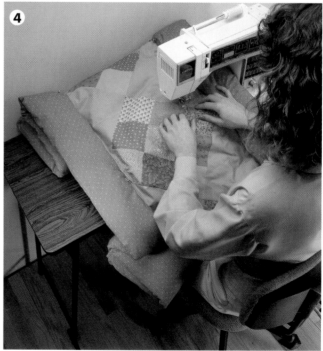

2. Roll or fold other side, as in step 1, if the sewing surface is not large enough to hold remaining width of quilt flat.

3. Fold quilt loosely along length, accordion-style, into lap-size bundle. Place bundle on your lap.

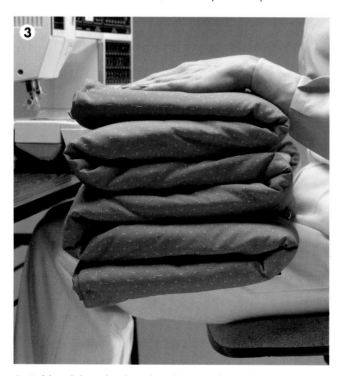

4. Pull quilt up from lap, section by section, so it is level with needle as you stitch. Do not allow quilt to hang over back or side of sewing table.

MACHINE-TYING A QUILT

When using a high-loft batting, machine-tie the quilt to preserve the loft. A quilt can be machine-tied by using a zigzag or decorative stitch, or by attaching ribbons or yarns.

Mark the placement of the ties on the quilt top before basting it to the batting and backing. Stagger the rows of ties for greater interest and strength. Space the ties approximately 5" (12.5 cm) apart.

Three Ways to Tie a Quilt by Machine

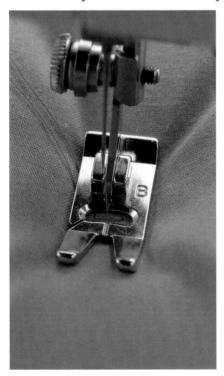

Zigzag stitch. Adjust stitch length and width to 0. Holding threads behind needle, stitch several times through all layers. Adjust stitch width to a wide setting; stitch 8 to 10 times. Return stitch width to 0; stitch several times. Clip threads.

Decorative stitch. Use a decorative stitch instead of a zigzag stitch to secure quilt layers; adjust stitch length and width for an attractive design. Stitch in place at beginning and end of decorative stitch.

Ribbon or yarn. Cut one 3" to 6" (7.5 to 15 cm) length of ribbon for each tie. Tie into bow. Center bow over placement mark; stitch bow in place, using zigzag stitch, left.

BINDING A QUILT

There are several methods for finishing the edges of a quilt. For mock binding, fold the backing fabric over the raw edges to the quilt top. For double binding with lapped corners, attach a separate strip of binding fabric to each edge and overlap the binding at the corners. Double binding can also be applied in one continuous strip, forming miters at each corner.

Mock binding is an easy way to finish the edges of a quilt and makes use of the excess backing fabric needed during basting and quilting. Choose a backing fabric that coordinates with the quilt top. Double binding is cut on the straight of grain and has two layers of fabric to provide a durable edge. The binding can either match or complement the quilt top. For all three methods, the finished binding is ½" (1.3 cm) wide.

Double binding with mitered corners.

Mock binding (top) and double binding with lapped corners (bottom).

How to Bind a Quilt with Mock Binding

1. Machine-baste through all layers of the quilt, ⅛" (3 mm) from raw edges of quilt top.

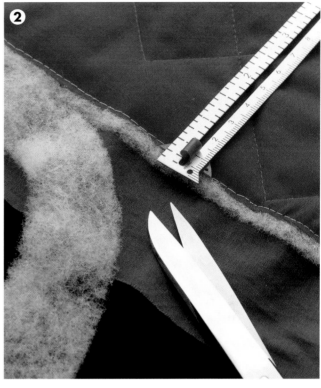

2. Trim batting only, ¼" (6 mm) from edge of quilt top, ⅜" (1 cm) from basting stitches.

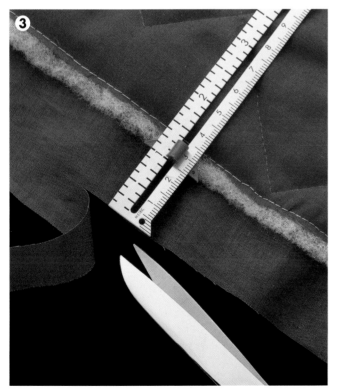

3. Trim backing 1" (2.5 cm) from cut edge of batting.

4. Fold backing diagonally at corner of batting; press foldline.

(continued)

5. Fold backing so edge of backing meets edge of batting; press.

6. Fold backing over edge of batting and quilt top, covering stitching line; pin.

7. Cut out square of excess fabric at each corner. Pin corners.

8. Edgestitch along fold to secure. Remove basting stitches on quilt back. Slipstitch corners, if desired.

How to Bind a Quilt with Double Lapped Binding

1. Fold fabric in half on lengthwise grainline (page 39). Cut strips 3" (7.5 cm) on crosswise grainline.

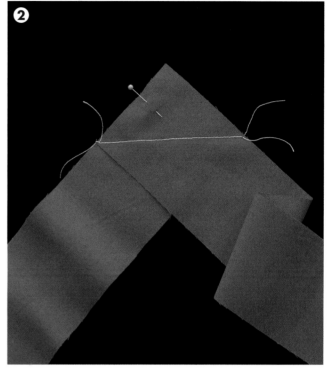

2. Pin strips, right sides together, at right angles; strips will form a "V." Stitch diagonally across strips.

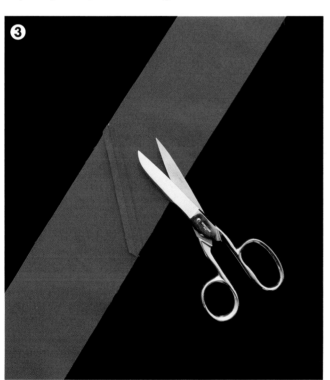

3. Trim the seam allowances to ¼" (6 mm). Press seam open. Trim points even with edges.

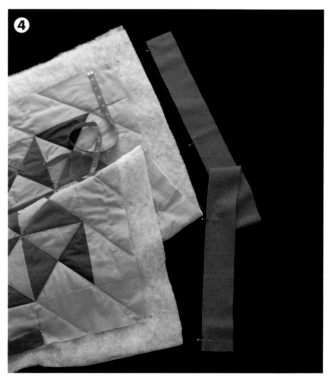

4. Measure one side of quilt; cut binding this length plus 2" (5 cm). Mark binding 1" (2.5 cm) in from each end; divide section between pins in quarters; pin-mark. Divide sides of quilt in quarters; pin-mark. (continued)

5. Fold binding in half lengthwise, wrong sides together. Place binding on quilt top, matching raw edges and pin-marks; binding will extend 1" (2.5 cm) beyond quilt top at each end.

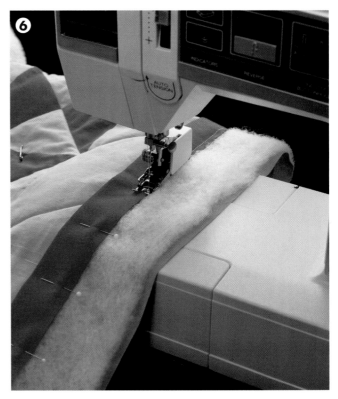

6. Stitch binding to quilt ¼" (6 mm) from raw edges of binding.

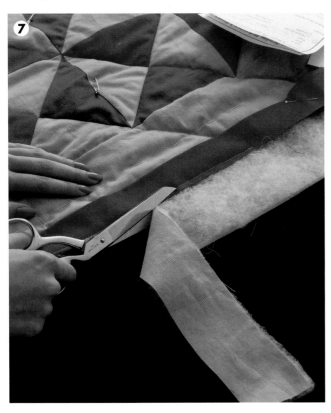

7. Cut excess batting and backing to ½" (1.3 cm) from stitching line.

8. Wrap binding around edge of quilt, covering stitching line on back of quilt; pin.

9. Stitch in the ditch on the right side of quilt, catching binding on back of quilt.

10. Repeat steps 4 to 9 for opposite side of quilt. Trim ends of binding even with edges of quilt top.

11. Repeat steps 4 to 7 for remaining two sides. Trim ends of binding to extend ½" (1.3 cm) beyond finished edges of quilt.

12. Fold binding down along the stitching line. Fold ½" (1.3 cm) end of binding over finished edge; press in place. Wrap binding around edge and stitch in the ditch as in steps 8 and 9. Slipstitch end by hand.

How to Bind a Quilt with Double Mitered Binding

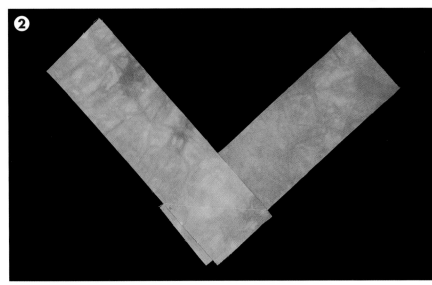

1. Trim the batting and backing even with the edges of the quilt top. Measure perimeter of quilt; add 12" (30.5 cm). Divide the measurement by 40" (101.5 cm) to calculate the number of strips needed. Cut 2¼" (5.7 cm) wide strips from selvage to selvage (crosswise grain).

2. Pin strips, right sides together, at right angles; strips will form a "V." Stitch diagonally across strips.

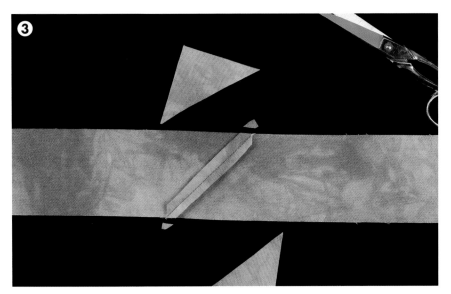

3. Trim seam allowances to ¼" (6 mm). Press seam open. Trim points even edges.

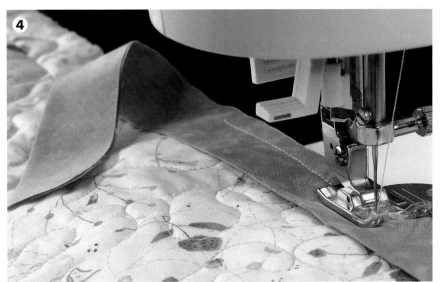

4. Fold binding in half lengthwise, wrong sides together; press. Lay binding along the edge of the quilt top. Leave an 8" tail, stitch the binding in place with about ¼" (6 mm) seam allowance.

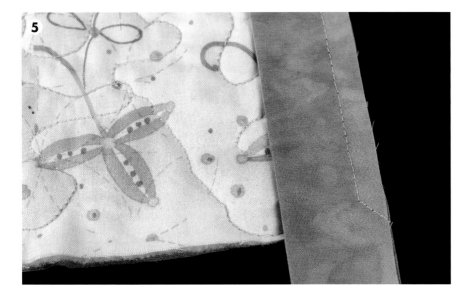

5. Stop sewing ¼" (6 mm) from the corner of the quilt. With needle in down position, pivot quit top and stitch diagonally to the corner of the quilt. Clip the thread.

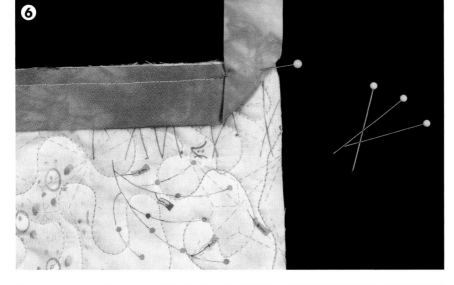

6. Fold the binding up and away from the quilt top.

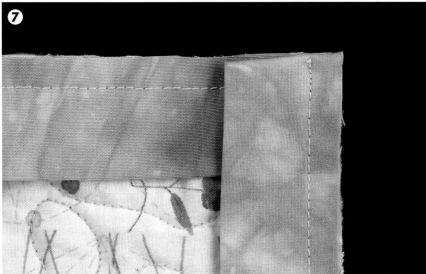

7. Fold the binding back down onto itself; keeping the fold aligned with the edge of the quilt top. Begin stitching from the upper fold, and continue to the next corner.

8. Repeat steps 5 to 7 for the remaining edges.

(continued)

9. Stop sewing 8" (20.3 cm) from the starting point; remove the quilt from the sewing machine and lay quilt on flat surface. Fold the two tail ends back on themselves so they meet in the middle of the unsewn edge. Clip ⅛" (3 mm) notches into bindings at the meeting point.

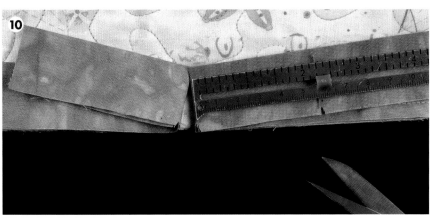

10. On the end tail, measure 2¼" (5.7 cm) from notch and cut a second set of notches.

11. Position the quilt to the left, and binding and quilt edge on the right. With your left hand, open the end tail so the right side is facing you. With your right hand, open the start tail with wrong side facing you. Lay the start tail on top of the end tail at a diagonal; right sides together; notches matching on raw edges of binding.

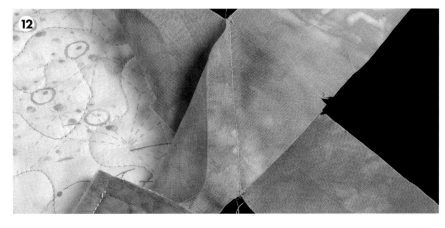

12. Pin in place; mark diagonal line. Sew on marked edge. Finger press the seam open; check for accuracy before trimming seam to ¼" (6 mm).

13. Finish stitching the binding to the quilt top.

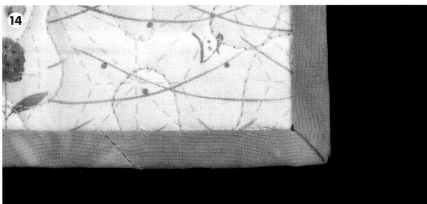

14. Fold the binding over the raw edges to the back. Blindstich binding in place, with the folded edge covering the line of machine stitching. A miter will form at each corner. Blindstich the mitered corner in place.

Quilt Care

Whether you value your quilt as a family heirloom or a work of art, you will want to take care of it so that it retains its beauty for a long time. Even quilts that are handled and used daily will last longer if you clean and store them with care.

CLEANING QUILTS

The care of a quilt depends on how it is used. If you are making a quilt to hang on the wall, it may only need to be vacuumed or shaken out occasionally. If you are making a quilt to be used on the bed, it will be laundered periodically. The less a quilt is handled, the longer it will last. Fabrics are easily damaged by abrasion and stress.

Dust and dirt abrade the fibers and shorten the life of a quilt. Quilts may be cleaned by vacuuming them, or by laundering them by machine or by hand. Dry cleaning is not recommended for washable fabrics, especially cottons; the chemicals used in dry cleaning may react with some dyes, resulting in color changes.

Vacuuming keeps quilts clean and minimizes the need to wash them. It is recommended that you lay the quilt on a flat, padded surface and vacuum it gently, using an upholstery brush and low suction. To protect the quilt from abrasion, you may place a fiberglass screen over the quilt and vacuum it through the screen.

Wash and dry quilts only when absolutely necessary, because washing and drying place stress on the fabric, particularly when done by machine. Before washing a quilt, test all dark and vivid fabrics for colorfastness (page 27).

Hand washing is gentler on the fabric, but quilts made of washable fabrics and battings may be washed and dried by machine. Whether you wash a quilt by hand or by machine, use mild soap, without perfumes and other additives, such as dishwashing soap. Avoid soaps and detergents recommended for washing fine woolens; they may yellow cotton fabrics.

Thoroughly dissolve the soap and fill the machine or tub with lukewarm water before adding the quilt. Be sure there is enough water to cover the quilt, to help disperse any excess dye and aid in cleaning and rinsing. It is important to rinse all the soap out of the fabric; soap residue can coat the fibers, attracting dirt and discoloring the fabric.

Use extra care in handling a quilt while it is wet. Water adds weight, so, rather than pick up a wet quilt by a corner or edge, support the entire quilt in your arms or in a towel. Lay the quilt flat to air-dry instead of hanging it. Quilts may also be dried by machine. Machine drying fluffs the batting, but air drying is less abrasive to the fabric.

TIPS FOR WASHING AND DRYING QUILTS

Machine Washing and Drying

- Use large washing machine and high water level.

- Wash on gentle or delicate cycle.

- Remove quilt from washing machine immediately after washing, or wet fabrics may bleed.

- Dry on cool to warm setting. Place dry terrycloth towel in dryer with quilt to shorten drying time.

- Remove quilt from dryer before it is completely dry; spread flat on clean cloth, smoothing out wrinkles, to finish drying. Do not press.

Hand Washing and Drying

- Use large tub, to keep quilt as flat as possible; for large quilts, use bathtub.

- Place quilt flat in tub, or in loose folds, as necessary.

- Wash gently by hand, using a kneading motion; do not bunch, swirl, or twist.

- Drain water, and refill tub with clear water; do not lift quilt. Repeat process until soap is rinsed out completely.

- Press out remaining water, gently squeezing quilt against tub, working toward the drain. Blot with clean towels or mattress pad to remove excess water.

- Lay quilt flat on clean sheets or mattress pad to dry. If drying quilt outdoors, avoid direct sunlight and cover quilt with clean sheet to protect it. If drying quilt indoors, use a fan to shorten drying time.

STORING QUILTS

The best way to store a quilt is to keep it flat on a bed. Quilts usually suffer less damage from use than from storage. The most common forms of damage are fading, fabric deterioration, staining, and permanent creasing.

Fading of fabrics is caused primarily by exposure to light. Light also damages fabric over a period of time, making it brittle and weak.

Mold and mildew can cause staining, so quilts should be stored at a humidity of 45 to 50 percent. Staining and deterioration can also occur when quilts come in contact with storage materials such as paper and wood. As these materials age, they release chemicals that destroy fabrics. Acid-free papers and boxes are available for storing quilts. Permanent creases are cause by folding and by pressure. When a quilt is folded for storage, the fibers along the folded edge are weakened and may break; the sharper the fold, the greater the damage. Putting weight on top of folded quilts increases the damage. Therefore, if you stack quilts in storage, refold and rotate the order occasionally.

Pad folds of quilt with acid-free tissue paper or with washed, unbleached cotton fabric, to prevent sharp creases. Refold quilts every few months, changing the placement of fold lines.

TIPS FOR STORING QUILTS

- Clean quilts thoroughly (page 117) before storing.

- Store quilts in washed, unbleached muslin or cotton pillowcases or sheets. Acid-free tubes, tissue paper, or boxes may also be used; these may be obtained from archival storage mail-order sources or from some quilt stores.

- Seal wood that will come in contact with quilts, using paint or polyurethane varnish.

- Avoid exposing quilts to direct sunlight, to keep fabrics from fading and becoming brittle.

- Avoid storing quilts in places where the humidity is high or where the temperature fluctuates greatly, such as attics or basements. Dry quilts thoroughly if they have become damp.

- Do not store quilts in plastic bags.

- Keep quilts away from direct heat sources, such as radiators, heat registers, or sunlight.

Personalized Quilts

A quilt can be personalized in many ways. You can design a quilt around a subject of personal interest by making a commemorative, friendship, theme, or signature quilt. A memory quilt can be made for someone by using fabric from articles of clothing worn by that person from birth to adulthood. Photos can be transferred to fabric and used for pieces of the quilt. Or you can personalize a quilt by simply signing and dating it.

Signing and dating a quilt can be done during the piecing of the quilt by embroidering or machine-stitching the name and date in the corner block, or during the quilting by using freehand quilting. You can use a preprinted custom label or make your own label from fabric, using stitching or a permanent fine-line pen. The label can be sewn into the binding at a corner on the back of the quilt and then hand-stitched on the two remaining sides, or it can be attached completely by hand.

There are several products on the market that allow you to transfer photos to fabric using your home scanner and computer. Be sure to choose a product that is compatible with your computer and printer, and follow the manufacturer's directions. Print shops also offer this service. Take care in sizing the photos so they will fit the dimensions of your quilt block.

Theme quilts are designed around a central theme or idea, such as the outdoor theme, shown above, with pine trees, spider webs, and loons quilted into the blocks.

Signature quilts contain quilt blocks autographed by others, such as family members or the members of a church or community group.

Old photos transferred to fabric are showcased at the center of each star block in this holiday memories quilt.

Friendship quilts have blocks designed and sewn by friends or family members. They are usually made to celebrate an occasion such as a wedding, an anniversary, or the birth of a child.

A baby quilt becomes a cherished memento when pieces are signed by family members.

BLOCK-PIECED QUILTS

Block piecing is by far the most popular way to make a quilt. The history of block-pieced quilts is a fascinating story of pioneer women who used small pieces of whatever fabrics they had to make quilts for their families. Original designs were shared for generations before patterns were ever published in magazines. Today there are hundreds of recognized quilt blocks.

Pine Trees

The Pine Trees design is a popular motif for wall hangings. The blocks can be arranged in several ways for a variety of looks.

The grid-piecing method (page 126) is used to piece the triangle-squares in the Pine Trees quilt block, allowing you to cut and piece them in one easy operation; a triangle-square is two triangles stitched together on their longest sides to form a square. This grid-piecing method may be used for any quilt that has several triangle-squares.

For easier construction, the tree trunk and base at the corner of the quilt block is made from rectangles, then trimmed to the correct size after piecing.

The instructions that follow are for a wall hanging made from four 12" (30.5 cm) quilt blocks. The finished quilt measures about 24" (61 cm) square.

Block Arrangements

Sawtooth effect is created by arranging the blocks with the tops of the trees toward the center of the quilt.

Starburst effect is created by arranging the blocks with the trunks of the trees toward the center of the quilt.

YOU WILL NEED

- ½ yd. (0.5 m) fabric for the top of the tree.
- ½ yd. (0.5 m) fabric for the background.
- ¼ yd. (0.25 m) fabric for the tree trunk.
- ¾ yd. (0.7 m) fabric for the backing.
- ⅜ yd. (0.35 m) fabric for the binding.
- Batting, about 28" (71 cm) square.

CUTTING DIRECTIONS ✂

- Cut one 18" (46 cm) square from background fabric and one from tree fabric to be used for grid-pieced triangle-squares (A).

- Cut two 8⅞" (22.8 cm) squares from tree fabrics; cut squares diagonally into triangles (B).

- Cut eight 2½" (6.5 cm) squares (C) and eight 4" x 5½" (10 x 14 cm) rectangles (D) from background fabric.

- Cut four 2" x 4" (5 x 10 cm) rectangles (E) and four 3" x 5" (7.5 x 12.5 cm) rectangles (F) from trunk fabric.

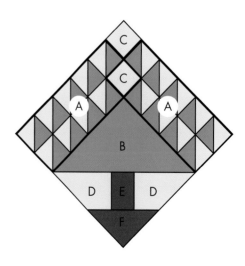

How to Make Triangle-squares Using the Grid-piecing Method

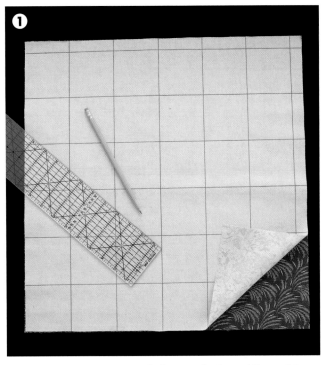

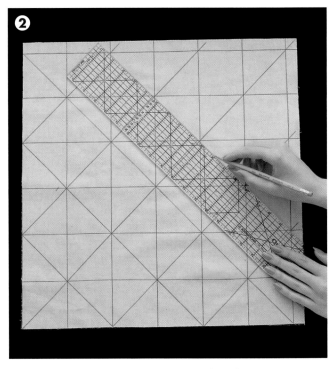

1. Cut one square or rectangle from each of two different fabrics. Draw grid of squares on wrong side of lighter-colored fabric, making the grid squares ⅞" (2.2 cm) larger than finished triangle-square; each square of grid makes two triangle-squares.

2. Draw diagonal lines through the grid as shown. Draw diagonal lines through grid in opposite direction as shown; there will be one diagonal line through each square.

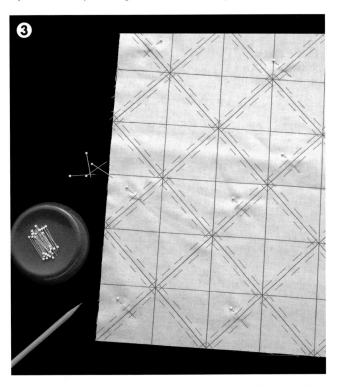

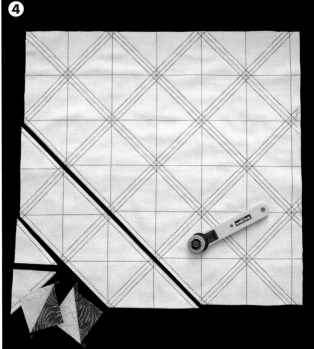

3. Mark dotted stitching lines ¼" (6 mm) from both sides of all diagonal lines. Pin the fabric layers, right sides together.

4. Stitch on all dotted lines. Cut on all solid lines to make triangle-squares. Press seam allowances toward darker fabric. Trim points extending beyond edges of triangle-squares.

How to Make a Pine Trees Wall Hanging

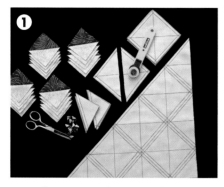

1. Make 72 triangle-squares from 18" (46 cm) squares of fabric, following steps 1 to 4, above; in step 1, draw a grid of 2⅞" (7.2 cm) squares, six across and six down.

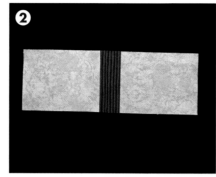

2. Stitch short sides of two 4" x 5½" (10 x 14 cm) rectangles cut from background fabric to long sides of 2" x 4" (5 x 10 cm) rectangle cut for tree trunk, with right sides together and raw edges even.

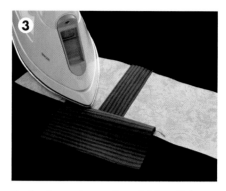

3. Stitch one long edge of 3" x 5" (7.5 x 12.5 cm) rectangle for tree base to one long edge of pieced rectangles, right sides together; match centers of rectangles. Press seam allowances toward tree base.

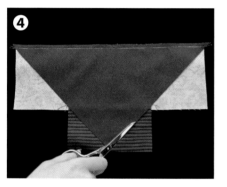

4. Stitch the large triangle cut from tree fabric to the opposite edge of the trunk unit, with right sides together and raw edges even. Trim the excess background and trunk fabrics to match the triangle. Press seam allowances toward darker fabric.

5. Stitch two rows of four triangle-squares as shown. Stitch rows together; attach to large triangle as shown.

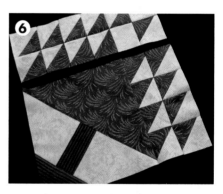

6. Stitch two rows of triangle-squares and two background squares as shown. Stitch rows together; attach to opposite side of triangle, positioning background squares at top of tree.

7. Repeat steps 2 to 6 to make three more blocks. Arrange blocks as desired. Stitch blocks together to form two rows; stitch the rows together. Press quilt top.

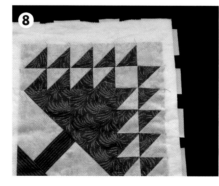

8. Cut backing 28" (71 cm) square; press. Layer and baste quilt top, batting, and backing (pages 92 to 97).

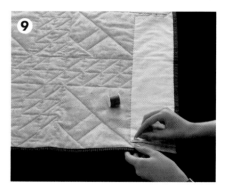

9. Quilt (pages 102 to 107). Cut and apply binding (pages 111 to 116); cut width of binding is 2½" (6.5 cm). Attach fabric sleeve (page 171); to hang quilt on point, attach second sleeve to adjacent side.

MORE PINE TREES DESIGNS

Corner triangles may be added to the sides of each tree in a Pine Trees quilt, as shown below, setting the trees vertically and making 17" (43 cm) quilt blocks. To cut the triangles for the corners, cut 9⅜" (24 cm) squares from four fabrics in half diagonally; one triangle of each color is used for each block.

The quilt below has 16 blocks, four across and four down. With a 4" (10 cm) border, the finished quilt measures about 76" (193 cm) square, a size suitable for a bed quilt.

The Pine Trees design is fun to make in seasonal colors. Make one with a Christmas theme, or change the colors for a spring, summer, fall, or winter quilt. Combine the seasonal blocks for a four-season quilt that can be displayed year-round.

Even though this design is called Pine Trees, it need not resemble trees at all. With the use of unexpected colors and a block arrangement that radiates out from the center, a four-block quilt can create a colorful starburst effect.

Starburst effect is created by the arrangement of the blocks and by using nontraditional colors. For the 16 triangle-squares of the inner rows, mark the 2⅞" (7.2 cm) grid, four across and four down, on 12" (30.5 cm) square of fabric. For the 20 triangle-squares of the outer rows, mark the 2⅞" (7.2 cm) grid, five across and four down, on 15" x 12" (38 x 30.5 cm) rectangle of fatbric.

Seasonal theme (left) can be created by using different fabrics for each block. Sashing (pages 66 to 69) has been added to set the blocks apart, and a lapped border (page 84) frames the quilt. To make the 18 triangle-squares necessary for each block, use the grid-piecing method on page 126, marking the 2⅞" (7.2 cm) grid, three across and three down, on 9" (23 cm) square of fabric.

Holiday fabrics can make a festive wall hanging for the Christmas season. A lapped border (page 84) frames the quilt. The triangle-squares are grid-pieced as for the quilt with a starburst effect, above.

Bow Ties

Bow Ties is a versatile quilt design that lends itself to many block arrangements. The Bow Ties design is shown here in four different arrangements. In the traditional pattern (below), the blocks are arranged in rows, with each bow tie facing in the same direction. As shown in the quilts (opposite), the blocks may also be turned alternately for a zigzag pattern, arranged in units of four blocks for an octagonal pattern, or arranged in a staggered pattern.

Traditionally, templates were used to make a Bow Ties quilt. But this design can now be made using a simplified method that enables quick cutting and chainstitching. The easy method for constructing a single Bow Ties block is on page 132. To make enough blocks for an entire quilt, construct them quickly and efficiently, using chainstitching (page 40).

The instructions that follow are for a wall hanging made from sixty-four 4" (10 cm) quilt blocks. The finished quilt measures about 37" (94 cm) square.

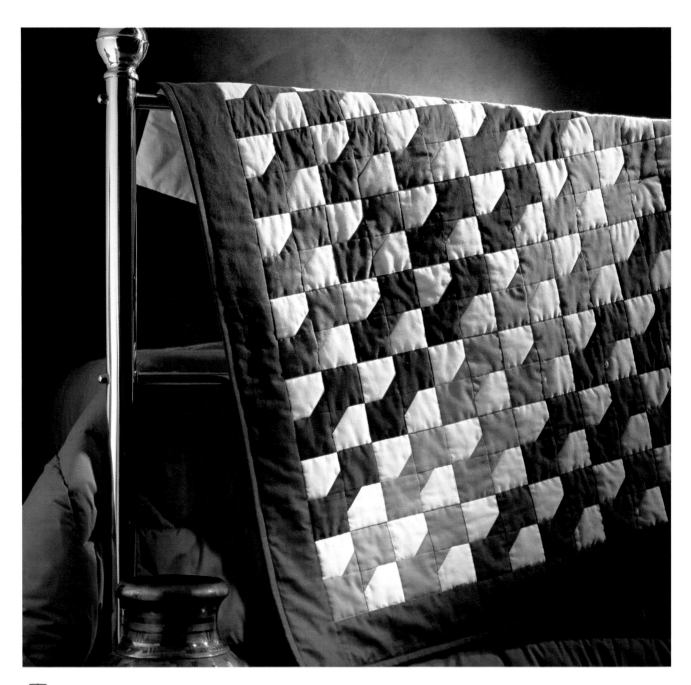

Block Arrangements

Octagonal pattern is created by arranging the quilt blocks in units of four.

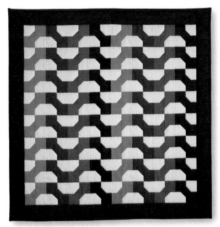

Zigzag pattern has the quilt blocks turned in alternate directions.

Staggered pattern of quilt blocks forms diagonal rows.

YOU WILL NEED

- ⅜ yd. (0.35 m) fabric in each of four colors for bow ties.
- ¾ yd. (0.7 m) fabric for background.
- ¾ yd. (0.7 m) fabric for border and binding.
- 1¼ yd. (1.15 m) fabric for backing.
- Batting, about 41" (104 cm) square.

CUTTING DIRECTIONS ✂

- Each block requires two 2½" (6.5 cm) squares (A) from background fabric and two 2½" (6.5 cm) squares (B) from bow-tie fabric, cut from 2½" (6.5 cm) fabric strips.

- Each block also requires two 1½" (3.8 cm) squares from bow-tie fabric, which will be pieced and trimmed to make triangles (C); cut the 1½" (3.8 cm) squares from 1½" (3.8 cm) fabric strips.

- The Bow Ties project requires 16 blocks of each bow-tie color. Cut eight 2½" (6.5 cm) strips from background fabric, cutting each strip into squares to make 128 background squares.

- Cut two 2½" (6.5 cm) strips from each of four bow-tie fabrics, cutting each strip into squares to make 32 squares from each fabric.

- Cut two 1½" (3.8 cm) strips from each bow-tie fabric, cutting each strip to make 32 squares from each fabric.

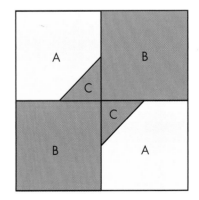

How to Make a Bow Ties Quilt Block

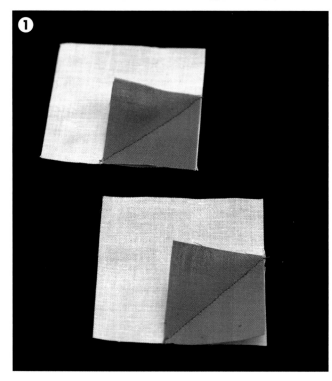

1. Place 1½" (3.8 cm) square in one corner of a background square, with right sides together and raw edges even. Stitch diagonally from corner to corner as shown. Repeat for a second pieced square.

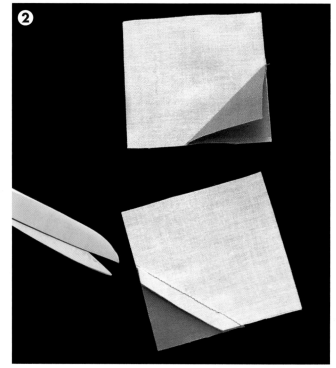

2. Press small square in half along stitched line, matching outer edges to large square. Trim fabric at stitched corner, leaving ¼" (6 mm) seam allowance. Repeat for second pieced square.

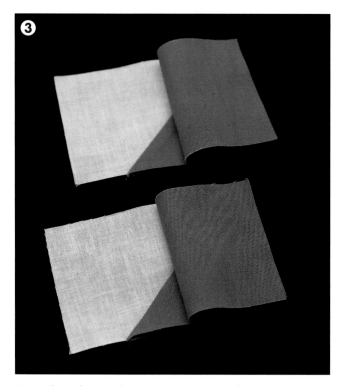

3. Stitch each pieced square to one square from bow-tie fabric, as shown, to make two half-block units.

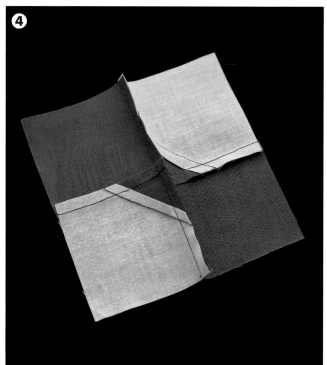

4. Stitch two units together to form a bow tie, finger-pressing center seam allowances in opposite directions.

How to Make a Bow Ties Quilt

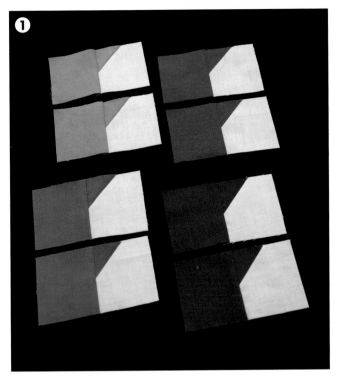

1. Piece blocks for each color, following steps 1 to 4, opposite; for staggered pattern (page 131), construct two half-block units of each color, following steps 1 to 3, opposite.

2. Arrange blocks, eight across and eight down, as shown in the quilts on pages 130 and 131. For staggered pattern, use half-block units to complete design.

3. Stitch the blocks into rows; stitch rows together, finger-pressing seam allowances in opposite directions. Press quilt top. Cut and attach border strips (pages 83 to 87); cut width of border strips is 3" (7.5 cm).

4. Cut backing 4" (10 cm) larger than quilt top; press. Layer and baste the quilt top, batting and backing (pages 92 to 97).

5. Quilt (pages 102 to 107). Cut and apply binding (pages 111 to 116); cut width of binding is 2½" (6.5 cm). For wall hanging, attach fabric sleeve (page 171).

MORE BOW TIES DESIGNS

The fabric and color selection can dramatically change the look of a Bow Ties quilt. Fabrics that resemble those used in men's neckties give an authentic look. Colors in the Amish tradition have a more striking effect, and subtle variations of graduated colors result in a more subdued quilt. Add variety to a Bow Ties quilt by choosing fabric scraps with different colors and textures for each block.

Many cotton prints resembling necktie fabrics give the Bow Ties quilt a traditional menswear look. An old-fashioned plaid fabric is used for the background of the quilt.

Gradations of warm colors are used to achieve a soft look. Make a sketch of the quilt to determine how many blocks of each color you will need.

Amish colors used in the traditional pattern create a wall hanging with heirloom appeal. In the Amish tradition of intentionally making the quilt imperfect, one quilt block has been turned in the opposite direction, adding an interesting design element.

Scraps can be used to create an eclectic look, with muslin used for the background squares. The octagonal pattern is interrupted with narrow sashing strips.

Houses

Pieced picture quilts depicting houses were first developed in the 1800s. They remain popular today because of the versatility of the design. This version of a traditional house block is also quick and easy to cut and piece.

By varying the use of color, you can create a nighttime effect, as shown opposite, using dark fabrics for the houses and sky, and yellow to illuminate the windows and doors. Or create a

daytime effect, using bright colors for the houses and black for the windows and doors, as shown in the quilt on page 141.

The instructions that follow are for a wall hanging made from nine 8" (20.5 cm) quilt blocks. Sashing with interrupted corners frames the blocks and unifies the overall design. The finished quilt with a single lapped border measures about 36" (91.5 cm) square.

YOU WILL NEED

- ⅜ yd. (0.35 m) fabric in each of three colors for houses and gables.
- ⅛ yd. (0.15 m) fabric for doors and windows.
- ⅛ yd. (0.15 m) fabric for roofs.
- ⅛ yd. (0.15 m) fabric or scraps in each color for chimneys, sky, and ground.
- ⅓ yd. (0.32 m) fabric for 1½" (3.8 cm) sashing.
- ½ yd. (0.5 m) fabric for 3" (7.5 cm) border.
- ⅓ yd. (0.32 m) fabric for binding.
- 1⅛ yd. (1.05 m) fabric for backing.
- Batting, about 40" (102 cm) square.

CUTTING DIRECTIONS ✂

- Cut the correct number of pieces for each of nine quilt blocks, using the dimensions in the chart below. From each of the three house fabrics, cut enough house and gable pieces for three quilt blocks, making enough for a total of nine blocks.

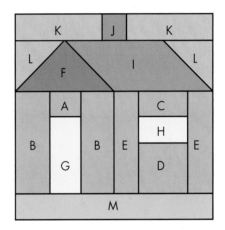

Pieces to Cut for Each Quilt Block

	Pieces	Number and Size
House	A	One 1½" x 1¾" (3.8 x 4.5 cm) rectangle.
	B	Two 1⅞" x 4½" (4.7 x 11.5 cm) rectangle.
	C	One 1½" x 2½" (3.8 x 6.5 cm) rectangle.
	D	One 2½" (6.5 cm) square.
	E	Two 1½" x 4½" (3.8 x 11.5 cm) rectangles.
Gable	F	One 5¼" (13.2 cm) square, cut diagonally in both directions; use one triangle for each quilt block.
Door	G	One 1¾" x 3½" (4.5 x 9 cm) rectangle.
Window	H	One 1½" x 2½" (3.8 x 6.5 cm) rectangle.
Roof	I	One parallelogram (page 56), cut from 2½" (6.5 cm) strip.
Chimney	J	One 1½" (3.8 cm) square.
Sky	K	Two 1½" x 4" (3.8 x 10 cm) rectangles.
	L	One 2⅞" (7.2 cm) square, cut in half diagonally for two triangles.
Ground	M	One 1½" x 8½" (3.8 x 21.8 cm) rectangle.

How to Make a Houses Quilt

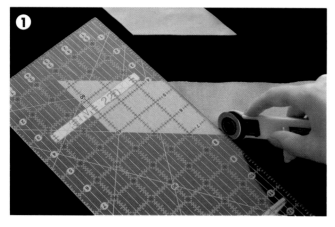

1. Cut 45° angle on one end of fabric strip for roof. Place 3¼" (8.2 cm) mark on ruler along angle-cut; cut strip to make parallelogram. Repeat for eight more roof pieces.

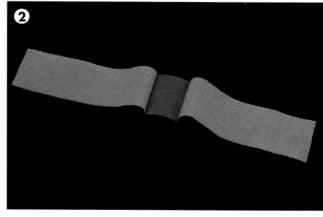

2. Stitch fabric strips for the sky to each side of the chimney piece.

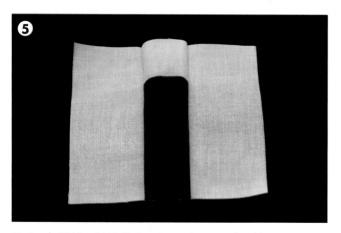

3. Stitch gable piece to roof piece as shown; use a gable color that will contrast with the house color. Finger-press seam allowance toward roof.

4. Stitch long edge of one sky triangle to one side of roof; stitch long edge of second sky triangle to gable. Finger-press seam allowances toward sky. Trim points extending beyond edges of unit.

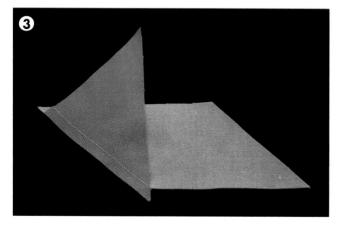

5. Stitch 1½" x 1¾" (3.8 x 4.5 cm) rectangle of house fabric to top of door. Stitch one 1⅞" x 4½" (4.7 x 11.5 cm) rectangle of house fabric to each side of pieced door section as shown.

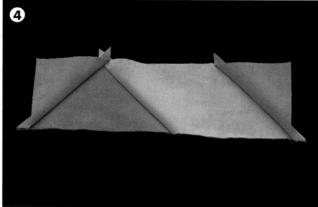

6. Stitch 1½" x 2½" (3.8 x 6.5 cm) rectangle of house fabric to the top of the window; stitch 2½" (6.5 cm) square to the bottom of the window. Stitch one 1½" x 4½" (3.8 x 11.5 cm) rectangle to each side of pieced window section.

7. Stitch pieced door section and pieced window section together. Stitch pieced strips and ground strip together. Press quilt block.

8. Repeat steps 2 to 7 for remaining quilt blocks. Arrange blocks in rows of three.

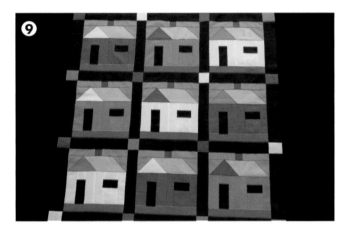

9. Cut sashing strips with connecting squares (page 69) and attach to the quilt blocks; you will need 24 sashing pieces with a cut width of 2" (5 cm) and sixteen 2" (5 cm) connecting squares.

10. Cut and attach border strips (pages 83 to 87); cut width of border strips is 3½" (9 cm).

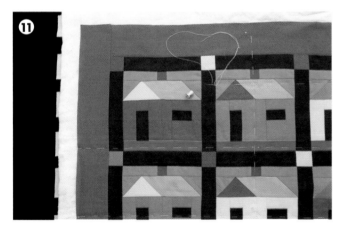

11. Cut 40" (102 cm) square of backing fabric. Layer and baste quilt top, batting, and backing (pages 92 to 97).

12. Quilt, using stitch-in-the-ditch method (page 103) around blocks, sashing, and borders; quilt houses as desired. Cut and apply binding (pages 111 to 116); cut width of binding is 2" (5 cm). For wall hanging, attach fabric sleeve (page 171). (Contrasting thread was used to show detail.)

MORE HOUSES DESIGNS

Houses designs allow you to have fun experimenting with colors and textures. Select colors to suggest a mood or time of day. Or choose colors or fabrics to depict a particular type of house.

Bright crayon colors create a cheerful coverlet for a child's room. The twin-size bed quilt shown above consists of 48 quilt blocks, six blocks across and eight down. The finished size of the quilt including a 3½" (9 cm) border, is about 65½" x 85½" (166.8 x 217.3 cm).

Houses quilt blocks can be embellished with appliqués, embroidery, or decorative buttons to add landscaping or architectural details.

Daytime effect is created by using sunny colors for the houses and black for the doors and windows.

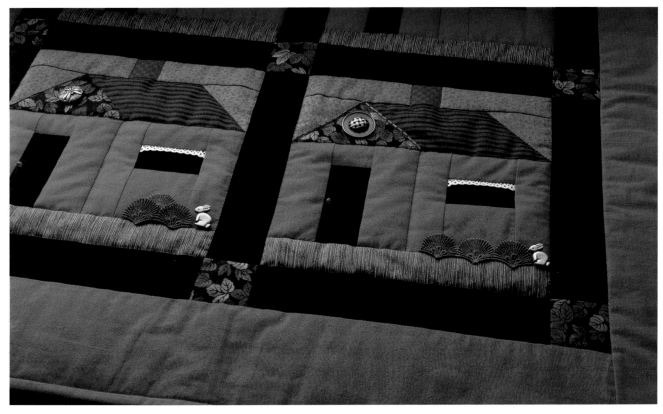

Embellished houses are decorated with lace, trims, beads, and buttons for a whimsical effect.

Ocean Waves

The Ocean Waves design is a traditional quilt design with rows of triangles that create a gentle flowing motion. Planning the color scheme for an Ocean Waves quilt can look difficult, but is actually simple to do.

The waves portion of an Ocean Waves block is made from ten triangle-squares plus four additional small triangles. Two large triangles in opposite corners complete the block. The grid-piecing method (page 126) is used to construct the triangle-squares. If you are unfamiliar with this type of construction, you may want to make the smaller Pine Trees project (page 124) before making the more challenging Ocean Waves project. The large

triangles at the corners form the squares in the design when the blocks are stitched together.

For the quilt shown opposite, choose one dark-colored solid fabric, which will be used for one half of each triangle-square; repeating one fabric in each triangle-square gives the quilt a unified color scheme. Choose eight light-colored solid fabrics, which will be used for the remaining half of the triangle-squares, choose a printed fabric for the large triangles.

The instructions that follow are for a wall hanging or lap quilt made from twenty-four 8" (20.5 cm) quilt blocks. The finished quilt with a double lapped border measures about 40" x 56" (102 x 142 cm).

YOU WILL NEED

- 1⅛ yd. (1.05 m) dark-colored solid fabric for one half of each triangle-square.

- ⅓ yd. (0.32 m) each of eight light-colored solid fabrics, or eight fat quarters, for remaining halves of triangle-squares.

- ½ yd. (0.5 m) printed fabric for large triangles.

- ¼ yd. (0.25 m) fabric for 1" (2.5 cm) inner border.

- ⅔ yd. (0.63 m) fabric for 3" (7.5 cm) outer border.

- ½ yd. (0.5 m) fabric for binding.

- 2½ yd. (2.3 m) fabric for backing.

- Batting, about 44" x 60" (112 x 152.5 cm).

CUTTING DIRECTIONS ✂

- For grid-pieced triangle-squares (A), cut eight 9½" x 15" (24.3 x 38 cm) rectangles from dark-colored solid fabric, and cut one 9½" x 15" (25.3 x 38 cm) rectangle from each of the eight light-colored solid fabrics.

- Cut twenty-four 2⅞" (7.2 cm) squares from dark-colored solid fabric; cut squares in half diagonally to make 48 small triangles (B).

- Cut three 2⅞" (7.2 cm) squares from each of eight light-colored solid fabrics; cut squares in half diagonally to make 48 more small triangles (C).

- Cut twenty-four 4⅞" (12.2 cm) squares from printed fabric; cut squares in half diagonally to make 48 large triangles (D).

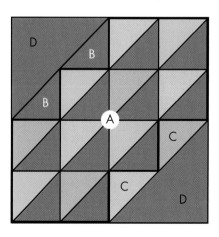

How to Make an Ocean Waves Quilt

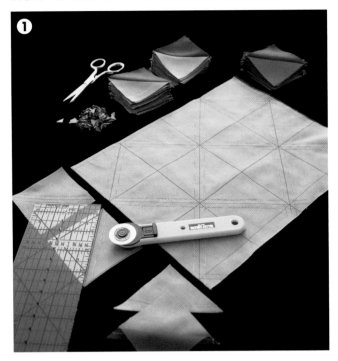

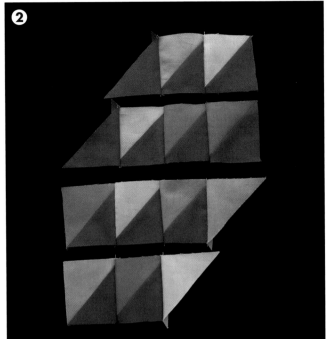

1. Assemble triangle-squares from 9½" x 15" (24.3 x 38 cm) rectangles, as on page 126, steps 1 to 4; in step 1, draw grids of 2⅞" (7.2 cm) squares, five across and three down. Make separate stacks of triangle-squares from each grid.

2. Stitch triangle-squares and small triangles into four rows as shown; use a triangle-square from each stack, using two of the colors twice. This will evenly distribute colors throughout the block.

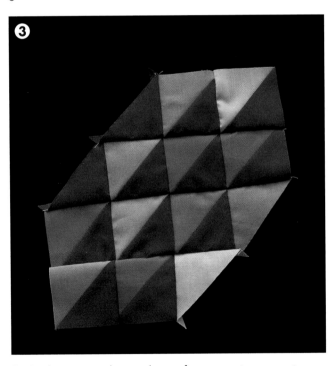

3. Stitch rows together as shown, finger-pressing seams in opposite directions. Do not press.

4. Stitch one large triangle to the diagonal edge of pieced section, taking care not to stretch bias edges. Repeat on opposite edge. Press block, pressing seam allowances toward large triangles. Trim points that extend beyond block.

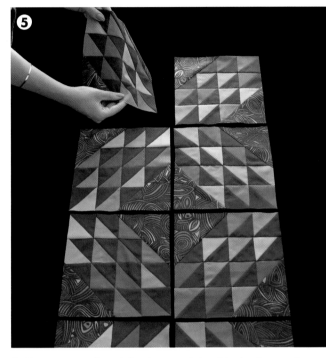

5. Repeat steps 2 to 4 for the remaining blocks; in step 2, randomly select two colors to be used twice. Arrange blocks, six across and four down, making sure that dark-colored triangles are next to light-colored solid triangles.

6. Stitch blocks into rows; stitch rows together, finger-pressing seam allowances in opposite directions. Press quilt top. Cut and attach border strips (pages 83 to 87); cut width of inner border strips is 1½" (3.8 cm) and cut width of outer border is 3½" (9 cm).

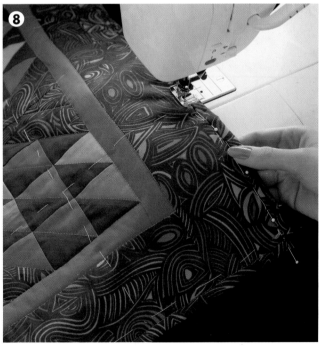

7. Cut backing about 4" (10 cm) larger than quilt top. Layer and baste quilt top, batting , and backing (pages 92 to 97). Quilt (pages 102 to 107).

8. Cut and apply binding (pages 111 to 116); cut width of binding is 2½" (6.5 cm). For wall hanging, attach fabric sleeve (page 171).

MORE OCEAN WAVES DESIGNS

The Ocean Waves design illustrates how different color combinations can be used to create different effects. For a subtle look, combine a light-colored solid fabric in each triangle-square with a softly contrasting solid. For a more random effect, use eight light-colored and eight sharply contrasting dark-colored fabrics for the grid-pieced triangle-squares.

Design squares that are formed between the quilt blocks can be made from various fabrics, as shown in this quilt. The triangle-squares consist of a single light color and eight dark colors.

Subtle color variation is achieved in this quilt by using hand-dyed fabrics. A soft pink is used in each triangle-square, and eight shades of pinks, blues, and lavenders are used for the contrasting fabrics. The printed fabric unifies the design, and stipple quilting (page 104) adds texture throughout the quilt.

Vibrant pattern is created in this quilt by using scraps of eight light-colored and eight dark-colored fabrics for the triangle-squares.

Contemporary Crazy Quilts

This contemporary variation of crazy quilting looks intricate, but is actually quick and easy to piece. For a gradation of colors in the rows of the quilt blocks, hand-dyed fabrics work well for the background fabrics. Solid-colored and printed fabric strips that match the border fabrics are used for contrasting strips in the blocks.

The instructions that follow are for a wall hanging made from sixty-four 3" (7.5 cm) quilt blocks. The finished quilt with a double lapped border measures about 32" (811.5 cm) square.

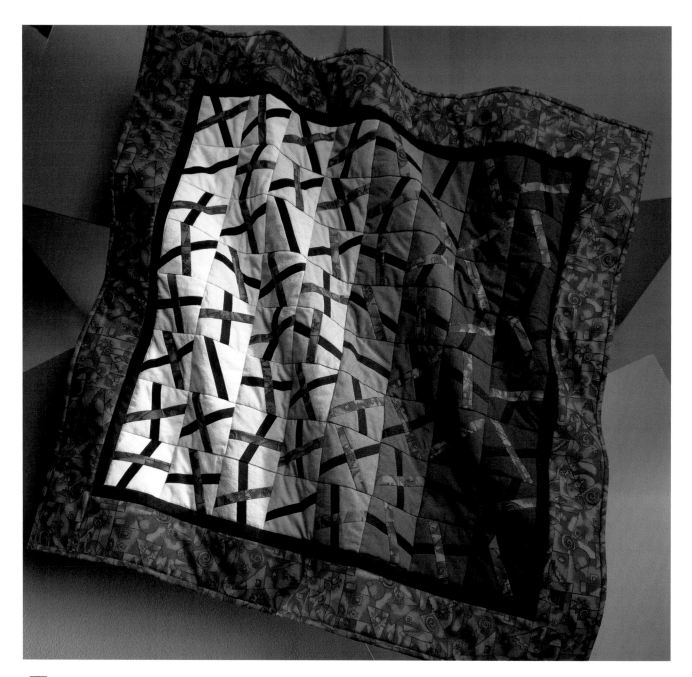

YOU WILL NEED

- One hand-dyed fabric packet of eight fat quarters.

- ⅔ yd. (0.63 m) solid-colored fabric to be used for ¾" (2 cm) inner border and contrasting insert strip.

- 1 yd. (0.95 m) printed fabric to be used for 3" (7.5 cm) outer border and for contrasting insert strip.

- 1 yd. (0.95 m) fabric for backing.

- Batting, about 36" (91.5 cm) square.

- Heavy cardboard or plastic for template.

CUTTING DIRECTIONS ✂

- Cut four 2¼" x 18" (6 x 46 cm) strips from each hand-dyed fabric.

- Cut eight 1" (2.5 cm) crosswise strips from the fabric for the inner border; cut strips at the center foldline of the fabric to make 16 strips.

- Cut eight 1" (2.5 cm) strips from the fabric for the outer border.

- Cut one 3½" (9 cm) square template from heavy cardboard or plastic.

How to Make a Contemporary Crazy Quilt

1. Stitch two hand-dyed strips of the same color to each side of 1" (2.5 cm) strip from inner border fabric, right sides together. Repeat for remaining 15 strips. Press seam allowances toward center strip.

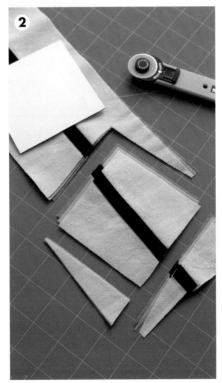

2. Cut four squares from each pieced strip, using template and rotary cutter; vary the angle of the strip on each square. Strips may be cut with three or four layers stacked together.

3. Set aside eight squares, one of each fabric color.

(continued)

4. Slash an angled cut through each remaining square, using straightedge; cut across insert strip and vary angle. Arrange corresponding portions in order, separating them in two stacks. Squares will be rejoined in step 7.

5. Stitch slashed edge of one portion from each square to edge of 1" (2.5 cm) strip from outer border fabric, right sides together; chainstitch portions together, extending the strip ½" (1.3 cm) beyond edges.

6. Press seam allowances toward strip. Trim ends of strip even with edges of squares, using strightedge or template as a guide.

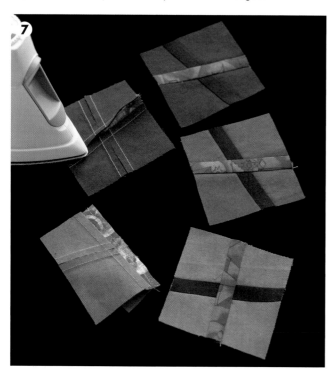

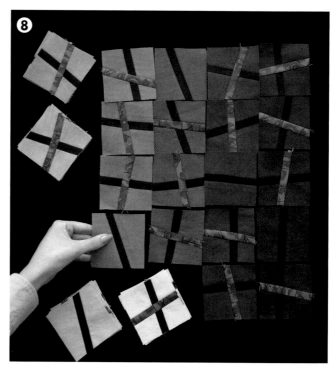

7. Stitch corresponding portions of squares to the opposite edge of strips to make blocks. Press seam allowances toward center of strip, taking care not to stretch bias edges.

8. Arrange blocks into vertical rows of each color, turning contrasting strips in different directions; include blocks set aside in step 3, placing them in random positions within each row.

9. Stitch blocks of each color into rows; stitch rows together, finger-pressing seam allowances in opposite directions. Press quilt top.

10. Cut and attach border strips (pages 82 to 87); cut width of inner border strips is 1¼" (3.2 cm), and cut width of outer border strips is 3½" (9 cm).

11. Cut 36" (91.5 cm) square of backing fabric. Layer and baste quilt top, batting, and backing (pages 92 to 97).

12. Quilt around blocks and borders, using stitch-in-the-ditch method (pages 103). Cut and apply binding (pages 111 to 116); cut width of binding is 2" (5 cm) For wall hanging, attach fabric sleeve (page 171).

Tumbling Blocks

The Tumbling Blocks quilt design, also called Building Blocks and Baby's Blocks, allows for optical effects that are simple to achieve through the use of fabrics in light, medium, and dark colors. The blocks are placed with the light sides facing in the same direction for a three-dimensional look.

Tumbling Blocks are constructed using 60° diamonds. They can be cut quickly using a tool such as an Easy-Six, designed for 60° diamonds. This tool eliminates any calculations and has markings for several sizes.

Three diamonds are stitched together to form a block unit. The blocks are joined at the sides in rows, and the rows are then stitched together. This quilt design does not lend itself to chainstitching; the blocks must be accurately pieced, one seam at a time, making this a more challenging project. For this reason, the Tumbling Blocks quilt design is usually used for smaller projects, such as wall hangings and crib quilts.

Tumbling Blocks quilts can be made with as few as three fabrics in light, medium, and dark colors or with a different fabric for every diamond in the quilt.

The instructions that follow are for a quilt made from diamonds with a finished quilt with a double lapped border measures about 25" x 40" (63.5 x 102 cm), a size suitable for a wall hanging or a crib quilt.

YOU WILL NEED

- ⅜ yd. (0.35 m) fabric each in light, medium, and dark colors; or scraps of fabrics in light, medium, and dark colors.
- ¼ yd. (0.25 m) fabric for inner border.
- ½ yd. (0.5 m) fabric for outer border.
- ⅜ yd. (0.35 m) fabric for binding.
- 1¼ yd. (1.15 m) fabric for backing.
- Batting, about 29" x 44" (73.5 x 112 cm).

CUTTING DIRECTIONS ✁

- Cut 60° diamonds (below) from fabrics in light (A), medium (B), and dark (C) colors; use the markings on the tool for a finished width of 2" (5 cm). You will need 66 light-colored diamonds, 55 medium-colored diamonds, and 55 dark-colored diamonds.

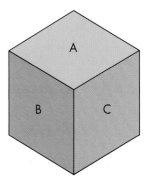

How to Cut 60° Diamonds

1. Cut the diamonds, using a tool designed for 60° diamonds. Cut fabric strips, using the marking for the desired finished size; strips will not measure finished size. To cut printed fabric, the tool and the fabric must be right sides up.

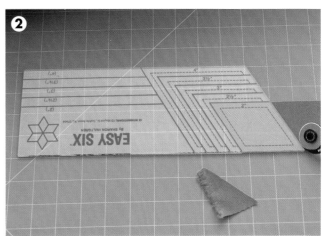

2. Trim selvage, using angled edge of tool. Rotate the tool, and place it at marking for desired finished size; cut along the angled edge of the ruler. Continue cutting additional diamonds from fabric strip.

How to Make a Tumbling Blocks Quilt

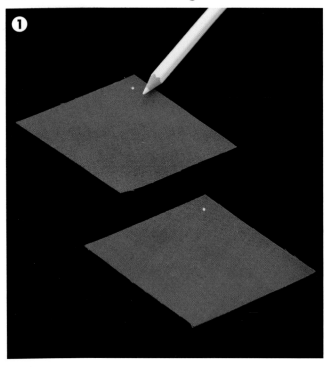

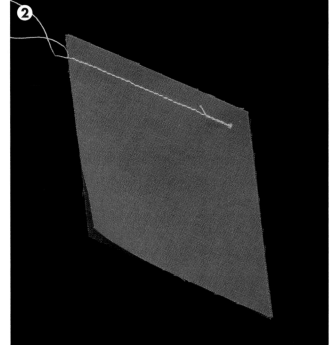

1. Mark wrong side of medium-colored diamonds where the ¼" (6 mm) seams will intersect, placing a dot at one wide-angle corner of each diamond.

2. Align one medium-colored and one dark-colored diamond, right sides together, matching corners. Stitch from sharply pointed end exactly to the dot, with medium-colored diamond facing up; back-stitch to secure ends of stitching.

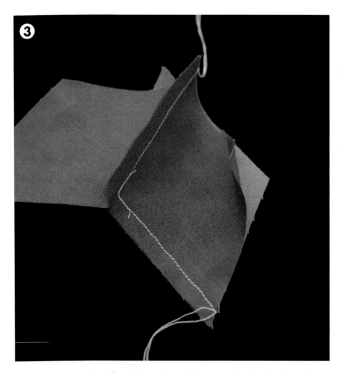

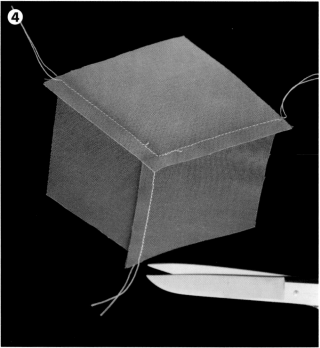

3. Align one side of a light-colored diamond to dark-colored diamond, right sides together, matching the edges and corners. Stitch from the pointed end exactly to the seam intersection, dark-colored diamond facing up; backstitch at ends.

4. Align light-colored diamond to medium-colored diamond, right sides together; stitch seams as in step 3, with light-colored diamond facing up. Press lightly, pressing seams toward darker fabric. Trim points that extend beyond block.

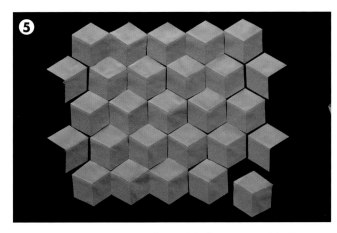

5. Repeat steps 1 to 4 to make 50 blocks. Arrange blocks into rows, with light-colored diamond at top of each block. Piece the remaining diamonds into partial blocks, as shown, to complete the quilt top, making sure to use diamonds of correct colors.

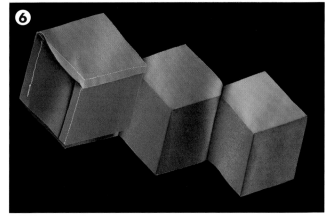

6. Join the blocks side-by-side, beginning and ending all seams ¼" (6 mm) from edges; do not catch seam allowances in stitching. Backstitch at ends.

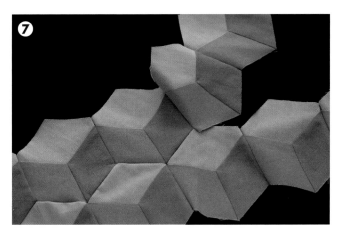

7. Join the rows in zigzag manner, stitching each individual seam and making sure not to catch the seam allowances in stitching; backstitch at ends.

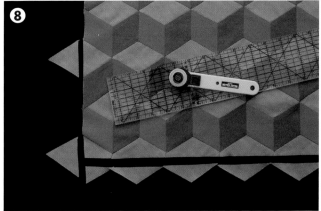

8. Piece remaining light-colored diamonds at lower edge, as shown. Press quilt top, pressing seams toward darker fabric. Trim outer edges even, using straightedge and rotary cutter; allow ¼" (6 mm) seam allowances.

9. Cut and attach border strips (pages 82 to 87); cut width is 1¼" (3.2 cm) for inner border and 3½" (9 cm) for outer border. Cut backing 4" (10 cm) larger than the quilt top. Layer and baste the quilt top, batting, and backing (pages 92 to 97).

10. Quilt, using stitch-in-the-ditch method (pages 103); quilting may be done in horizontal rows, defining blocks. Cut and apply binding (page 111 to 116). For wall hanging, attach fabric sleeve (page 171).

MORE TUMBLING BLOCKS DESIGNS

The Tumbling Blocks design, with its dimensional quality, has many variations. Try turning some of the quilt blocks to create motion in the quilt design. Add subtle visual interest by using unexpected fabrics randomly.

Tumbling blocks can be built around six-pointed stars (pages 158 and 159). The stars and blocks are made individually, then arranged as desired before they are stitched together. The arrangement of the stars may be either symmetrical or random. You may want to experiment with different arrangements to create illusions, such as blocks suspended in space.

A design alternative it to stitch blocks into motifs, such as pyramids, and appliqué the motifs onto a quilt top, as on page 159. This is a faster way to incorporate Tumbling Blocks into larger quilts.

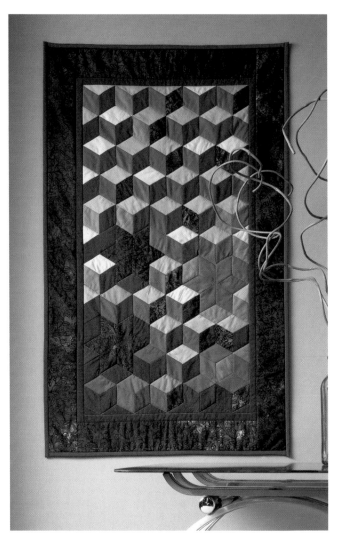

Three random stars, interspersed among the blocks, create an interesting visual effect. Scraps of solids, with an occasional print, are used to add variety.

Stars and blocks in the quilt at right are arranged symmetrically in rows. Stipple quilting embellishes the stars and accentuates the three-dimensional quality of the blocks. The design is appliquéd onto a background fabric, forming an irregular border.

Drunkard's Path Placemats & Table Runners

Enhance a table with a set of quilted placemats and a table runner, using the Drunkard's path design (page 178). For quick construction, the placemats and table runner are assembled using an easy stitch-and-turn method.

Each placemat is made from one sixteen-patch quilt block. Make all four placemats with the same sixteen-patch design, or add variety to the table setting by making each placemat with a different block design. Border strips, stitched to opposite sides of the block, are used to create a banded effect. The finished placemats measures about 12" x 18" (30.5 x 46 cm).

The table runner can be made in several lengths, depending on the number of Drunkard's Path blocks that are stitched together; a border strip is stitched to each end of the runner.

The table runner is most attractive when it is made from one block design, since the sixteen-patch block arrangements form interesting designs when placed end to end. Experiment to see which design you like best by arranging the units in different ways before stitching the blocks. The instructions that follow are for a table runner of five sixteen-patch blocks. The finished table runner measures about 12" x 66" (30.5 x 168 cm).

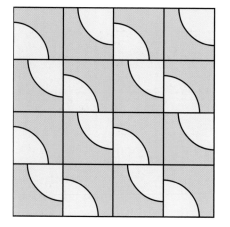
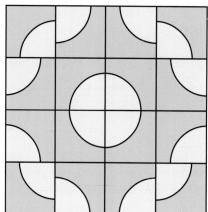

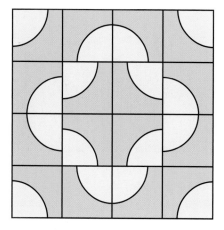
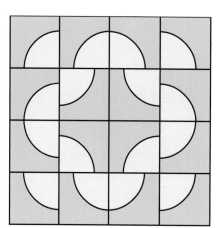

CUTTING DIRECTIONS
(For Four Placemats) ✂

- Cut three 3½" (9 cm) strips from border fabric; cut the strips to make eight 3½" x 12½" (9 x 31.8 cm) rectangles for the border strips.

- Cut three 7" (18 cm) strips from background fabric; cut the strips to make sixteen 7" (18 cm) squares.

- Make the circle template, and cut sixteen 5" (12.5 cm) circles from fabric, as on page 179, steps 1 and 2.

- Cut two 12½" (31.8 cm) strips from backing fabric; cut the strips to make eight 9½" x 12½" (24.3 x 31.8 cm) rectangles.

- Cut four 14½" x 20½" (36.8 x 52.3 cm) rectangles from batting.

CUTTING DIRECTIONS
(For One Table Runner) ✂

- Cut two 3½" x 12½" (9 x 31.8 cm) rectangles from border fabric.

- Cut four 7" (18 cm) strips from background fabric; cut the strips to make twenty 7" (18 cm) squares.

- Make the circle template, and cut twenty 5" (12.5 cm) circles from fabric, as on page 179, steps 1 and 2.

- Cut the backing fabric to make two 12½" x 34" (31.8 x 86.5 cm) strips.

- Cut one 14½" x 70" (36.8 x 178 cm) rectangle from batting.

How to Sew a Drunkard's Path Placemat

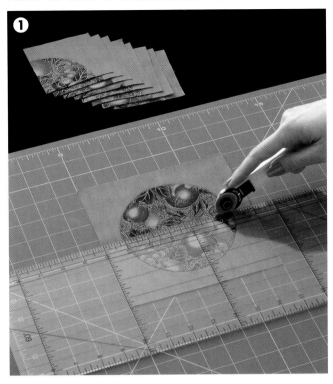

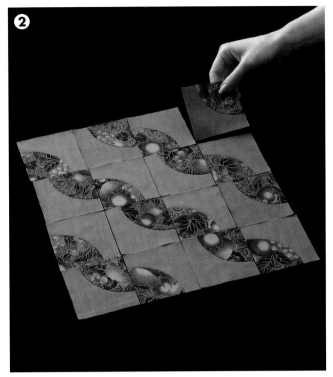

1. Make the Drunkard's Path units as on pages 179 to 180, steps 3 to 6.

2. Arrange 16 units, four across and four down, in the desired block arrangement, as shown on page 182.

3. Assemble the 16-patch block, using chainstitching (page 40).

4. Stitch a border strip to each end of block. Press the seam allowances toward borders. (continued)

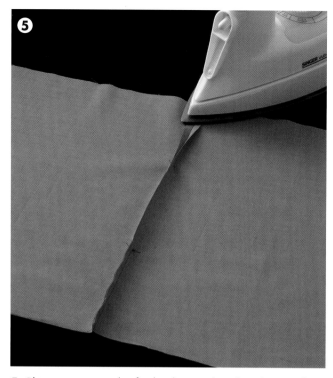

5. Place two rectangles for backing with right sides together and raw edges even; stitch ¼" (6 mm) seam on one long edge, leaving a 4" to 5" (10 to 12.5 cm) center opening for turning. Press seam open.

6. Place backing and placemat top right sides together. Center fabrics on batting, baking side up; pin or baste layers together.

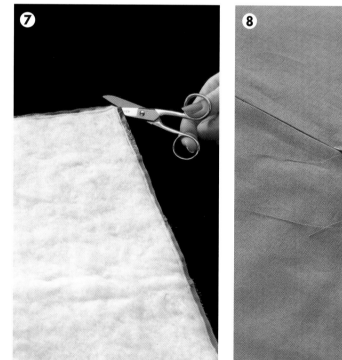

7. Stitch around the placemat, ¼" (6 mm) from raw edges of fabric. Trim batting ⅛" (3 mm) from seam; trim corners diagonally.

8. Turn the placemat right side out; press lightly. Hand-stitch the opening closed.

9. Pin-baste layers together. Quilt placemat, using stitch-in-the-ditch method to define the borders and block (page 103).

How to Sew a Drunkard's Path Table Runner

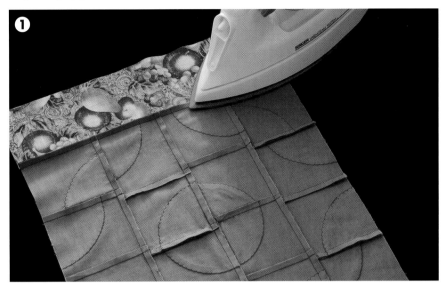

1. Follow steps 1 to 3, page 183, to make five 16-patch blocks in desired arrangement. Stitch blocks together end to end. Press seams open. Stitch a border strip to each end of the runner; press the seam allowances toward borders.

2. Follow step 5, opposite. Trim the backing to the length of the table runner top.

3. Complete the table runner as in steps 6 to 9, opposite. (Contrasting thread was used to show detail.)

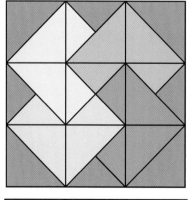

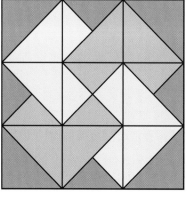

Card Trick Design

Three different pieced squares are used to make the Card Trick quilt block. The corner squares of the block are made from two triangles. The middle square on each side of the block is made from three triangles. And the center square of the block is made from four triangles.

The instructions that follow are for Card Trick blocks in two sizes. The 9" (23 cm) finished block is made using a background fabric and a different fabric for each of the four "cards." The 6" (15 cm) finished block is made using a background fabric and two card fabrics. Both block styles are used in the sampler quilt on page 230 and in the wall hanging on page 190.

How to Sew a 9" (23 cm) Card Trick Block Using Four Fabrics for the Cards

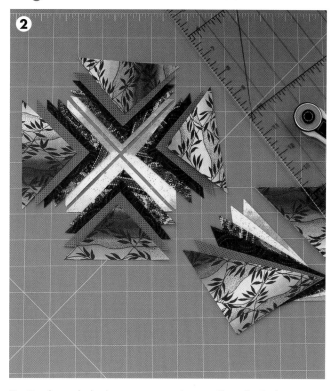

1. Cut one 4¼" (10.8 cm) square each from the background fabric and four card fabrics. Cut two

2. Cut through the large squares diagonally in both directions. Cut through the small squares diagonally in one direction.

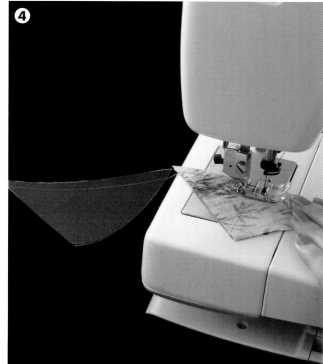

3. Arrange triangles from background and card fabrics as shown. There will be two triangles remaining from each of the four card fabrics.

4. Stitch background and card triangles of corner square, right sides together, on long sides, using chainstitching (page 40). Repeat for remaining corner squares. (continued)

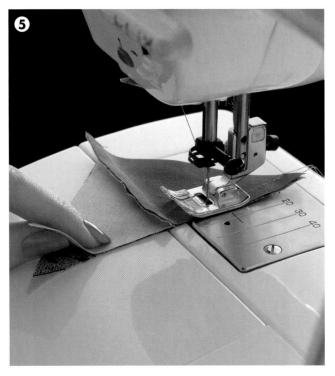

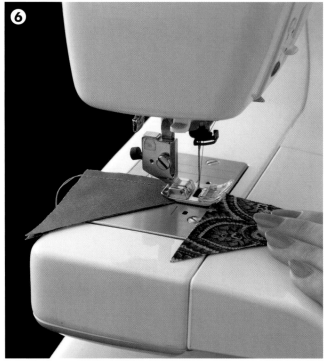

5. Make middle square for side of block by stitching small background triangle to small card triangle on one short side. Then stitch pieced triangle to the remaining triangle for the middle square, stitching right sides together on long side. Repeat for remaining middle squares.

6. Stitch two small triangles for center square of block, right sides together, along one short side. Repeat for two remaining small triangles.

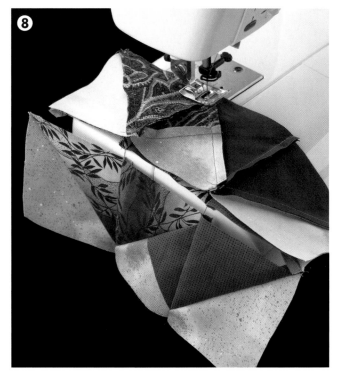

7. Complete center square of block by stitching pieced triangle sets right sides together, on long side, finger-pressing seam allowances in opposite directions. Trim off points.

8. Assemble block, using chainstitching (page 40). Press block.

How to Sew a 6" (15 cm) Card Trick Block Using Two Fabrics for the Cards

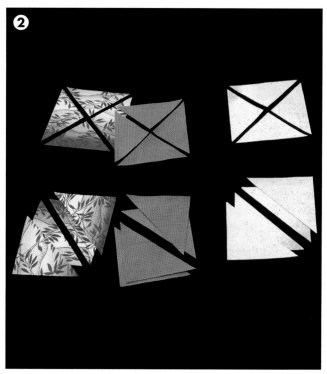

1. Cut one 3¼" (8.2 cm) square each from the background fabric and two card fabrics. Cut two 2⅞" (7.2 cm) squares each from background fabric and two card fabrics.

2. Cut through the large squares diagonally in both directions. Cut through the small squares diagonally in one direction.

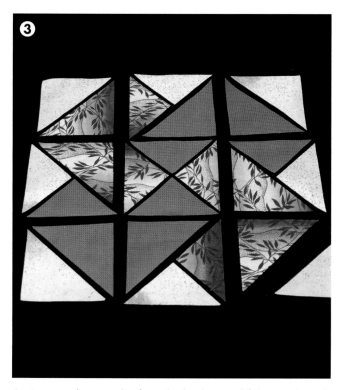

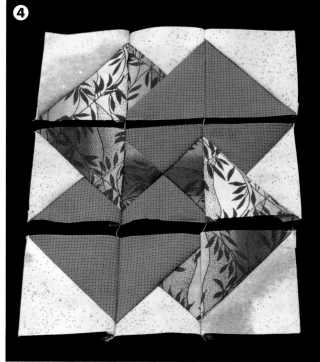

3. Arrange the triangles from the background fabric and card fabrics as shown. Assemble as on pages 187 and 188, steps 4 to 7.

4. Assemble block, using chainstitching (page 40). Press block.

CARD TRICK WALL HANGINGS

This contemporary quilt, made using the Card Trick design (page 186), incorporates two quilt block sizes. Sashing pieces, cut from a coordinating fabric, are arranged for a random look and add interest to the block arrangement.

The wall hanging is made from six 9" (23 cm) Card Trick blocks and nine 6" (15 cm) Card Trick blocks. The finished quilt measures about 33" x 51" (84 x 129.5 cm), making it suitable for a wall hanging, baby quilt, or small lap quilt.

To add interest to the quilt, choose a narrow-striped fabric for the sashing pieces. This gives vertical and horizontal movement to the design. To unify the quilt design, you may want to use one of the card fabrics for the border of the quilt.

YOU WILL NEED

- ½ yd. (0.5 m) each of four fabrics, for cards of Card Trick blocks.
- ⅝ yd. (0.6 m) fabric, for background of Card Trick blocks.
- ½ yd. (0.5 m) fabric, for sashing.
- ½ yd. (0.5 m) fabric, for border.
- 1½ yd. (1.4 m) fabric, for backing.
- ½ yd. (0.5 m) fabric, for binding.
- Batting, about 39" x 55" (99 x139.5 cm).

CUTTING DIRECTIONS ✂

- For the 9" (23 cm) finished blocks, cut the following strips across the width of the fabric: one 4¼" (10.8 cm) strip each from the background fabric and the four card fabrics two 3⅞" (9.7 cm) strips from the background fabric; and one 3⅞" (9.7 cm) strip each from the four card fabrics. Cut the strips to make six 4¼" (10.8 cm) squares from the background fabric, three 4¼" (10.8 cm) squares from each of the card fabrics, twelve 3⅞" (9.7 cm) squares from the background fabric, and six 3⅞" (9.7 cm) squares from each of the card fabrics. Cut the squares diagonally as on page 187, step 2, cutting the large squares in both directions and cutting the small squares in one direction.

- For the 6" (15 cm) finished blocks, cut the following strips: one 3¼" (8.2 cm) strip each from the background fabric and the four card

fabrics; two 2⅞" (7.2 cm) strips from the background fabric; one 2⅞" (7.2 cm) strip each from the four card fabrics. Determine the desired arrangement of card fabrics for each of the nine 6" (15 cm) blocks. Cut strips into the necessary triangles for each block as on page 189, steps 1 and 2.

- For the sashing, cut four 3½" (9 cm) strips. Cut the strips to make nine 3½" x 6½" (9 x 16.3 cm) rectangles and nine 3½" x 9½" (9 x 24.3 cm) rectangles.

- For the border, cut five 3½" (9 cm) strips. The strips will be cut to size for the border strips in step 9, right.

- For the binding, cut four 2½" (6.5 cm) fabric strips.

How to Sew A Card Trick Wall Hanging

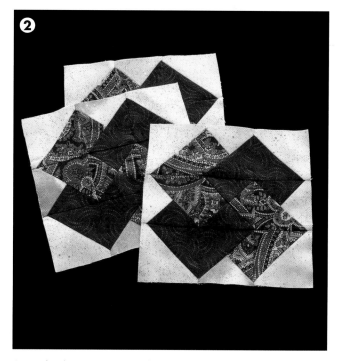

1. Make six 9" (23 cm) finished Card Trick blocks as on pages 187 and 188, steps 3 to 7.

2. Make three 6" (15 cm) finished Card Trick blocks as on page 189, steps 3 and 4.

(continued)

3. Repeat step 2 twice, using a different combination of card fabrics for each set of three blocks. This gives you three sets of three blocks.

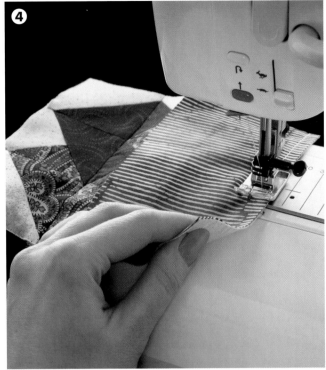

4. Stitch one short sashing strip to one side of one small block, right sides together; press seam allowances toward sashing strip. Repeat for remaining small blocks.

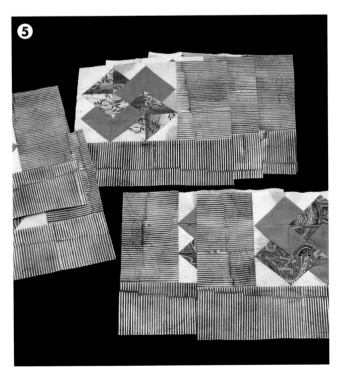

5. Stitch one long sashing strip to lower edge of one small block-and-sashing unit, right sides together; press seam allowances toward sashing strip. Repeat for six additional blocks. This gives you seven square units and two rectangular units.

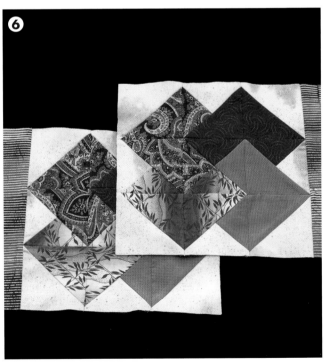

6. Stitch one long sashing strip to one side of one large block, right sides together; press seam allowances toward sashing strip. Repeat for a second block and long sashing strip.

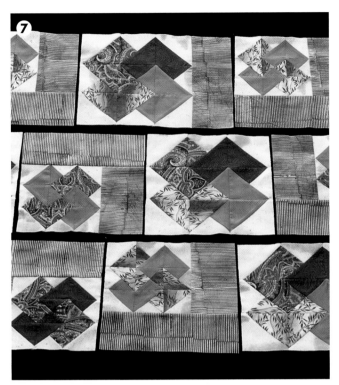

7. Arrange blocks into three rows as shown. Reposition or turn blocks as necessary for pleasing overall design.

8. Stitch the units together to make three rows; press seam allowances toward sashing strips. Stitch rows together; press seam allowances to one side. Press quilt top.

9. Cut and apply the border as for inner border on page 213, steps 3 to 5; consider short ends of this quilt to be upper and lower edges for this step.

10. Cut backing fabric 4" (10 cm) wider and longer than quilt top. Layer and baste quilt top, batting, and backing (pages 92 to 97). Quilt, using stitch-in-the-ditch method (page 103).

11. Apply binding as on pages 111 to 116.

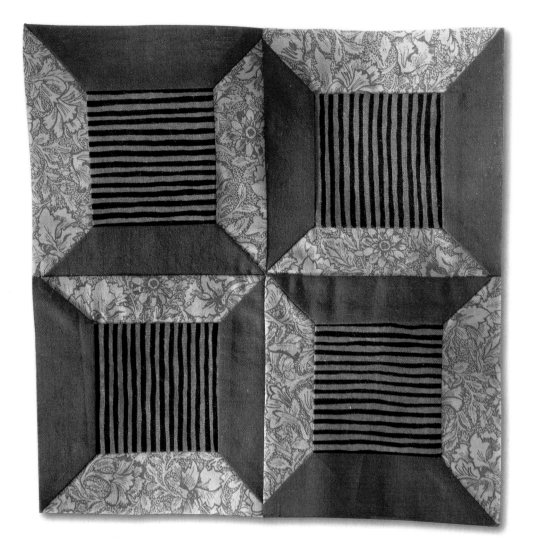

Spools Design

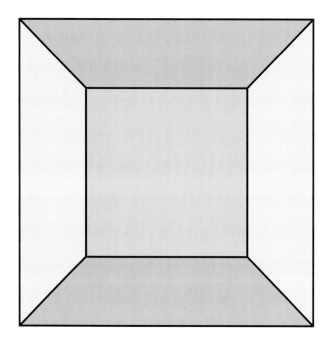

The four-patch Spools quilt block consists of four spool blocks. Each spool block is made from four trapezoids and one center square. Two trapezoids become the upper and lower portions of the spool, and the remaining two trapezoids become the background in the block. The center square is cut from striped fabric to represent the thread on the spool.

For best results, cut the trapezoids for the spools and the squares for the thread from fabrics that are similar in color value. Cut the background trapezoids from a fabric that strongly contrasts with the fabrics used for the spools and thread. The trapezoids can be cut using a quilter's tool, such as the Companion Angle, or they can be cut using the template (opposite).

The instructions that follow are for a 9" (23 cm) finished four-patch block. The block is used in the sampler quilts (pages 228 and 230) and the Spools wall hanging (page 197).

Template for the Spools Design

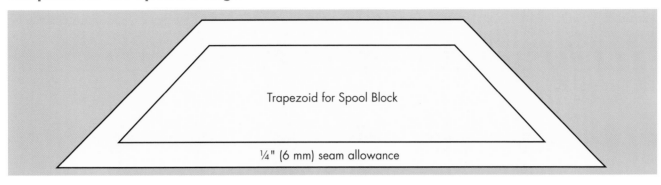

Trapezoid for Spool Block

¼" (6 mm) seam allowance

How to Sew a Four-patch Spools Block

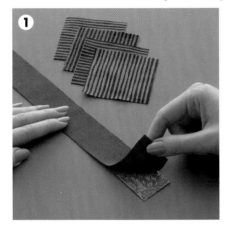

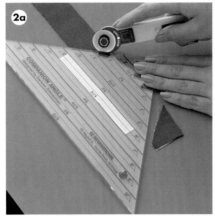

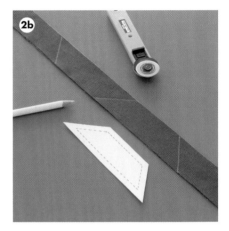

1. Cut four 3" (7.5 cm) squares from striped fabric for thread. Cut one 1½" (3.8 cm) strip each from spool fabric and background fabric; layer strips, matching raw edges.

2a. Quilter's tool. Align 5" (12.5 cm) dotted line on Companion Angle with one long side of layered strips; cut along angled edges of tool. To cut second set of trapezoids, rotate tool and align it with diagonal cut edge of fabric; cut. Repeat to cut eight trapezoids from each color.

2b. Template. Make the template (opposite) from cardboard or from template material. Align template with raw edges of fabric strips; mark along angled sides, using chalk or marking pencil. To mark second set of trapezoids, rotate and realign the tool. Repeat to mark eight sets of trapezoids. Cut on marked lines.

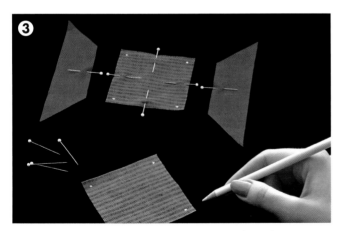

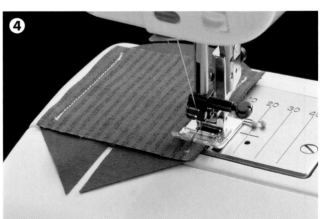

3. Mark wrong side of each thread square where the ¼" (6 mm) seams will intersect, placing a dot at each corner. Pin-mark center of each side of thread square. Pin-mark center of shortest long edge of spool and background trapezoids.

4. Align spool trapezoid to thread square, matching pin marks, with edge of trapezoid parallel to stripes of the thread square. Stitch exactly between the dots, backstitching at beginning and end of stitching. Repeat on opposite side of square. (continued)

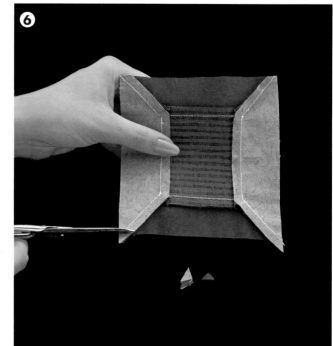

5. Finger-press seam allowances toward the trapezoids. Repeat step 4 to stitch the background trapezoids to the thread square.

6. Align angled ends of two adjacent trapezoids, right sides together. Stitch from the pointed end exactly to the seam intersection; backstitch. Repeat at remaining corners. Press seams of background trapezoids toward spool trapezoids and thread square; trim points.

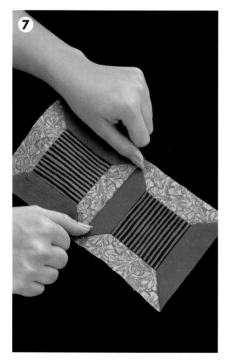

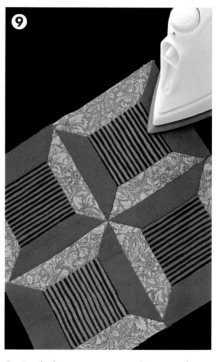

7. Repeat steps 3 to 6, to make four spool blocks. Stitch two blocks together, in a vertical-horizontal arrangement as shown. Finger-press seam allowances to one side.

8. Stitch remaining two squares together in a horizontal-vertical arrangement as shown. Finger-press seam allowances in opposite direction from first row.

9. Stitch the two rows together, matching seamlines. Finger-press seam allowances to one side. Press the quilt block.

SPOOLS WALL HANGINGS

A decorative wall hanging, made from the Spools design (page 194), can have a country or homespun look. It may have special appeal to a person who sews. For extra detail, the border incorporates a spool block at each corner. Striped fabric is used to represent the thread on the spools. To achieve several color variations with the same striped fabric, the fabric can be overdyed, using fabric dye according to the manufacturer's instructions.

The border of the wall hanging can be embellished, if desired, with buttons of various sizes, arranged randomly. The finished wall hanging measures about 42" (107 cm) square.

CUTTING DIRECTIONS ✂

YOU WILL NEED

- Striped fabric, for thread, one or more colors to total about ⅓ yd. (0.32 m).

- ½ yd. (0.5 m) fabric, for spools.

- ½ yd. (0.5 m) fabric, for background.

- ¼ yd. (0.25 m) fabric, for inner border and for background trapezoids of corner spool blocks.

- 1 yd. (0.95 m) fabric, for outer border and binding.

- 1½ yd. (1.4 m) fabric, for backing.

- Batting, about 46" (117 cm) square.

- Buttons, about 50 in various sizes and colors, optional.

- In the directions that follow, cut the strips across the width of the fabric. Cut ten 1½" (3.8 cm) strips from the spool fabric; cut the strips to make 80 spool trapezoids as on page 195; step 2a or 2b. Cut nine 1½" (3.8 cm) strips from the background fabric; cut the strips to make 72 background trapezoids. Cut one 1½" (3.8 cm) strip from the inner border fabric; cut the strip to make eight background trapezoids for the corner blocks of the border.

- Cut three 3" (7.5 cm) strips from thread fabric; cut the strips to make 40 thread squares, each 3" x 3" (7.5 x 7.5 cm).

- Cut four 2" (5 cm) strips from the inner border fabric; these will be cut to length in step 5, opposite. Cut four 5" (12.5 cm) strips from the outer border fabric; these will be cut to length for the borders in step 6.

- Cut four 2½" (6.5 cm) strips from the binding fabric.

How to Sew a Spools Wall Hanging

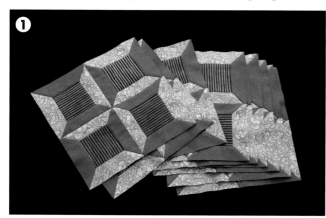

1. Complete nine four-patch Spools blocks as on pages 195 and 196.

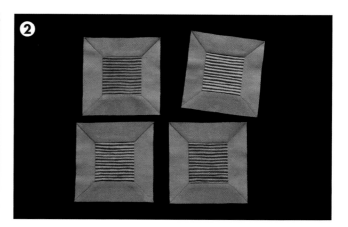

2. Stitch four spool blocks for border, using trapezoids cut from the inner border fabric for the background trapezoids; set aside.

3. Arrange four-patch blocks as desired into three rows of three blocks.

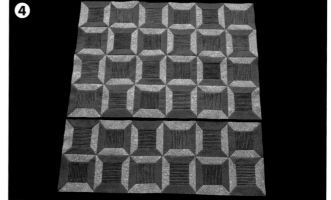

4. Stitch blocks into rows; then stitch rows together, finger-pressing seam allowances in opposite directions. Press quilt top.

198 ◆ THE QUILTING BIBLE, 3rd EDITION

5. Continue as on page 213, steps 3 to 5; in step 5, omit reference to piecing inner border.

6. Measure through middle of quilt in both directions to determine the shortest measurement. Trim four 5" (12.5 cm) outer border fabric strips to this length.

7. Attach the border as on page 169, steps 10 to 12, positioning corner spools upright.

8. Cut backing fabric 4" (10 cm) wider and longer than quilt top. Layer and baste the quilt top, batting, and backing (pages 92 to 97).

9. Quilt the wall hanging, using the stitch-in-the-ditch method (page 103). Stitch in the seamlines of inner and outer borders; then stitch between blocks and around the spools to define design. (Contrasting thread was used to show detail.)

10. Apply binding as on pages 111 to 116. Stitch buttons to border, placing buttons randomly. Attach fabric sleeve (page 171).

Shadowed Square Design

The Shadow Square quilt block, illustrated in the graphic at left, is made from two triangles. One triangle is cut from strip-pieced fabrics and the other from a coordinating fabric.

Four 6" (15 cm) blocks can be assembled to make a 12" (30.5 cm) diamond design as shown above. This design is used in the sampler quilt on page 230 and in the pillow on page 203. The Shadowed Square block and variations of it are also used in the lap quilt on page 206.

Strip piecing, stitching fabric strips together side by side, makes interesting striped fabric from which to cut triangles. A quilter's tool, such as the Companion Angle, can be used to cut the triangles quickly. Or, cut them using a template made from cardboard or template material. To save fabric, the tool or the template can be rotated to cut every other triangle. This produces two variations of strip-pieced triangles. For the diamond design, use four matching triangles.

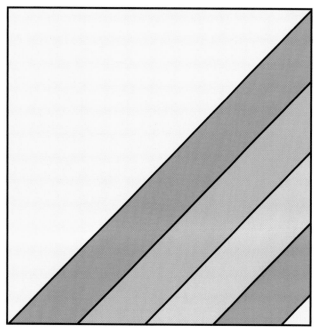

How to Sew Shadowed Square Quilt Blocks

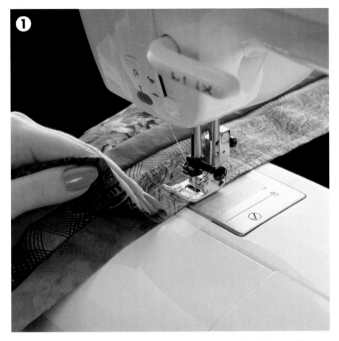

1. Cut one 1½" (3.8 cm) strip across the width of five different fabrics. Stitch strips right sides together, lengthwise, in desired sequence, using ¼" (6 mm) seam allowances.

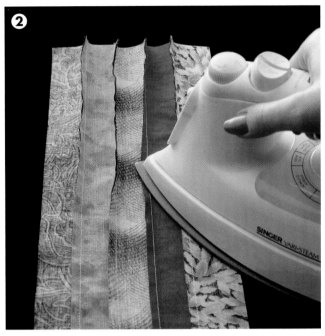

2. Place pieced strip across, rather than lengthwise, on ironing surface, to prevent distorting grainline during pressing. Press all the seam allowances in one direction, or, for a seam joining a light and a dark fabric, press seam allowances toward the dark fabric. Turn strip over, and press from the right side.

3a. Quilter's tool. Align 9" (23 cm) dotted line on Companion Angle with one long edge of the pieced strip; cut along angled edges of tool. Rotate tool and align with opposite raw edge to cut second triangle. Repeat to cut additional triangles.

3b. Template. Cut a 6⅞" (17.5 cm) square from cardboard or template material, and cut it in half diagonally to make triangle template. Align long edge of template with raw edge of pieced strip; mark along angled sides, using marking pencil. Rotate and realign template to mark second triangle. Repeat to mark additional triangles; cut triangles.   (continued)

4. Cut 6⅞" (17.5 cm) squares from coordinating fabric. Layer squares, and cut in half diagonally to make triangles.

5. Align coordinating fabric triangle and strip-pieced triangle, right sides together; stitch on long edge, taking care not to stretch bias edges. Finger-press seam allowance toward darker fabric.

How to Sew a Diamond Design from Shadowed Square Quilt Blocks

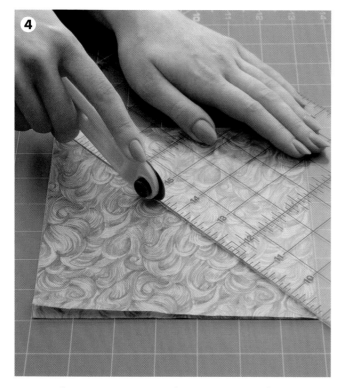

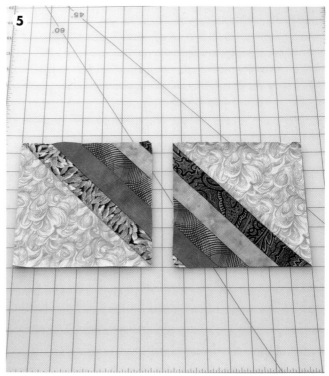

1. Follow steps 1 to 5, above; make four Shadowed Square blocks, using identical strip-pieced triangles. Arrange blocks to form a center diamond as shown.

2. Stitch blocks to form two rows; then stitch the rows together, finger-pressing seam allowances in opposite directions. Press block, pressing long seam allowances to one side.

SHADOWED SQUARE PILLOWS

For a quick quilting project, make a pillow using the Shadowed Square design on page 200. This pillow features a diamond design framed by a 3" (7.5 cm) coordinating border.

The pillow cover is designed to fit an 18" (46 cm) pillow form. For easy construction, the pillow cover back has an overlap closure, secured with hook and loop tape.

CUTTING DIRECTIONS ✂

- For the pillow cover front, cut two 3½" x 12½" (9 x 31.8 cm) border strips and two 3½" x 18½" (9 x 47.3 cm) border strips.

- Cut two 18½" x 13" (47.3 x 33 cm) rectangles, for the pillow cover back.

YOU WILL NEED

- ¼ yd. (0.25 m) each of four fabrics, stripes of diamond.

- ⅝ yd. (0.6 m) fabric, for one stripe of diamond, border strips, and pillow back.

- ¼ yd. (0.25 m) fabric, for background.

- ⅝ yd. (0.6 m) muslin, for pillow lining.

- Batting, about 20" (51 cm) square.

- One 18" (46 cm) square pillow form.

- 2" (5 cm) strip of hook and loop tape, ¾" (2 cm) wide.

How to Sew a Shadowed Square Pillow

1. Cut and assemble four Shadowed Square blocks into diamond design as on pages 201 and 202. Stitch one short border strip to one side of block, right sides together and raw edges even. Press seam allowances toward border. Repeat on opposite side.

2. Stitch remaining border strips to the remaining sides of block. Press seam allowances toward the border. Press pieced pillow top.

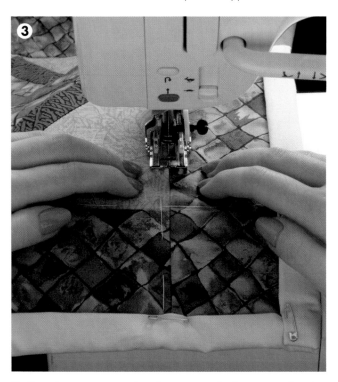

3. Place batting over muslin. Center pieced pillow top, right side up, over batting; baste layers together (pages 92 to 97). Quilt the block, using the stitch-in-the-ditch method (page 103).

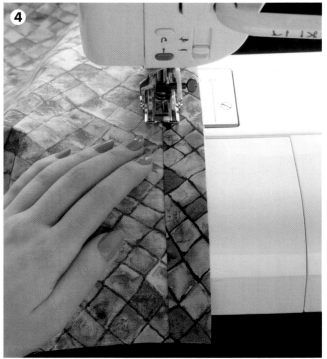

4. Press under 1" (2.5 cm) twice on one long edge of the rectangle for pillow back; stitch to make double-fold hem. Repeat for the remaining pillow back piece.

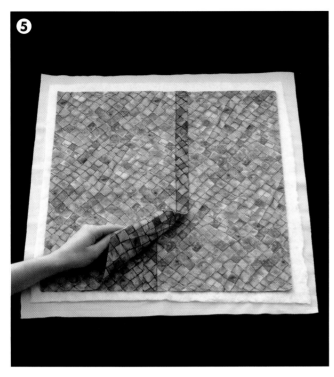

5. Position pillow back piece over the pillow front, right sides together, matching raw edges; hemmed edges of the back pieces overlap about 3" (7.5 cm) at center. Pin in place.

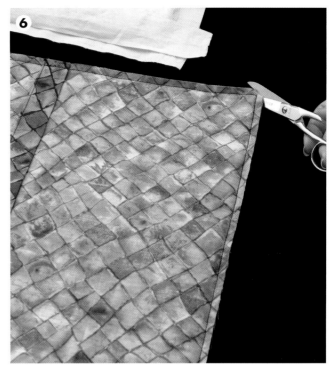

6. Stitch around pillow cover, ¼" (6 mm) from raw edges. Trim the batting ⅛" (3 mm) from seam. Trim muslin even with edges of pillow cover. Trim corners diagonally. Turn pillow right side out; press lightly.

7. Pin hook side of hook and loop tape to overlap, centering tape on hem; stitch around tape. Pin loop side of hook and loop tape to the underlap, directly under hook side of tape; stitch.

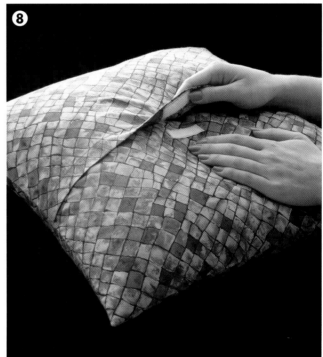

8. Insert the pillow form into pillow cover. Secure the hook and loop tape.

SHADOWED SQUARE LAP QUILTS

Although this lap quilt appears intricate, it is actually simple to sew. It is made using the Shadowed Square design with a diagonal strip-pieced triangle (page 200) and several variations; half of each block is a plain fabric triangle. Easy strip-piecing techniques are used to assemble the pieced triangle designs.

Choose a printed fabric for the plain fabric triangles in each of the blocks. Then choose eight or more coordinating fabrics to use for the pieced triangles. Printed fabrics and fabrics with color gradations will make the finished quilt appear more intricate. The finished quilt with a double border measures about 44" x 56" (112 x 142 cm).

CUTTING DIRECTIONS ✄

- In the directions that follow, cut the strips across the width of the fabric. Cut four 6⅞" (17.5 cm) strips from printed fabric; cut the strips to make twenty-four 6⅞" (17.5 cm) squares. Cut the squares diagonally as on page 201, step 3, to make 48 triangles. The fabric strips for the pieced triangles are cut on pages 209 to 212.

- Cut five 1½" (3.8 cm) strips from inner border fabric. Cut five 3½" (9 cm) strips from outer border fabric. The strips will be cut to length for the inner and outer borders on page 213.

- Cut five 2½" (6.5 cm) strips from binding fabric.

YOU WILL NEED

- 1 yd. (0.95 m) printed fabric, for plain triangles.

- ⅓ yd. (0.32 m) each of eight or more coordinating fabrics, for pieced triangles.

- ⅓ yd. (0.32 m) fabric, for inner border.

- ⅔ yd. (0.63 m) fabric, for outer border.

- ½ yd. (0.5 m) fabric, for binding.

- Batting, about 48" x 60" (122 x 152.5 cm) rectangle.

- 2⅔ yd. (2.48 m) fabric, for backing.

The Shadowed Square lap quilt (opposite) is made using the basic Shadowed Square block and several variations.

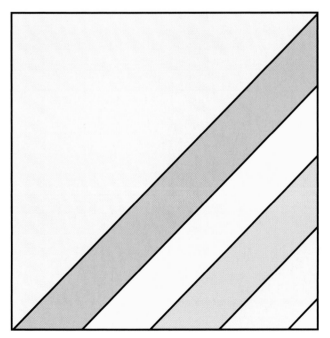

Block with diagonal strip-pieced triangle.

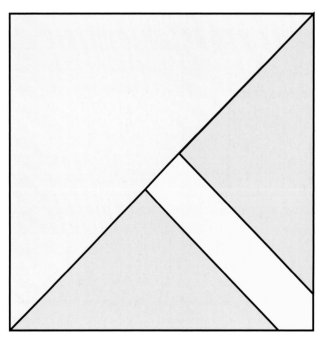

Block with interrupted triangle (version one).

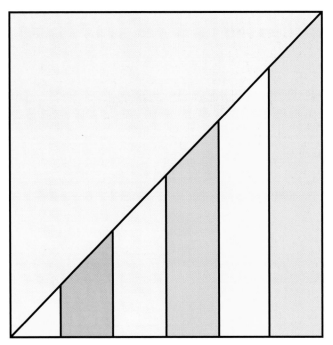

Block with vertical strip-pieced triangle.

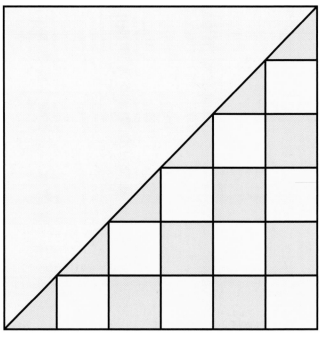

Block with 1" (2.5 cm) checkerboard triangle.

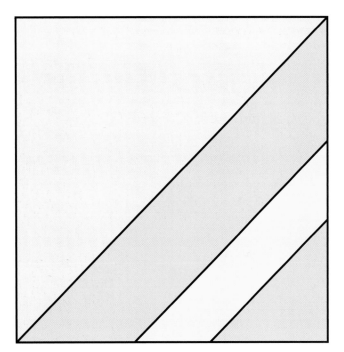

Block with interrupted triangle (version two).

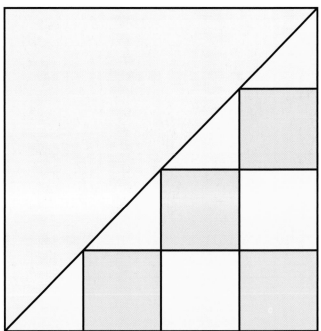

Block with 1½" (3.8 cm) checkerboard triangle.

How to Sew the Blocks for the Shadowed Square Lap Quilt

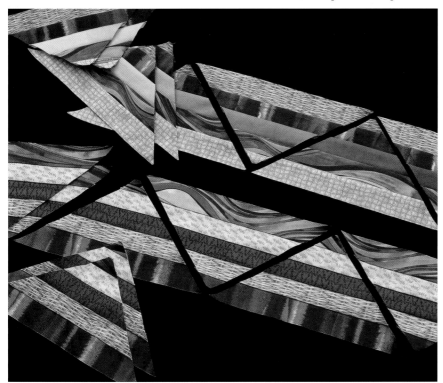

(Diagonal strip-pieced triangles) Cut and assemble eight strip-pieced triangles, as on page 201, steps 1 to 3. Repeat to make eight additional triangles, using different fabrics or a different arrangement of the fabrics for the pieced strip.

1. (Vertical strip-pieced triangles) Cut one 1½" (3.8 cm) strip each from six fabrics. Stitch the strips together lengthwise in scant ¼" (6 mm) seams in the desired sequence. Press seam allowances in one direction.

2. Cut eight triangles from pieced strip as on page 201, step 3a or 3b; align short edge of template with the raw edge of pieced strip. Point of triangle extends slightly beyond one edge of pieced strip. (continued)

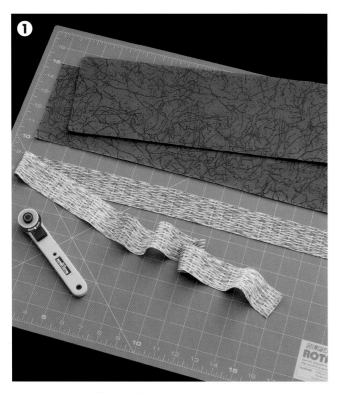

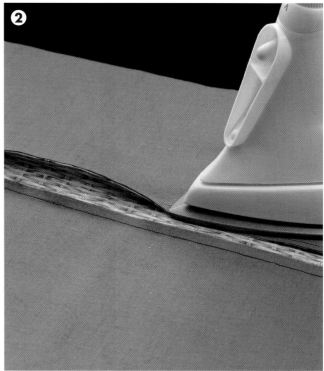

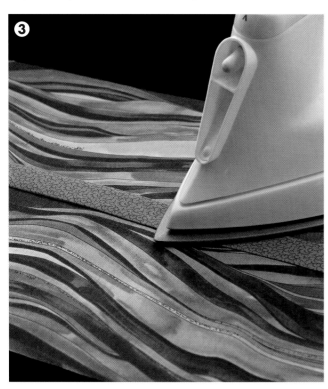

1. (Interrupted triangles) Cut one 5" (12.5 cm) strip from fabric; cut one 1½" (3.8) strip from a different fabric. Cut strips in half; discard one narrow strip.

2. Stitch a 5" (12.5 cm) strip to each side of narrow strip, with ¼" (6 mm) seams. Press seam allowances toward center strip.

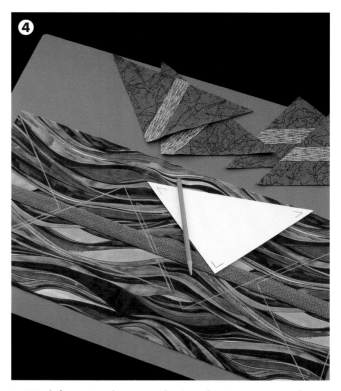

3. Repeat steps 1 and 2 to make a second pieced strip, using different fabrics.

4. Mark four triangles on each pieced strip, using template or tool; vary the position of the template so the narrow fabric strip runs both horizontally and vertically across the triangles. Cut triangles.

How to Sew the Blocks for the Shadowed Square Lap Quilt

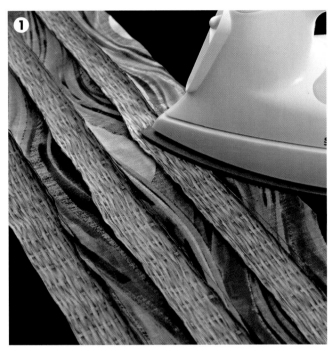

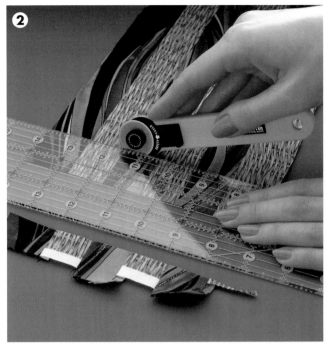

1. (1" [2.5 cm] checkerboard triangles) Cut two 1½" (3.8 cm) strips each from two contrasting fabrics; cut the strips in half. Stitch six strips together lengthwise, with scant ¼" (6 mm) seams, alternating fabrics. Press strip, pressing seam allowances in one direction.

2. Repeat step 1, using different fabrics, to make a second pieced strip. Trim the short end of each strip at a 90° angle. Cut 1½" (3.8 cm) strips across each pieced fabric strip.

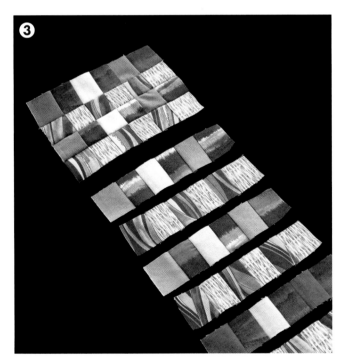

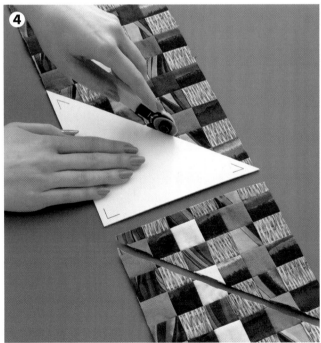

3. Stitch pieced strips together with scant ¼" (6 mm) seams, alternating them to form a checkerboard. Press seam allowances in one direction.

4. Mark eight triangles on strip, using a template or a tool, and aligning short edge of template with raw edge of pieced strip. Point of triangle extends slightly beyond pieced strip. Cut triangles.   (continued)

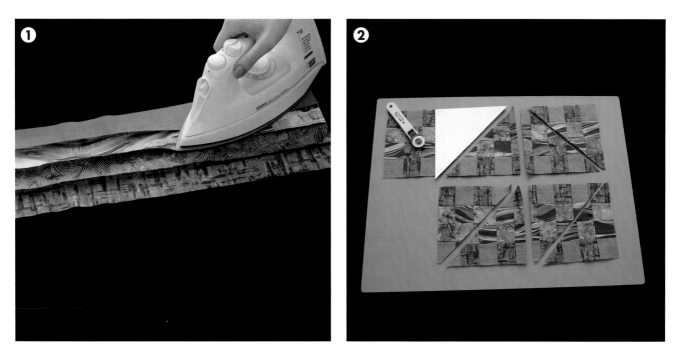

1. (1½" [3.8 cm] checkerboard triangles) Cut one 2" (5 cm) strip each from four fabrics. Stitch the strips together lengthwise in scant ¼" (6 mm) seams. Press seam allowances in one direction.

2. Cut 2" (5 cm) strips across pieced strip as on page 211, step 2. Reassemble strips, alternating fabrics to form a checkerboard. Cut eight triangles from strip as shown.

How to Assemble the Shadowed Square Lap Quilt

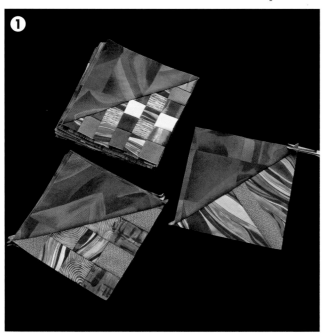

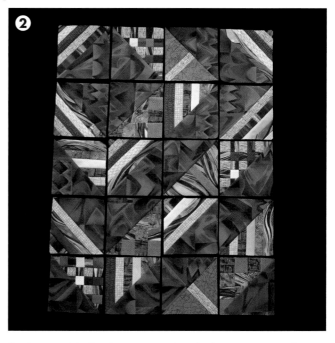

1. Place pieced triangle and plain fabric triangle right side together; stitch on long edge, taking care not to stretch bias edges. Press the seam allowances toward plain triangle; trim points. Repeat to make 48 blocks.

2. Arrange blocks six across and eight down, rotating plain triangles to create a radiating diamond pattern. Stitch the blocks into rows; then stitch rows together, finger-pressing seam allowances in opposite directions. Press quilt top.

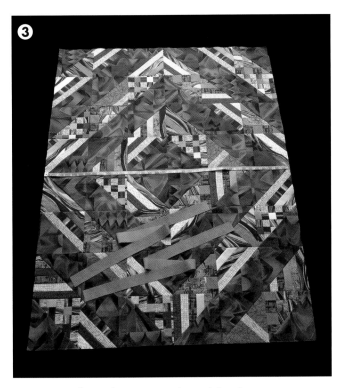

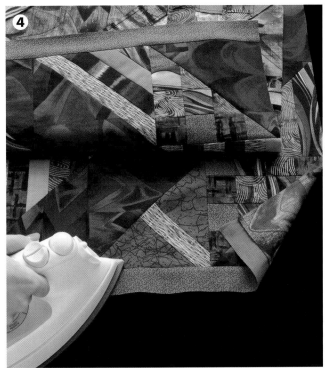

3. Measure the quilt top across the middle. Cut two inner border strips equal to this measurement, for upper and lower inner border.

4. Pin inner border strip to upper edge of quilt top at center and ends, right sides together; pin along length, easing in any fullness. Stitch; press seam allowances toward inner border. Press from right side. Repeat at lower edge.

5. Piece remaining inner border strips; trim seam allowances. Measure quilt top down the middle, including inner border strips. Cut two inner border strips for sides equal to this length. Pin and stitch the strips to sides of quilt top as in step 4.

6. Repeat steps 3 to 5 to apply the outer border. Cut backing fabric 4" (10 cm) wider and longer than quilt top, piecing as necessary.

7. Layer and baste the quilt as on pages 92 to 97. Quilt, using stitch-in-the-ditch method (page 103). Apply the binding as on pages 111 to 116.

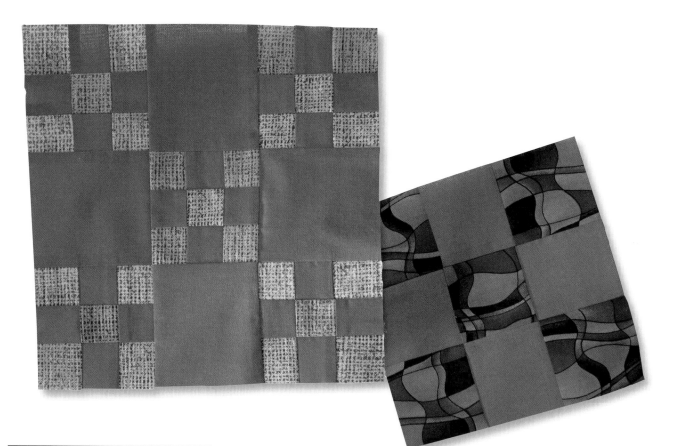

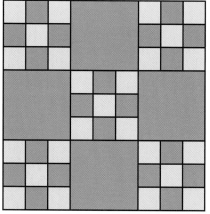

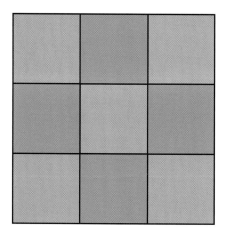

Nine-patch & Double Nine-patch Designs

A Nine-patch quilt block, made from nine squares, is one of the most basic quilt blocks. The Double Nine-patch block alternates squares and checkerboard pieced squares. Each of the checkerboard squares is made from nine smaller squares.

Both styles of blocks are used in the sampler quilts on pages 228 and 230. One of these blocks is also used to make the sleeping bag on page 218.

The checkerboard squares used in the Double Nine-patch block are made using a strip-piecing method that lets you create intricate designs quickly without individually seaming small pieces of fabric.

The instructions that follow are for a 6" (15 cm) Nine-patch block and a 9" (23 cm) Double Nine-patch block. At least two fabrics are needed to make each quilt block.

How to Sew a Nine-patch Quilt Block

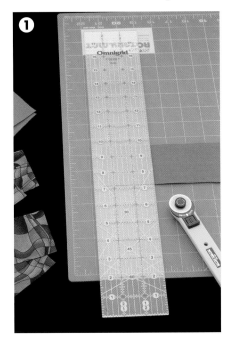

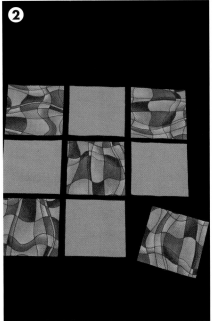

1. Cut five 2½" (6.5 cm) squares from Fabric A, and cut four 2½" (6.5 cm) squares from Fabric B.

2. Arrange the squares, alternating the fabrics, to form a nine-square checkerboard.

3. Assemble the quilt block, using chainstitching (page 40). Press the block.

How to Sew a Double Nine-patch Quilt Block

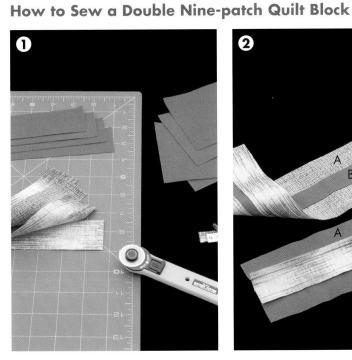

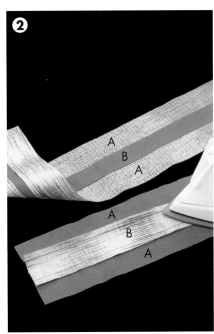

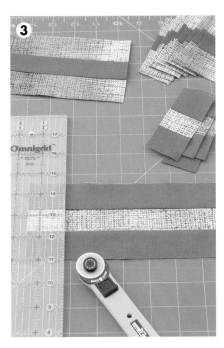

1. Cut four 3½" (9 cm) squares from Fabric A. Cut two 1½" (3.8 cm) strips across the width of both Fabric A and Fabric B; cut strips in half to make four strips of each.

2. Stitch one B-A-B unit and one A-B-A unit, right sides together. Discard remaining two strips. Press all the seams toward the darker fabric.

3. Trim short end of each pieced strip at a 90° angle. Cut ten 1½" (3.8 cm) strips across B-A-B unit and five 1½" (3.8 cm) strips across B-A-B unit and five 1½" (3.8 cm) strips across A-B-A unit. (continued)

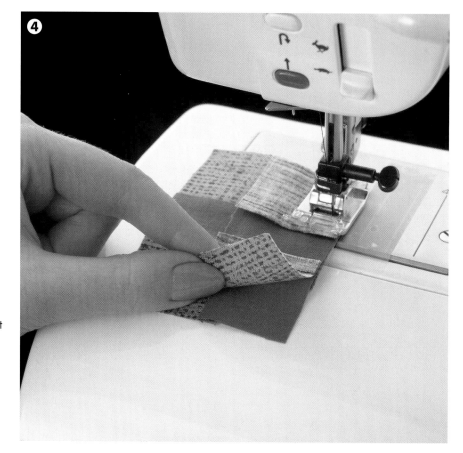

4. Stitch one B-A-B unit to one A-B-A unit on the long edges, right sides together. Then stitch B-A-B unit to the other long edge of A-B-A unit, right sides together, to form checkerboard. Repeat to make four more checkerboard units. Press the seam allowances toward the sides with the two darker squares.

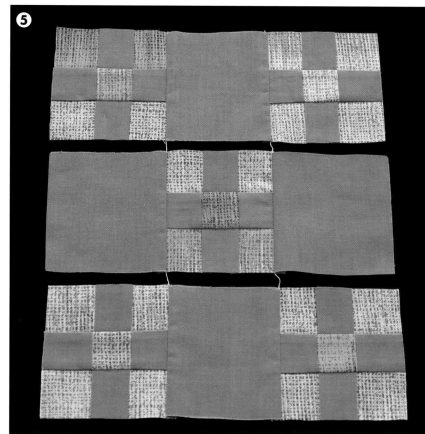

5. Alternate plain squares with checkerboard squares to form the Double Nine-patch block. Assemble block, using chainstitching (page 40).

NINE-PATCH SLEEPING BAGS

Children will love snuggling down into their own patchwork sleeping bag, made with the Nine-patch design (page 214). A generous side opening makes it easy to get in and out of the sleeping bag.

Novelty printed fabrics, combined with a solid coordinating fabric, work well for the Nine-patch design in this project. The Nine-patch quilt blocks are separated by sashing with connecting squares. The connecting squares of the sashing can be cut from the primary fabric in the block to create a dominant diagonal effect.

Several timesaving techniques are used to construct the sleeping bag. The Nine-patch blocks on the front of the sleeping bag are stitched together quickly, using strip-piecing. Simple stitch-in-the-ditch quilting is used on the front of the sleeping bag; however, to save time and give a more intricate look to the piecing, the stitching is continued from block to block by stitching through the sashing. The back of the sleeping bag is constructed from one fabric piece and features channel quilting.

The instructions that follow are for a finished sleeping bag that measures about 34" x 58" (86.5 x 147 cm). A shorter bag, about 50" (127 cm) in length, can be made by eliminating one row of blocks and sashing. For convenience, the sleeping bag features ties at the lower edges so the bag may be rolled up and tied in a neat bundle.

YOU WILL NEED

- ⅞ yd. (0.8 m) printed fabric, for primary fabric in block.
- ⅔ yd. (0.63 m) fabric, for secondary fabric in block.
- 1 yd. (0.95 m) fabric, for sashing.
- ¼ yd. (0.25 m) fabric, for connecting squares of sashing.
- 1¾ yd. (1.6 m) fabric, for back of sleeping bag.
- 3⅓ yd. (3.07 m) muslin, for inner lining.
- 3⅓ yd. (3.07 m) fabric, for lining.
- Batting, two pieces about 38" x 62" (96.5 x 157.5 cm).
- 2⅝ yd. (2.4 m) grosgrain ribbon, ⅝" (1.5 cm) wide, for ties.

CUTTING DIRECTIONS ✂

- Cut the following strips across the width of the fabric: eleven 2½" (6.5 cm) strips from the primary fabric in the block and eight 2½" (6.5 cm) strips from the secondary fabric in the block. These pieces will be strip-pieced and cut to make the Nine-patch blocks.

- Cut twelve 2½" (6.5 cm) strips from the sashing fabric; these will be cut to size for the sashing strips as on page 218, step 4. Cut two 2½" (6.5 cm) strips from the fabric for the connecting squares of the sashing; cut the strips to make forty 2½" (6.5 cm) squares.

- Trim the width of the fabric for the back to 38" (96.5 cm). Cut two 38" x 62" (96.5 x 157.5 cm) pieces from the inner lining fabric. The sleeping bag lining is cut after the outer bag is constructed.

How to Sew a Nine-patch Sleeping Bag

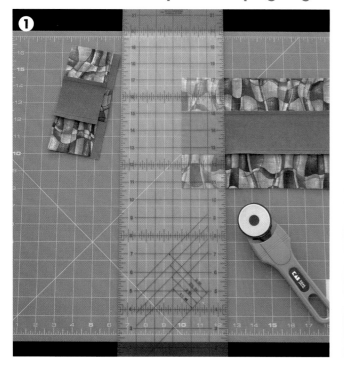

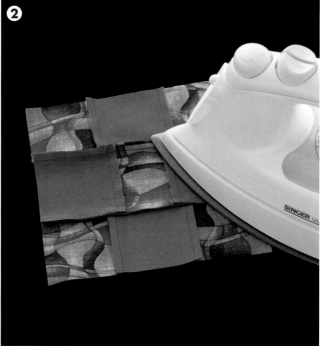

1. Stitch four B-A-B units and two A-B-A units, as for Double Nine-patch quilt block on page 215, step 2. Trim short end of each pieced unit at 90° angle. Cut 2½" (6.5 cm) strips across each pieced unit.

2. Stitch one B-A-B unit to one A-B-A unit on long edges, right sides together. Then stitch B-A-B unit to other long edge of A-B-A unit, right sides together, to form checkerboard. Press seam allowances toward the sides with the two darker squares.

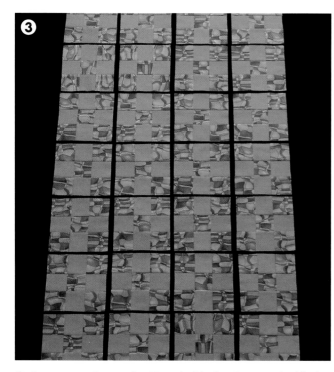

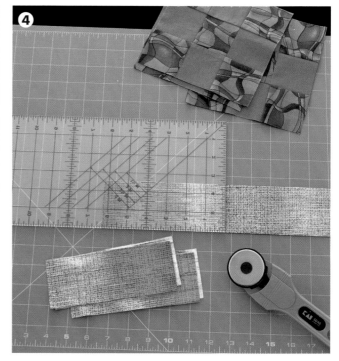

3. Repeat step 2 to make 28 quilts blocks. Arrange the blocks, four across and seven down.

4. Measure sides of several quilt blocks to determine shortest measurement; using 2½" (6.5 cm) sashing fabric strips, cut 67 sashing strips to this length.

5. Attach sashing with connecting squares as on page 168, steps 5 to 8.

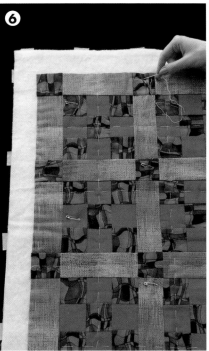

6. Layer and baste the sleeping bag front, batting, and inner lining (pages 92 to 97).

7. Quilt, using stitch-in-the-ditch method (page 103), stitching continuous rows through sashing.

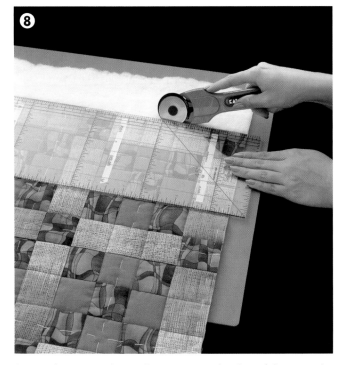

8. Trim batting and inner lining even with edge of the pieced top. Measure the front of the sleeping bag across and down the middle; record dimensions for use in step 14.

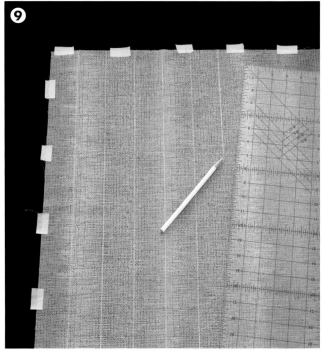

9. Tape the backing fabric to a hard, flat work surface, keeping fabric smooth and taut. Using a straightedge and quilting pencil, mark 2" (5 cm) parallel lines down length of fabric for backing. Remove tape. (continued)

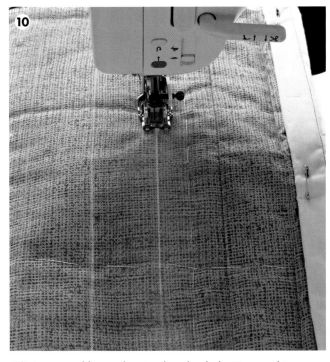

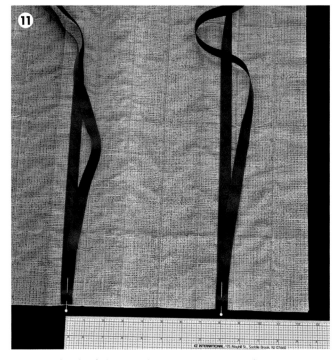

10. Layer and baste sleeping bag back, batting, and inner lining. Channel-quilt (page 103) on the marked lines; reverse the direction of stitching every other line to avoid distorting fabric.

11. Trim back of sleeping bag to same size as front. Cut two 46" (117 cm) lengths of ribbon; fold each length in half, and pin to lower edge of sleeping bag back, 4½" (11.5 cm) and 12½" (31.8 cm) from one side. Stitch ribbon to bag, scant ¼" (6 mm) from raw edge.

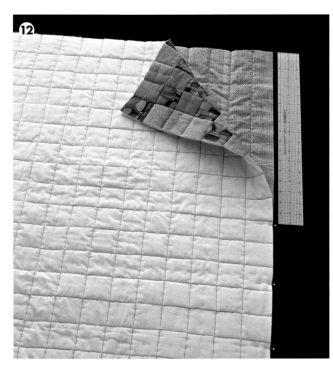

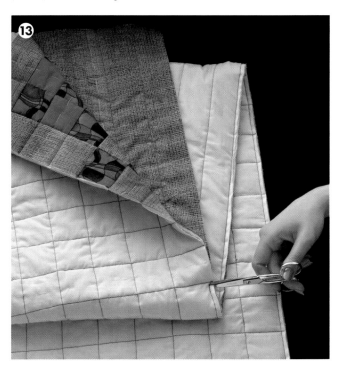

12. Pin the sleeping bag front to sleeping bag back, with right sides together and raw edges even. Pin-mark 18" (46 cm) from upper edge for opening on one side of sleeping bag.

13. Stitch around sides and bottom, backstitching at pin mark for opening. Clip the seam allowances at backstitching. Turn right side out.

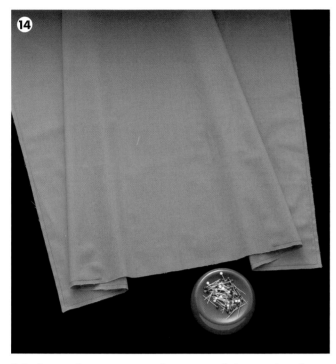

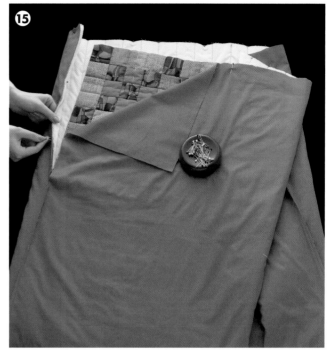

14. Cut two lining pieces to dimensions of sleeping bag front; pin right sides together. Pin-mark side opening, and stitch as for outer section, leaving a 12" (30.5 cm) center opening on lower edge for turning; do not clip seam allowances at backstitching. Do not turn right side out.

15. Insert outer bag inside lining, right sides together; pin along side opening and upper edge, with the raw edges even. Stitch, beginning and ending at bottom of side opening.

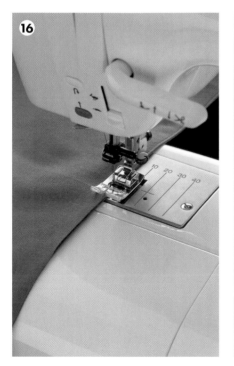

16. Turn the sleeping bag right side out through opening in bottom of lining. Edgestitch opening closed.

17. Insert lining inside the sleeping bag. Tack lining to bottom of outer bag at lower seam.

18. Press lightly on upper edge and side opening edges. Topstitch ¼" (6 mm) from upper and side edges. Stitch several times across bottom of side opening, to reinforce.

Log Cabin Design

Log Cabin remains one of the most popular traditional designs. The instructions that follow use chainstitching for quick and easy piecing of multiple blocks.

Choose three fabrics for each half of the block, and a fabric for the center square. Fabrics may graduate from light to dark, or from dark to light on each side of the center square, or they may be arranged in a random order.

The instructions that follow make a 7" (18 cm) finished block that is used in the sampler quilts (pages 228 and 230). A smaller Log Cabin block is used for the miniquilts (page 224).

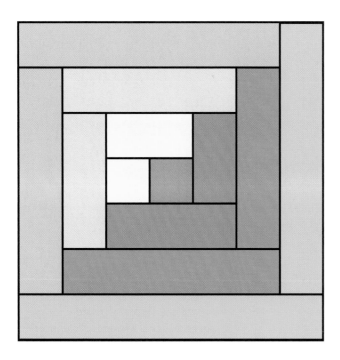

How to Sew a Log Cabin Quilt Block

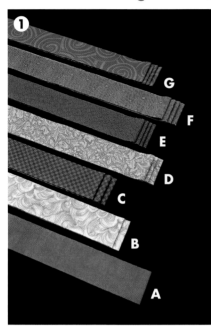

1. Cut 1½" (3.8 cm) strips across the width of seven different fabrics. Label strips from A to G, as shown.

2. Stitch Strips A and B, right sides together, along one long side. Press seam allowances away from strip A. Cut across the pieced strip at 1½" (3.8 cm) intervals.

3. Stitch pieced units to a second Strip B, using chainstitching (page 40) as shown.

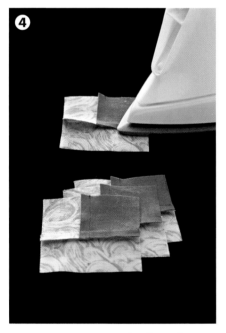

4. Trim Strip B even with edges of pieced units. Press seam allowances away from center squares.

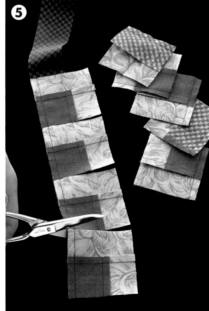

5. Stitch three-piece units to Strip C, using chainstitching; position units at 90° angle to most recent seam on side nearest center square. Trim Strip C even with edges of pieced units. Press seam allowances away from center squares.

6. Stitch four-piece units to a second Strip C, using chainstitching; position units at 90° angle to the most recent seam on side nearest center square. Continue in this manner, stitching two strips of each color to pieced units in sequence. Press the seam allowances away from center square.

LOG CABIN MINIQUILTS

This trio of quilts, made using the Log Cabin design (page 222), creates a stunning wall display. The blocks in each quilt are arranged in a different way to create three different designs.

For a subtle blending of colors with a contemporary feel, make the blocks using hand-dyed fabrics as shown in the quilt opposite. These solid-colored fabrics are available in packets of six or eight fabrics and can be purchased from quilting stores and mail-order suppliers. Choose a printed fabric for the border, binding, and center square of the quilt blocks.

The quilts can also be made using a combination of printed fabrics. For best results, select fabrics for one half of the block that contrast with the fabrics for the other half. This emphasizes the design created by the block arrangement.

The quilts are made from 3½" (9 cm) blocks. Each of the finished quilts measures about 18" x 25" (46 x 63.5 cm). The yardages and the cutting instructions below are for a set of three quilts.

YOU WILL NEED

- ½ yd. (0.5 m) bundle of six hand-dyed fabrics in a light to dark gradation; or ½ yd. (0.5 m) each of three light and three dark printed fabrics.

- 1 yd. (0.95 m) fabric, for borders and center square of each block.

- ½ yd. (0.5 m) fabric, for binding.

- 1⅞ yd. (1.75 m) fabric, for backing.

- Batting, three pieces, about 22" x 29" (56 x 73.5 cm) each.

CUTTING DIRECTIONS ✄

- Label the fabrics for the block design as on page 226, steps 1a or 1b. Cut the following strips across the width of the fabric: seven 1" (2.5 cm) strips each, from Fabrics B and C; eleven 1" (2.5 cm) strips each, from Fabrics D and E; and sixteen 1" (2.5 cm) strips each, from Fabrics F and G.

- Cut two 1" (2.5 cm) strips from the fabric for the center squares of the blocks; these are Strips A.

- Cut six 2½" (6.5 cm) strips from the fabric for the border; the strips will be cut to length as on page 226, steps 4 and 5.

Log Cabin quilt blocks can be made from either solid-colored or printed fabrics and sewn into three design arrangements to make miniquilts.

How to Sew a Log Cabin Miniquilt

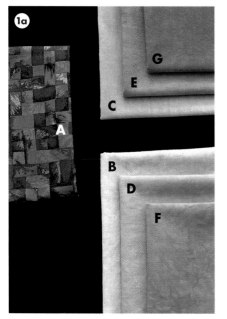

1a. Hand-dyed fabrics. Arrange and label six hand-dyed fabrics from B to G, graduating from dark to light and light to dark as indicated. Fabric for center square is Fabric A.

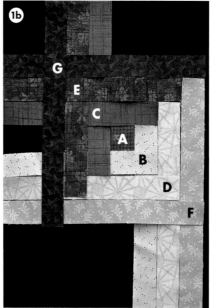

1b. Printed fabrics. Determine the arrangement of the fabrics, cutting narrow strips, if necessary; position three light fabrics on one half of the block and three dark fabrics on the other half. Label fabrics from A to G as indicated.

2. Assemble 72 Log Cabin blocks as on page 223, steps 2 to 6; in step 2, cut across pieced strip at 1" (2.5 cm) intervals.

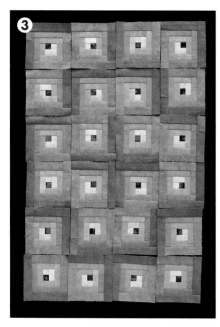

3. Arrange blocks four across and six down, as shown in the quilts on pages 224 and 225.

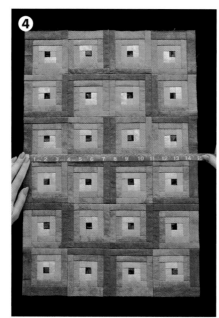

4. Stitch the blocks into rows; stitch rows together, finger-pressing seam allowances in opposite directions. Press quilt top. Measure each quilt top across the middle; determine shortest measurement.

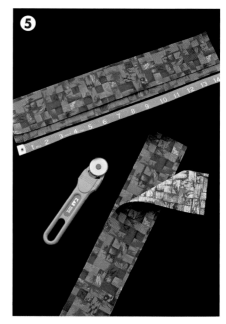

5. Layer fabric strips for borders and cut six strips to measurement determined in step 4 for upper and lower borders; remainder of border strips will be trimmed to size for side borders in step 6.

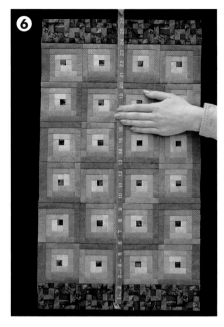

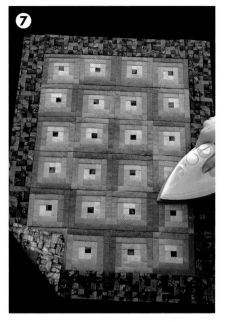

6. Stitch upper and lower border strips to each quilt top as on page 84. Measure each quilt top down the middle, including border strips; determine shortest measurement. From remaining border strips, cut six side borders to this length.

7. Stitch border strips to sides of each quilt top. Press seam allowances toward borders. Press quilt top.

8. Cut backing fabric for each quilt 4" (10 cm) wider and longer than quilt top. Layer and baste the quilt top, batting, and backing (pages 92 to 97).

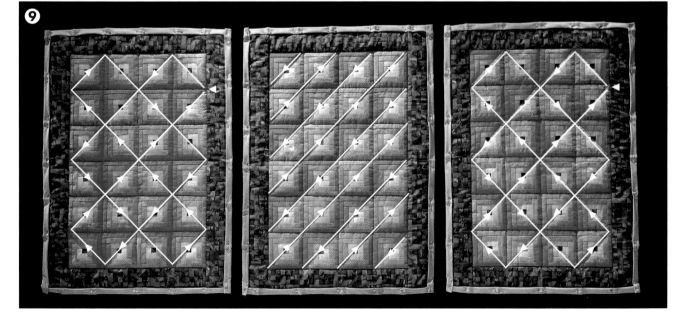

9. Quilt wall hangings, using stitch-in-the-ditch method (page 103), stitching in seamlines joining blocks and borders. Stitch additional diagonal lines through centers of blocks to accentuate design as indicated by arrows. Apply binding to quilts as on pages 111 to 116. Attach fabric sleeve to each quilt (page 171).

Sampler Quilt

Sampler quilts are made from a variety of quilt blocks, united through color and size. The instructions that follow are for a 56" x 77" (142 x 195.5 cm) sampler quilt that can be used as a wall hanging, lap quilt, or twin-size bed quilt. Although the quilt may appear complex and intricate, it is easily assembled from the nine quilt blocks, plain fabric panels, quick-pieced checkerboards, and pieced-triangle strips.

The quilt is designed with four vertical columns that are separated by sashing strips. A narrow inner border frames the quilt, and Log Cabin blocks form a colorful outer border.

This sampler quilt is an attractive way to showcase a variety of quilting techniques. The example shown opposite has template quilting on the sashing strips, and the plain fabric blocks are embellished with free-motion stipple quilting, motif quilting, and template quilting.

Sampler quilts can be made using several fabrics, sometimes even as many as thirty. To simplify fabric selection, start with two or three multicolored fabrics to set the theme. Use the theme fabrics for the plain fabric panels; then incorporate them in some of the pieced blocks. The theme fabrics set the overall tone of the quilt. When choosing theme fabrics, think about scale. A larger print with many colors makes it easier to select the remaining fabrics.

Choose fabric colors with values that range from light to dark. Select a variety of fabrics, including solids, prints, checks, and stripes. You may want to keep swatches in a notebook and collect fabrics over a period of time. Multicolored prints work especially well when making the pieced checkerboard strips. Solid-colored fabrics are used for the sashing strips to separate and define the columns and the border of the quilt.

When piecing the quilt top, it is important to stitch scant ¼" (6 mm) seams. This allows for shrinkage resulting from multiple stitched seams and ensures that the pieced border will fit around the quilt top.

Sampler quilt incorporates nine quilt block designs and a variety of quilting techniques.

YOU WILL NEED

- Two or three multicolored theme fabrics.

- Assorted fabrics, for pieced blocks and pieced strips.

- ¼ yd. (0.25 m) each of three fabrics, for vertical sashing strips.

- ⅓ yd. (0.32 m) fabric, for inner border.

- Batting, about 60" x 81" (152.5 x 206 cm).

- Fabrics for Log Cabin border: ⅛ yd. (0.15 m) Fabric A, ¼ yd. (0.25 m) Fabric B, ⅜ yd. (0.35 m) Fabric C, ⅜ yd. (0.35 m) Fabric D, ½ yd. (0.5 m) Fabric E, ½ yd. (0.5 m) Fabric F, ⅝ yd. (0.6 m) Fabric G.

- 3½ yd. (3.2 m) fabric, for backing.

- ⅝ yd. (0.6 m) fabric, for binding.

Diagram of the Sampler Quilt

Log Cabin blocks	
Ohio Star blocks	
Pieced-triangle strips	
Checkerboard strips	
Theme fabrics (choose 2 or 3)	
Shadowed Square blocks	
Drunkard's Path units	
Pieced Heart blocks	
Card Trick blocks	
Double Nine-patch block	
Spools block	
Nine-patch block	
Sashing strips (choose three)	
Inner border	
Binding	

CUTTING DIRECTIONS ✄

- For Column One of the sampler quilt, cut one 7½" x 12½" (19.3 x 31.8 cm) rectangle and one 6½" x 12½" (16.3 x 31.8 cm) rectangle from theme fabric for the plain fabric panels.

- For Column Two, cut one 6½" x 9" (16.3 x 23 cm) rectangle, one 6½" x 9½" (16.3 x 24.3 cm) rectangle, and one 6½" x 11½" (16.3 x 29.2 cm) rectangle from theme fabric for the plain fabric panels.

- For Column Three, cut one 9½" x 10" (24.3 x 25.5 cm) rectangle and one 9½" x 11" (24.3 x 28 cm) rectangle from theme fabric for the plain fabric panels.

- For Column Four, cut one 6½" x 10½" (16.3 x 27.8 cm) rectangle, and one 6½" x 12½" (16.3 x 31 .8 cm) rectangle from theme fabric for the plain fabric panels.

- For pieced blocks and pieced strips, cut the as on pages 232 to 225.

- For the vertical sashing strips, cut fabric strips across the width of the fabric. Cut two 3½" (9 cm) strips from first sashing fabric, to join Columns One and Two. Cut two 2½" (6.5 cm) strips from second sashing fabric, to join Columns Two and Three. Cut two 2½" (6.5 cm) strips from third sashing fabric, to join Columns Three and Four.

- For the inner plain border, cut six 1½" (3.8 cm) strips across the width of the fabric. For the outer Log Cabin border, cut 1½" (3.8 cm) strips across the width of seven fabrics. Light-colored fabrics may be used for one half of the block and dark-colored fabrics for the other half. Cut the number of fabric strips as follows: Fabric A, two strips for center squares; Fabric B, four inner light strips; Fabric C, six inner dark strips; Fabric D, eight middle light strips; Fabric E, ten middle dark strips; Fabric F, eleven outer light strips; and Fabric G, thirteen outer dark strips.

- For the binding, cut seven 2½" (6.5 cm) strips.

How to Sew Column One of the Sampler Quilt

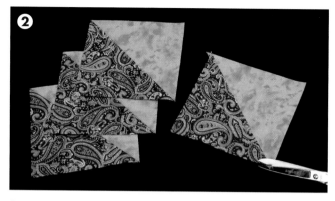

1. Sew one 12" (30.5 cm) block each of the following: Ohio Star (page 172), Drunkard's path (page 178), and Shadowed Square (page 200). Set aside two of the remaining strip-pieced triangles from the Shadowed Square design for use in Column Two.

2. Cut two 6⅞" (17.5 cm) squares each from two fabrics for pieced-triangle strips. Layer squares and cut once diagonally. Stitch one triangle from each fabric, right sides together, along long edge. Finger-press seam allowances to one side; trim points. Repeat with remaining triangles to make four squares.

3. Stitch two pieced squares right sides together as shown, to make a pieced-triangle strip. Finger-press seam allowances to one side. Repeat to make a second pieced-triangle strip for Column Four; set aside.

4. Cut two 1½" x 20" (3.8 x 51 cm) strips each from two fabrics. Stitch strips together lengthwise, alternating fabrics, to make a 4½" x 20" (11.5 x 51 cm) pieced strip. Press seam allowances in one direction.

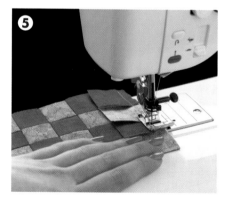

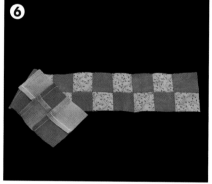

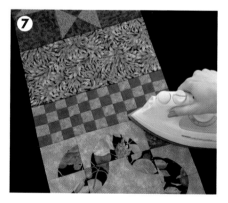

5. Trim short end of pieced strip at 90° angle. Cut twelve 1½" (3.8 cm) strips across the pieced strip. Stitch pieced strips together, alternating fabrics to make a 4½" x 12½" (11.5 x 31.8 cm) checkerboard strip.

6. Cut one 1½" x 20" (3.8 x 51 cm) strip from each of two fabrics; make a 2½" x 12½" (6.5 x 31.8 cm) checkerboard strip as in steps 4 and 5.

7. Stitch blocks, checkerboard strips, pieced-triangle strip, and the theme-fabric rectangles into a column as desired. Press the pieced column, pressing seam allowances in one direction.

How to Sew Column Two of the Sampler Quilt

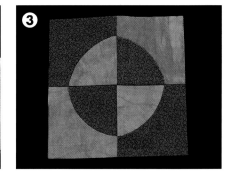

1. Make one 6" (15 cm) Pieced Heart block (page 162); set aside the remaining heart units for use in Column Four. Using the strip-pieced triangles set aside from Column One, make two Shadowed Square blocks as on page 202, steps 4 and 5; in step 4, cut one 6⅞" (17.5 cm) square. Stitch blocks together as shown to make a vertical strip.

2. Cut one 7" (18 cm) square each from two fabrics. Using circle template with 5" (12.5 cm) diameter, cut one circle each from two fabrics, adding scant ¼" (6 mm) seam allowance. Continue to make a total of eight Drunkard's Path units as on pages 179 to 180, steps 3 to 6.

3. Arrange four Drunkard's Path units as shown. Stitch units together to form two rows; stitch rows together. Set aside remaining units for use in Column Four.

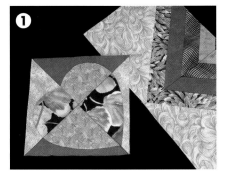

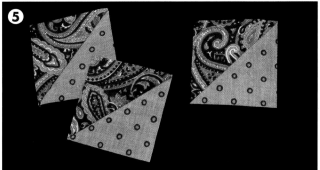

4. Cut three 1½" x 11" (3.8 x 28 cm) strips from each of two fabrics. Continue as on page 232, steps 5 and 6; in step 5, press seam allowances in one direction, and, in step 6, cut six strips across each pieced strip. Stitch strips together, alternating fabrics to make two 3½" x 6½" (9 x 16.3 cm) checkerboard strips.

5. Cut two 2⅞" (7.2 cm) squares from two fabrics for pieced-triangle strip; cut the squares in half once diagonally. Stitch one triangle from each fabric, right sides together, along long edge. Repeat with the remaining triangles to make three pieced-triangle squares.

6. Stitch the pieced-triangle squares together, side by side, to make a 2½" x 6½" (6.5 x 16.3 cm) strip. Finger-press seam allowances to one side.

7. Stitch blocks, checkerboard strips, pieced-triangle strip, and theme fabric rectangles into a column as desired. Press the pieced column, pressing the seam allowances in one direction.

How to Sew Column Three of the Sampler Quilt

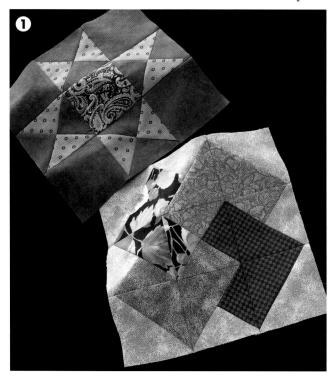

1. Make one 9" (23 cm) Ohio Star block (page 162) and one 9" (23 cm) Card Trick block (page 186).

2. Make one 9" (23 cm) Spools block (page 194) and one Double Nine-patch block (page 214).

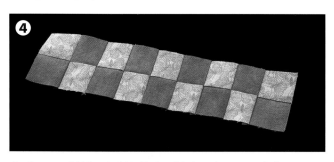

3. Cut two 3⅞" (9.7 cm) squares from each of two fabrics for pieced-triangle strip. Make a 3½" x 9½" (9 x 24.3 cm) strip as on page 233, steps 5 and 6; in step 5, omit reference to 2⅞" (7.2 cm) squares.

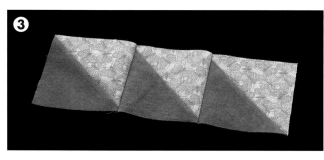

4. Cut one 1½" x 15½" (3.8 x 39.3 cm) strip each from two fabrics. Make 2½" x 9½" (6.5 x 24.3 cm) checkerboard strip as on page 232, steps 4 and 5; in step 5, cut nine strips across pieced strip.

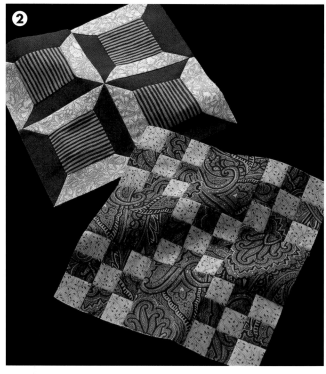

5. Stitch blocks, checkerboard strip, pieced-triangle strip, and theme-fabric rectangles into a column as desired. Press pieced column, pressing seam allowances in one direction.

How to Sew Column Four of the Sampler Quilt

1. Make one 6" (15 cm) Card trick block (page 186) and one 6" (15 cm) Nine-patch block (page 214).

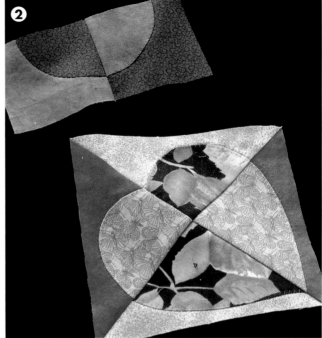

2. Stitch two remaining Drunkard's Path units from Column Two together as shown to make a two-patch block; discard remaining units. Complete second 6" (15 cm) Pieced Heart block from units remaining from Column Two.

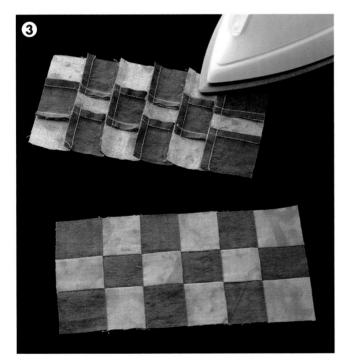

3. Make two 3½" 6½" (9 x 16.3 cm) checkerboard strips as on page 233, step 4.

4. Stitch blocks, pieced-triangle strip, checkerboard strips, two-patch Drunkard's Path block, and theme-fabric rectangles into a column as desired. Press pieced column, pressing seam allowances in one direction. Assemble quilt as on pages 236 and 237.

How to Assemble the Sampler Quilt

1. Stitch short ends of corresponding vertical sashing strips together. Trim the seam allowances; finger-press to one side. Trim each sashing strip to measure 61½" (156.3 cm).

2. Mark centers of vertical sashing strips and columns. Pin one sashing strip to one column, right sides together, matching the centers and ends. Pin along length, easing in any excess fullness; stitch. Repeat to join all sashing strips and columns. Press the seam allowances toward sashing.

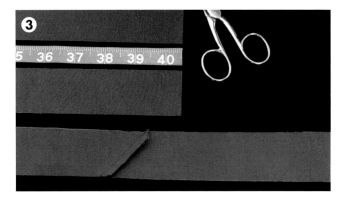

3. Stitch short ends of two strips for inner border together. Trim the seam allowances; finger-press to one side. Repeat to make a second pieced strip. Trim pieced strips to 63½" (161.3 cm), for side strips of inner border. Trim remaining strips to 40½" (103 cm), for upper and lower strips of inner border.

4. Pin inner border strip to upper edge of the quilt top at the center and ends, right sides together; pin along length, easing in any fullness. Stitch; press the seam allowances toward the inner border. Repeat at lower edge.

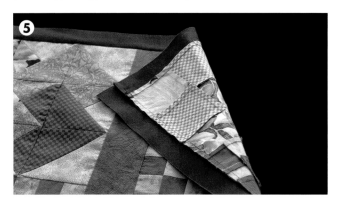

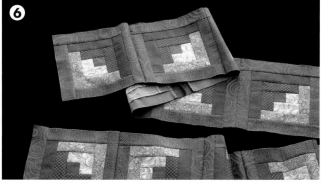

5. Pin and stitch pieced strips to sides of quilt top as in step 4. Press seam allowances toward the inner border.

6. Assemble 34 Log Cabin blocks, as on page 223, steps 2 to 6. Stitch six Log Cabin blocks together for the upper border strip, placing the color values as shown in diagram on page 231. Finger-press the seam allowances to one side. Repeat to stitch strip for lower edge.

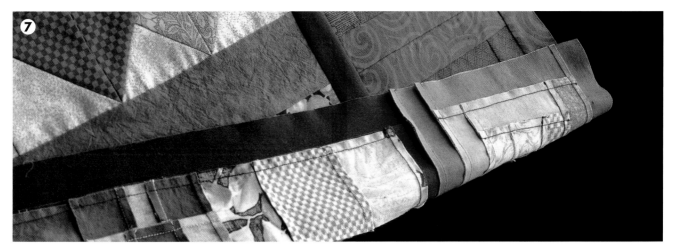

7. Pin the light-colored side of Log Cabin strip to upper edge of quilt top at center and ends, right sides together; pin along length, easing in any fullness. Stitch; press seam allowances toward the inner border. Repeat at lower edge.

8. Stitch 11 Log Cabin blocks together for the side border strip, placing the color values as shown in the diagram on page 231. Repeat for remaining side strip. Pin and stitch pieced strips to sides of quilt top as in step 7. Press the seam allowances toward the border.

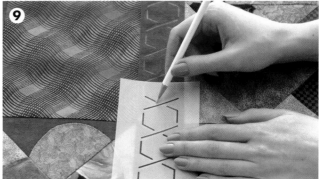

9. Mark quilting lines for template quilting as desired (page 100). Cut backing 4" (10 cm) wider and longer than quilt top, piecing the fabric as necessary. Layer and baste quilt top, batting, and backing (pages 92 to 97).

10. Quilt along sashing and inner border as on page 103, using the stitch-in-the-ditch method; then complete free-motion and template quilting within the theme fabrics and sashing strips as on page 104.

11. Stitch-in-the-ditch along seams of pieced blocks as on page 103. Stitch in the ditch between the Log Cabin blocks, and stitch through blocks diagonally in both directions, making a X; use continuous stitching, and pivot the stitching ¼" (6 mm) from raw edge at seams between blocks. Apply binding as on pages 111 to 116.

ALTERNATE
PIECING METHODS

very avid quilter has a stash. Fabrics accumulate over time. Some are leftovers from past projects; some are irresistible pieces purchased for undetermined future projects. The quilt methods and projects in this section give you lots of ways to use fabrics from your stash. Quilting and scraps have always gone together. Reclaim the tradition of using what you have.

Traditional Crazy Quilts

Crazy quilting allows you to use scraps of all kinds to make quilts in an unplanned, nonprecise pattern. Crazy quilting was popular during the Victorian Era when scraps of silk were used to complement the lavish decorating style. Patches were basted on a foundation fabric and secured with hand embroidery stitches.

Today, machine embroidery makes these quilts faster to sew. Experiment with decorative threads, such as metallics and rayons, for embroidery stitches. Mix a variety of fabrics, such as silks, satins, denims, and bits of old table or bed linens.

For the traditional method of crazy quilting, the patches are basted to a foundation fabric with the edges turned under, then secured with decorative stitches, such as feather and herringbone stitches.

Use a lightweight fabric, such as muslin, for the foundation, in a light color that will not show through the fabrics in the quilt top. The foundation fabric is usually cut into blocks, and the completed blocks sewn together to make the quilt top. For small quilts, the patches can be applied to one large foundation.

Traditionally, batting was not used with crazy quilts. To secure the quilt top to the backing, the quilts were tacked at the seamlines. If batting is used, the blocks should be tacked or quilted at frequent intervals to keep the batting from shifting.

TIPS FOR MAKING A CRAZY QUILT

- Use machine embroidery thread for smooth, even decorative stitching with sheen.

- Control slippery fabrics, suck as some silks, by fusing them to lightweight interfacing.

- Use woven lamé for a decorative effect. Preshrink the lamé with a steam iron, and fuse it to knitted interfacing for strength and to prevent raveling.

- Use a larger needle and loosen the needle thread tension when stitching with metallic thread. Check to see that the needle does not have burrs.

YOU WILL NEED

- Fabric scraps for quilt blocks.

- Lightweight muslin for foundation fabric.

- Fabric for borders, if desired, yardage determined as on page 83.

- Fabric for backing, yardage determined as on page 31.

- Fabric for binding.

- Batting, if desired, about 4" (10 cm) larger than quilt.

- Machine embroidery thread for crazy quilt made by traditional method.

How to Make a Crazy Quilt Using the Traditional Method

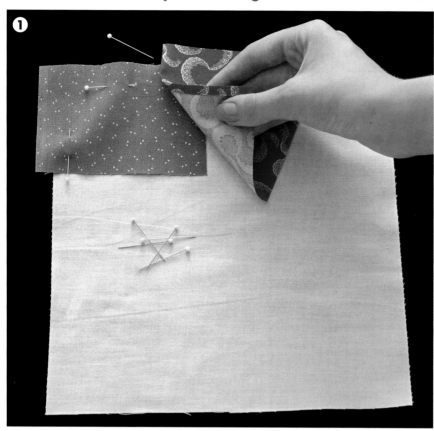

1. Cut the foundation fabric slightly larger than the finished block size plus ½" (1.3 cm) for seam allowances. Cut a patch for one corner; pin in place. Cut another patch to overlap first patch; turn under ¼" (6 mm) on edge that will overlap. Pin or baste in place.

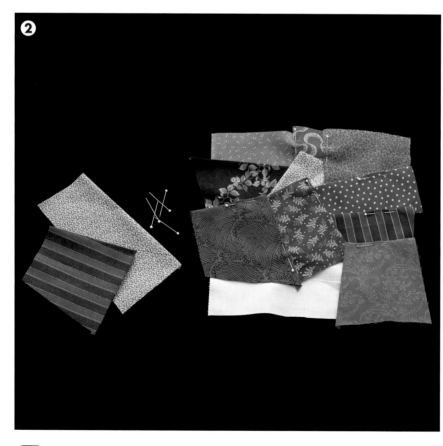

2. Continue to attach patches until foundation is covered. Turn under ¼" (6 mm) on all edges except those on outside of the block; pin or baste in place.

3. Stitch along pressed edges, using decorative stitches, working from center to edges; pull needle thread to underside, and knot.

4. Trim blocks to finished size plus ½" (1.3 cm) for seam allowances using a square ruler.

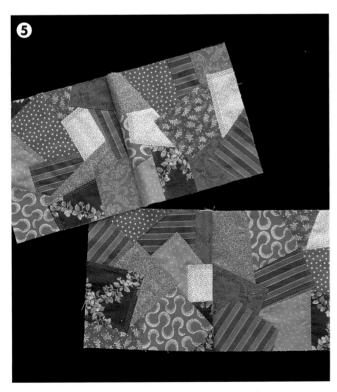

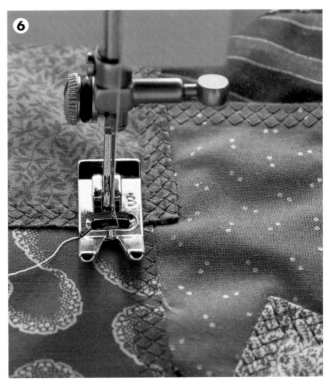

5. Arrange blocks as desired; stitch blocks together into rows. Stitch rows together, finger pressing seam allowances in opposite directions. Press quilt top. Cut and attach border strips (pages 84 to 87).

6. Cut backing (page 31). If batting is desired, cut batting 4" (10 cm) larger than quilt top, batting, and backing (pages 92 and 93). Machine quilt at frequent intervals. Cut and apply binding (pages 111 to 116).

Stitch-and-Flip Crazy Quilt

Crazy quilts can be sewn using stitch-and-flip method. For this method, the patches are secured without decorative stitching, and raw edges are concealed as each new piece is added. This method works well for quilts with a contemporary look.

How to Make a Crazy Quilt Using the Stitch-and-Flip Method

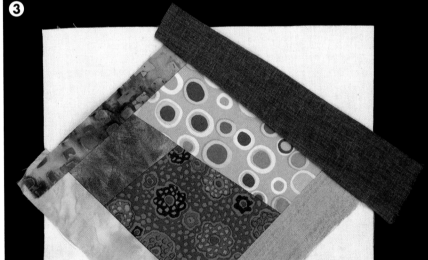

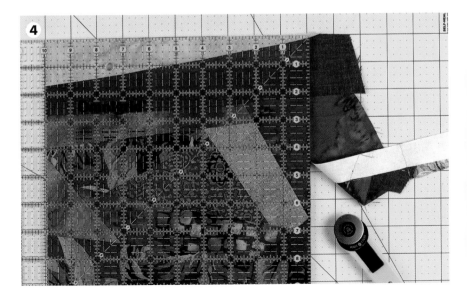

1. Cut the foundation fabric slightly larger than the finished block size plus ½" (1.3 cm) for seam allowances. Cut a patch, and place in center or corner of foundation. Pin in place. Place a second patch on first patch, right sides together, aligning one edge. The second patch must be slightly longer than the center patch. Stitch ¼" (6mm) seam along aligned edges.

2. Flip the second patch right side up; press.

3. Pin in place. Working clockwise around the center patch, continue to attach patches until foundation is covered.

4. Trim blocks to finished size plus ½" (1.3 cm) for seam allowances using a square ruler.

5. Arrange blocks as desired; stitch blocks together into rows. Stitch rows together, finger pressing seam allowances in opposite directions. Press quilt top. Cut and attach border strips (pages 84 to 87).

6. Cut backing (page 31). If batting is desired, cut batting 4" (10 cm) larger than quilt top, batting, and backing (pages 92 and 93). Machine quilt at frequent intervals. Cut and apply binding (pages 111 to 116).

YOU WILL NEED

- Muslin for foundation.
- Scraps, cotton, silk, or specialty fabric.
- Lightweight fusible interfacing to stabilize silk.
- Iron.
- Square ruler to square up blocks.
- Thread.

String-Pieced Quilts

String piecing is an easy way to use your scraps to create interesting and lively fabric arrangements. Traditionally used to make utility quilts, string piecing also lends itself to many contemporary designs.

String piecing is done on a foundation of fabric, usually muslin. Strips of fabric in various widths are stitched to the foundation. For unexpected accents, add silks, brocades,

and other specialty fabrics to your string-pieced quilts. To stabilize specialty fabrics, fuse lightweight interfacing to the back of the fabric. The completed blocks can be arranged for a variety of effects.

Basic instructions are given for making string quilts of any size or shape. This technique is used for making all styles of string-pieced quilts.

How to Make a String Pieced Quilt Block

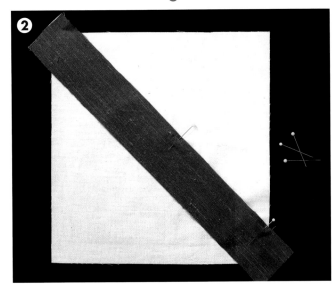

YOU WILL NEED

- 1⅔ yd. (1.63 m) lightweight muslin for foundation fabric.

- Variety of fabric strips, 2 to 3 yd. (2 to 3 m) total.

- 1½ yd. (2.5 m) fabric for backing.

- ⅜ yd. (.5 m) for binding.

- Batting, about 34" x 54" (117 x 168 cm).

1. Cut muslin foundation 1" (2.5 cm) larger than finished block size. Cut strips of fabric, varying the width as desired; the cut length should extend beyond the edges of the foundation.

2. Place one strip, right side up, in the middle of the foundation at the desired angle. The ends of the strips must extend beyond edges of foundation. Pin in place.

3. Place second strip, right side down, along one long edge of first strip; pin. Stitch ¼" (6mm) from aligned raw edges.

4. Fold strip right side up; press. Continue adding strips until half of foundation is covered. If desired, change angle of some strips, and stitch ¼" (6 mm) from raw edge of top strip; trim edges of strips even.

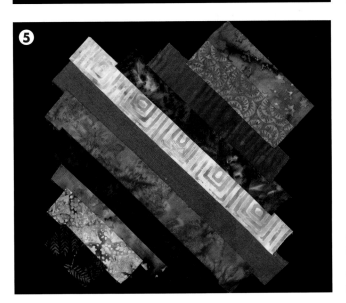

5. Repeat steps 3 and 4 for the opposite side of the foundation.

6. Trim block to finished size plus ½" (1.3 cm) for seam allowances.

More String-Pieced Quilts

Bold, contrasting colors have a strong impact in this modern string-pieced quilt. The arrangement of the center eight blocks creates a three-dimensional effect.

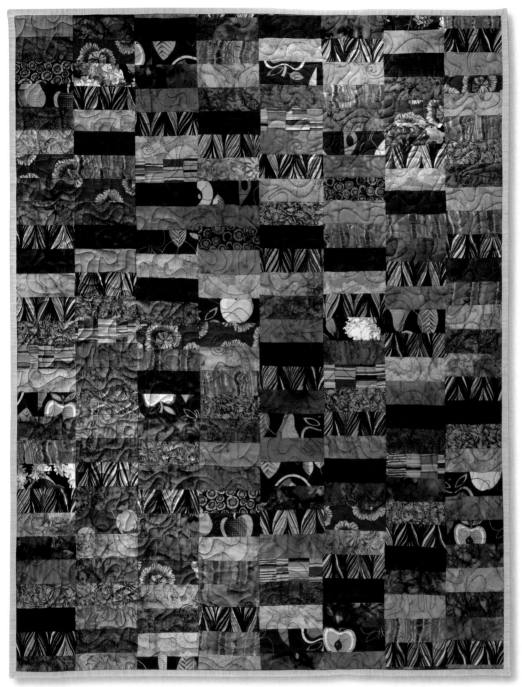

The linear design of this quilt is achieved by string-piecing long foundation strips instead of blocks. The quilt measures about 30" x 50" (76 x 127cm), making it suitable for a wall hanging or lap quilt.

How to Make a String-pieced Block Quilt

1. Cut fifteen 11" (28cm) squares out of the muslin. Cut strips of fabric, varying the width as desired; the cut lengths must extend beyond the edges of the muslin foundation. Make fifteen string-pieced blocks (page 247). Trim blocks to 10½" (27 cm).

2. Determine the desired block arrangement. A flannel board (page 37) is very helpful for this step.

3. Stitch each row of three blocks together. Stitch rows together, pressing seams in opposite directions.

4. Cut batting 4" (10 cm) larger than quilt top; press. Layer and baste quilt top, batting, and backing (pages 92 to 97). Quilt on all seam-lines, using the stitch-in-the-ditch method (page 103).

5. Bind quilt (page 111). Add a hanging sleeve (page 171), if desired.

Sunburst Wall Quilt

Use colorful scraps to make the Sunburst Wall Quilt, an updated version of Grandmother's Fan. Add dupioni silk and other speciality fabrics to add sparkle and unite the scraps. Use a colorful border fabric to help select colors for the quilt.

The wall hanging comes together quickly using a muslin foundation. Wedge shaped pieces are stitched and flipped, creating a radiating sunburst.

Two sizes of blocks, large and small, are made using the stitch-and-flip technique (page 245) on a muslin foundation. Blocks are cut and pieced together to create the sunburst effect.

All of the seam allowances are ¼" (6 mm). The finished size is about 40" (102 cm) square.

YOU WILL NEED

- 1 yd. (1 m) muslin for foundation.

- 2 to 3 yds. (2 to 3 m) of fabric scraps (cottons, silks, brocades).

- Lightweight interfacing for stabilizing silks and brocades.

- 1⅛ yd. (1 m) fabric for the outer border.

- ¼ yd. (0.25 m) fabric inner border.

- Batting, about 42" (106.7 cm) square.

- ½ yd. (0.5 m) fabric for binding.

- 1¼ yd. (1.25 m) fabric for backing.

- Cut A Round Circle Cutter Ruler, large.

- Small 28 mm straight rotary cutter and mat.

- Large 15" Square Ruler.

- Thread.

CUTTING DIRECTIONS ✂

- Cut muslin squares for foundation, four 14½" x 14½" (37 x 37 cm), and four 7½" x 7½" (19 x 19 cm) blocks.

- Cut four 6" crosswise strips for the borders and set aside. The remainder can be incorporated in with the scraps. Prepare silks and brocades by applying fusible interfacing to the back of the fabric, following manufacturer's instructions.

The colorful border fabric for this quilt provided inspiration and guidance for selecting the scrap fabrics in the quilt.

How to Make a Sunburst Quilt

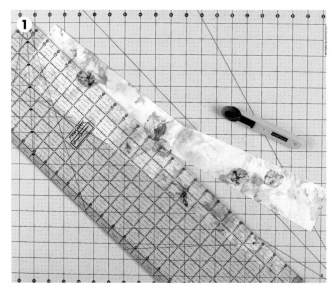

1. Cut scraps in to various sized wedges about 20" (51 cm) long and 3" (7.5 cm) at the wide end and 1" (2.5 cm) at the narrow end. To cut quickly, take a 4" x 20" (10 cm x 51 cm) scrap; place a ruler at an angle and cut two wedges using rotary cutter.

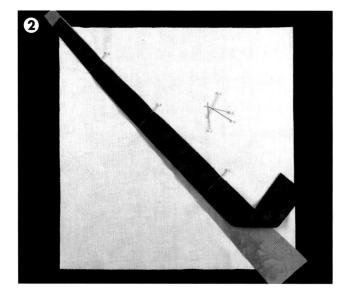

2. Place a wedge diagonally in the center of one of the 14½" (37 cm x 37 cm) square muslin foundations, covering the entire length of the foundation block. Pin in place. Place a second wedge on first wedge, right sides together, wide ends in one corner, aligning one long edge of the wedges. Stitch ¼" (6 mm) seam along aligned edges.

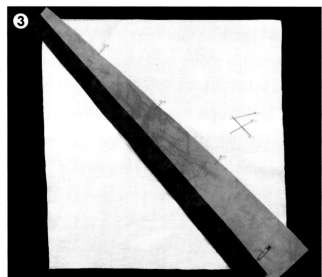

3. Flip the second wedge right side up; press. Pin in place. Place a safety pin in the corner as a visual reminder. The wide end of the wedges will always start in this corner.

4. Place a third wedge (right sides together) on top of the second wedge; pin in place; sew and press. Working outward from the center patch, continue to attach wedges until foundation is covered.

5. Flip the second patch right side up; press. Working outward from the center patch, continue to attach wedges (right sides together) until foundation is covered.

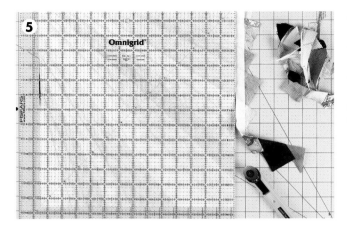

6. Repeat with the additional three 14½" (37 cm) square muslin foundations.Trim blocks to 13½" (34.5 cm) square using a square ruler.

7. Repeat steps 4-10 using the four 7½" x 7½" (19 x 19 cm) foundation blocks, using appropriate sized and colored scraps. In the sample shown, the small blocks where done in a blue scraps.

8. Trim the center sunburst blocks to 7" (17.5 cm) square using a square ruler.

9. (For steps 9 and 10, you may want to first practice using muslin.) Lay the circle cutter ruler on top of the 13½"(34.5 cm) (large) sunburst blocks. Cut out at the 12" (34.5 cm) mark.

10. Lay the circle cutter ruler on top of the 7" (17.5 cm) (small) sunburst block at cut on the 13" (33 cm) mark.

(continued)

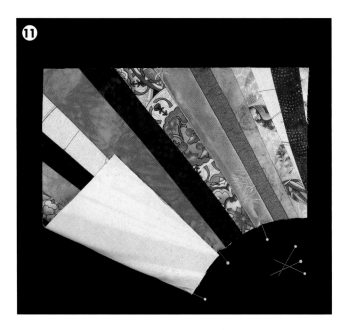

11. Fold the 13½" (large) sunburst block in half. Mark with a pin. Fold ends into pin. Mark the folds with pins.

12. Fold the 7" (17.5 cm) (small) Sunburst Block in half. Mark with a pin. Fold ends into pin. Mark the folds with pins.

13. Place the curved small blocks right sides together over the large blocks matching the three pins. Pin together, adding pins as needed and aligning the ends. Place under presser foot and slowly sew, removing pins as you approach them.

14. Arrange blocks as desired. Use a digital camera to get a different perspective. The sunburst illusion will change depending on the placement of the blocks.

15. Stitch two blocks together into rows. Stitch the rows together, finger pressing seam allowances in opposite directions. Press quilt top. Cut and attach border strips (pages 84 to 87).

16. Cut batting and backing 4" (10 cm) larger than quilt top. Machine quilt at frequent intervals. Cut and apply binding (pages 111 to 116).

17. For wall hanging, attach fabric sleeve (page 171).

Alternate method. If you do not have a circular ruler for cutting the arcs in steps 9 and 10, make templates from plastic or lightweight cardboard. For the large template, cut a 13½" (34.5 cm) square. Using a string-and-pencil compass, draw an arc in one corner with a 6¼" (16 cm) radius, and cut away. For the small template, cut a one-quarter-circle template with a radius of 6¾" (17 cm).

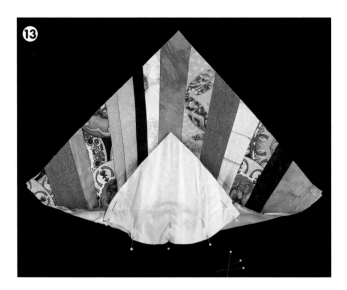

ANOTHER SUNBURST QUILT

This quilt showcases the Sunburst Pattern in the center surrounded by an inner border of silk dupioni. The second border includes string piecing and more circles. The scalloped outer border is the Wheel of Mystery block made using purchased templates by Omnigrid. The quilt was lined to the edge, encasing the batting to eliminate the need for binding. Machine quilting was the final step.

Modern Tumbler Baby Quilt

The Tumbler quilt design is a classic way to scrap quilt. Rows of trapezoids, alternating directions, create a lively overall design. The tumblers were traditionally cut using templates to ensure they were all the same size and shape. As long as the top and bottom of the trapezoid are parallel, and the side angles are the same, the scraps fit together in alternating directions to form straight rows. For this Modern Tumbler design, a Tri Tool is used to quickly and accurately cut the tumbler patches from fabric strips. Add more rows to create a larger quilt.

The instructions are for a baby quilt that is 45" x 56" (115 x 142 cm).

YOU WILL NEED:

- ¼ yd. (0.25m) each of ten fabrics for tumblers.
- ⅝ yd. (0.6m) fabric for the sashing.
- ½ yd. (0.5m) fabric for binding.
- Batting, crib size, 45" x 60" (115 x 142cm).
- 2½ yds. (2.3 m) fabric for the backing .
- Tri Rec tool by EZ Quilting.

CUTTING DIRECTIONS ✄

- Cut two 5" (12.7 cm) strips the width of the fabric from each of the ten fabrics.
- Cut eight 2½" (6.4 cm) strips the width of the fabric from the sashing fabric.
- Cut six 2½" (6.4 cm) strips the width of the fabric from binding fabric.

How to Make the Tumbler Baby Quilt

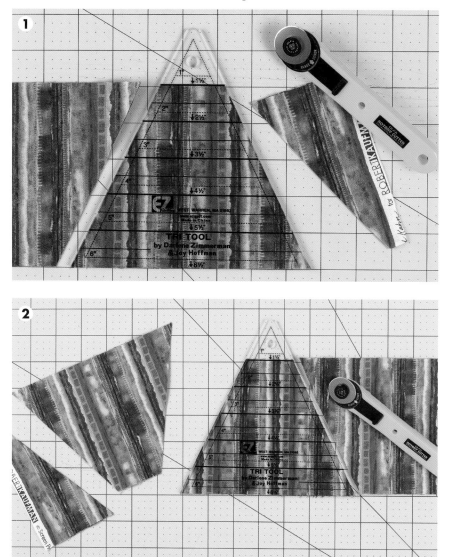

1. Place the Tri Tool with the 1½" (3.8 cm) line on top of the 5" strip and the 6½" (16.3 cm) line along the bottom of the strip. Cut along edges using rotary cutter.

2. Flip the Tri Tool around, aligning with freshly cut edge. Reposition yourself or the cutting board to safely cut new edge. Continue cutting pieces, alternating directions. You will get seven tumblers per strip.

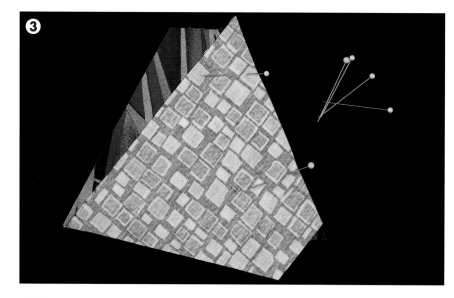

3. Pin two tumbler blocks right sides together, aligning the sides of the tumbler. There will be a ¼" (6 mm) equilateral triangle sticking out at each end. Sew using a ¼" (6 mm) seam allowance. Press and open. Check to see that top and bottom of tumbler are aligned. Repeat, adding tumblers in random order, until you have 18 tumblers in a row.

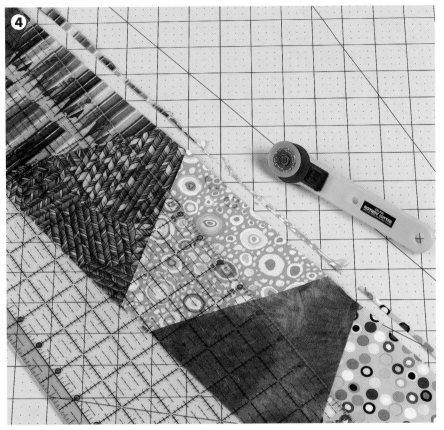

4. Repeat step 3 for the other seven rows. Square the row edges, if necessary.

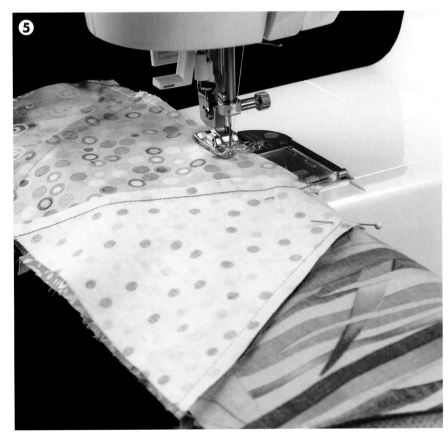

5. Place two rows together to make a mirror image. Pin at intersections, aligning seams. Stitch rows together. Press seam allowances in one direction.

6. Piece sashing to create the needed length. Sew sashing to the 4 mirror image rows and to the outer vertical edges.

7. Cut backing (page 31). Cut batting 4" (10 cm) larger than quilt top, batting, and backing (pages 92 and 93). Baste layers together. Machine quilt using stitch in the ditch or overall design. Cut and apply binding (pages 111 to 116).

TIP

Bias Edges

• Spray starch helps stabilize bias edges, especially on loosely woven fabrics.

EMBELLISHED QUILTS

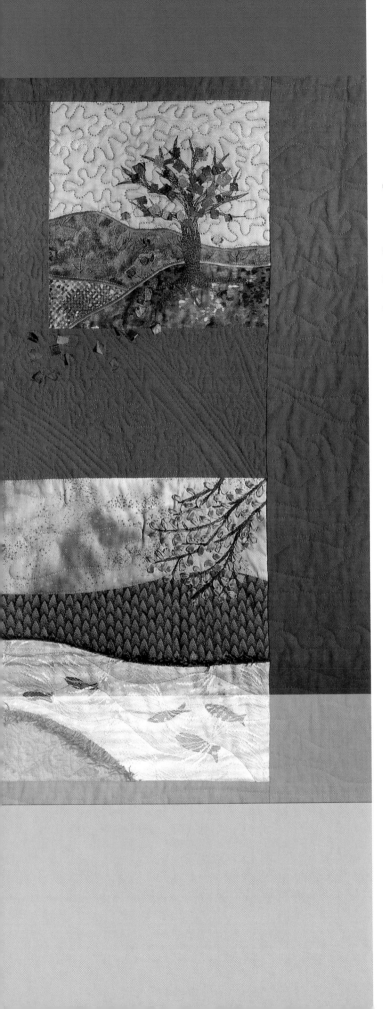

Take your quilting beyond the basics and add a personal, artistic touch. Add surface embellishments, textural interest, and surprising details to turn ordinary quilts into art quilts. The nine quilts in this section introduce you to a wide range of embellishment possibilities. Follow the directions from start to finish or use the ideas to embellish quilts of your own design.

Log Cabin Stripe Wall Hanging

Customize this simple wall hanging to go with any decorating style from country to contemporary, depending on the choice of fabrics. This quilt utilizes a combination of hand-dyed fabrics and a printed fabric. Beaded tassels embellish the centers of the Log Cabin blocks. And, for added interest, the wall hanging is quilted, using metallic thread, giving the quilt a shimmering look.

The hand-dyed fabrics used to produce the subtle color changes within the Log Cabin blocks are available in packets of eight coordinates at quilting shops and through mail-order suppliers.

The finished quilt measures about 45½" x 61½" (116 x 156.3 cm).

YOU WILL NEED

- ½ yd. (0.5 m) bundle of eight hand-dyed fabrics in a light to dark gradation, for Log Cabin blocks; or ¼ yd. (0.25 m) each of Fabrics B, C, D, E, and F, and ⅜ yd. (0.35 m) each of Fabrics G, H, and I, and ⅛ yd. (0.15 m) Fabric A, for centers of Log Cabin blocks.

- 1⅛ yd. (1.05 m) printed fabric.

- ⅓ yd. (0.32 m) fabric, for inner border.

- ⅞ yd. (0.8 m) fabric, for outer border.

- ⅝ yd. (0.6 m) fabric, for binding.

- 2⅞ yd. (2.65 m) fabric, for backing.

- Batting, about 50" x 64" (127 x 163 cm).

- Metallic sewing thread, for quilting and thread tassels.

- Embroidery thread, optional, for thread tassels.

- Beads.

CUTTING DIRECTIONS ✂

- Cut 1½" (3.8 cm) strips across the width of the fabric, for Fabrics A through I, for the Log Cabin blocks. Label the fabrics for the Log Cabin blocks as on page 226, step 1.

- Cut three 5¾" x 36½" (14.5 x 91.8 cm) strips from printed fabric.

- Cut six 1½" (3.8 cm) strips from the fabric for the inner border. Cut two strips to 36½" (91.8 cm) in length for the upper and lower inner borders. The side inner borders are cut on page 266, step 5. Cut six 4½" (11.5 cm) strips from the fabric for the outer border.

- Cut seven 2½" (6.5 cm) strips from the fabric for the binding.

How to Sew Log Cabin Quilt Blocks

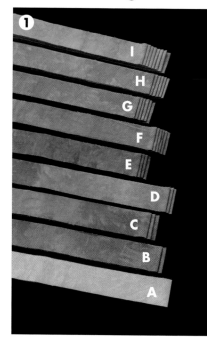

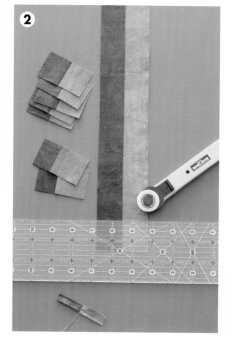

1. Cut fabrics for Log Cabin blocks as on page 263. Label strips from A to I as shown.

2. Stitch Strips A and B, right sides together, along one long edge. Press seam allowances away from Strip A. Cut across pieced strip at 1½" (3.8 cm) intervals to make sixteen units.

3. Stitch the pieced units to a second strip B, using chainstitching as shown.

4. Trim Strip B even with edges of pieced units. Press seam allowances away from center squares.

5. Stitch the three-piece units to Strip C, using chainstitching; position units at 90° angle to most recent seam on side nearest center square. Trim Strip C even with edges of pieced units. Press seam allowances away from center squares.

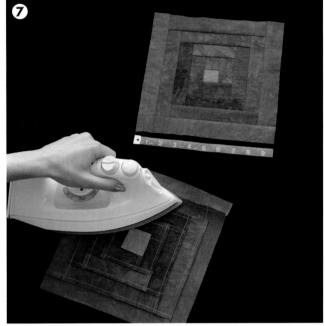

6. Stitch four-piece units to a second Strip C, using chainstitching; position units at 90° angle to the most recent seam on side nearest the center square. Trim Strip C even with edges of pieced units. Press seam allowances away from center squares.

7. Continue stitching two strips of Fabrics D, E, F, G, H, and I to pieced units in sequence.

How to Sew a Log Cabin Stripe Wall Hanging

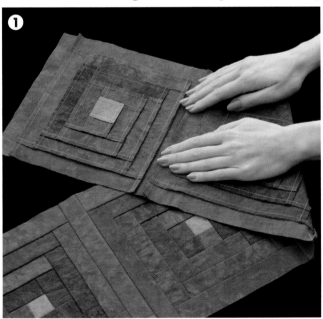

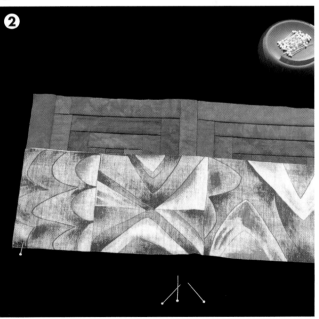

1. Stitch four Log Cabin blocks side by side, right sides together, to make a four-unit row. Finger-press seam allowances to one side. Repeat to make three more four-unit rows.

2. Pin printed fabric strip to lower edge of first Log Cabin row, at center and ends, right sides together; pin along the length, easing in any fullness. Stitch. Press seam allowances to one side. (continued)

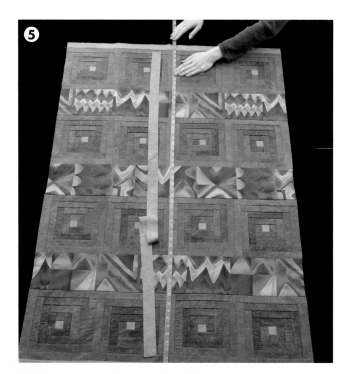

3. Continue stitching alternating rows of Log Cabin blocks and printed fabric strips together. Press the seam allowances to one side.

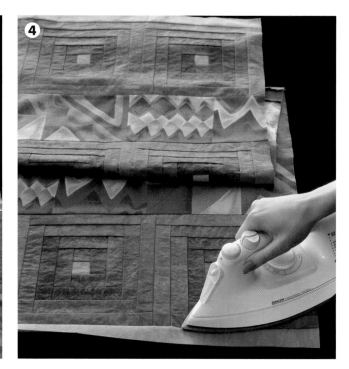

4. Pin the upper inner border strip to the upper edge of quilt top at center and ends, right sides together; pin along the length, easing in any fullness. Stitch. Repeat at lower edge. Press seam allowances toward inner borders.

5. Measure vertically through middle of quilt top, including inner border strips; cut two inner border strips for the sides equal to this length, piecing as necessary. Pin and stitch strips to sides of quilt top as in step 4.

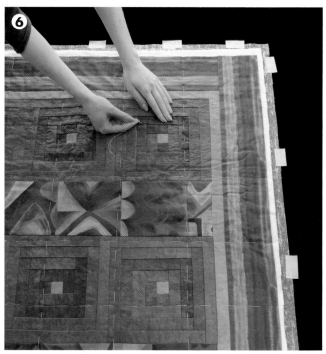

6. Apply the outer border as on page 272, steps 6 to 8. Cut backing fabric 4" (10 cm) wider and longer than quilt top, piecing as necessary. Layer and baste the quilt as on pages 92 to 97.

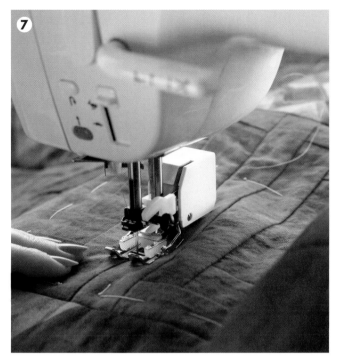

7. Quilt by stitching in the ditch (page 103) between rows of printed fabric and rows of Log Cabin blocks. Stitch in the ditch between Log Cabin blocks. Stitch in the ditch on each side of inner border.

8. Stitch diagonally in both directions through Log Cabin blocks by making an X. Begin with a stitch length; end by reducing the stitch length to near 0. Quilt design motifs in printed fabric strips as desired (pages 101 and 106).

9. Quilt the outer border by stitching between inner border and binding in a zigzag pattern, using machine-guided quilting and a walking foot (pages 100 and 104). Attach the fabric sleeve (page 171) and apply binding (pages 111 to 116).

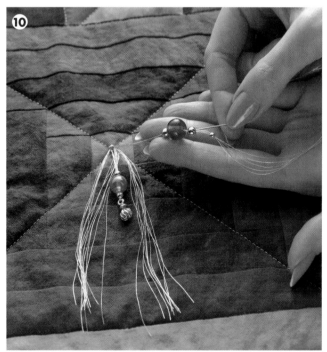

10. Thread several strands of metallic or embroidery thread through needle. Stitch through center of each Log Cabin block, and knot by taking a backstitch; leave thread tails. Attach dangling beads among thread tails, using metallic or embroidery thread; string several beads together for a tassel effect, if desired.

Woven Stars Wall Hanging

This quilt pattern is made up of three modified Ohio Star quilt blocks of graduated sizes. The star block in the center of the quilt serves as the center square for the next larger star block. That resulting block, in turn, becomes the center square for the third and final star block.

Triangles for the quilt can be easily cut from strips of fabric, using easy Angle cutting tools. Their use minimizes cutting time and effort. Instructions for traditional cutting methods are also given.

This quilted wall hanging is given an old-fashioned Victorian feel with lace, ribbons, and braid trims, buttons, and charms. The lace, ribbons, and braid trims are pinned randomly from edge to edge across the quilt; then they are quilted onto the quilt top before the binding is applied.

The completed wall hanging measures approximately 39" (99 cm) square.

YOU WILL NEED

- Fabric scrap, for center square.
- ⅛ yd. (0.15 m) fabric, for inner star background.
- ⅛ yd. (0.15 m) fabric, for inner star points.
- ¼ yd. (0.25 m) fabric, for middle star background.
- ¼ yd. (0.25 m) fabric, for middle star points.
- ⅝ yd. (0.6 m) fabric, for outer star background.
- ⅓ yd. 90.32 m) fabric, for outer star points.
- ½ yd. (0.5 m) fabric, for border.
- 1¼ yd. (1.15 m) fabric, for backing.
- Batting, about 43" (109 cm) square.
- ¼ yd. (0.25 m) fabric, for binding.
- 7 to 10 yd. (6.4 to 9.15 m) lace or ribbon, of desired width.
- Buttons or charms, for embellishing.
- Easy Angle cutting tool, optional.
- Easy Angle II cutting tool, optional.

CUTTING DIRECTIONS ✂

(without the Easy Angle cutting tools)

- Cut one 4½" (11.5 cm) square from the center fabric.

- Cut four 2⅞" (7.2 cm) squares each from the background fabric and the star point fabric for the inner star. Cut squares into triangles as on page 270. Cut four 2½" (6.5 cm) squares from the background fabric.

- Cut four 4⅞" (12.2 cm) squares each from the background fabric and the star point fabric for the middle star. Cut squares into triangles as on page 270. Cut four 4½" (11.5 cm) squares from the background fabric.

- Cut four 8⅞" (22.8 cm) squares each from the background fabric and the star point fabric for the outer star. Cut into triangles as on page 270. Cut four 8½" (21.8 cm) squares from the background fabric.

- Cut four 4" (10 cm) strips across the width of the border fabric.

- Cut four 2" (5 cm) strips from the binding fabric.

(with the Easy Angle cutting tools)

- Cut one 4½" (11.5 cm) square from the center fabric.

- Cut one 2½" (6.5 cm) strip across the width of the background fabric and the star point fabric for the inner star. Cut eight triangles from each fabric strip as on page 270, steps 1 and 2. Cut four 2½" (6.5 cm) squares from the background fabric.

- Cut one 4½" (11.5 cm) strip across the width of the background fabric and the star point fabric for the middle star. Cut eight triangles from each fabric strip as on page 270, step 3. Cut four 4½" (11.5 cm) squares from the background fabric.

- Cut two 8½" (21.8 cm) strips across the width of the background fabric and one 8½" (21.8 cm) strip across the width of the star point fabric for the outer star. Cut eight triangles from each fabric as on page 270, step 3. Cut four 8½" (21.8 cm) squares from the background fabric.

- Cut four 4" (10 cm) strips across the width of the border fabric.

- Cut four 2" (5 cm) strips from the binding fabric.

How to Cut Triangles for the Woven Stars Wall Hanging

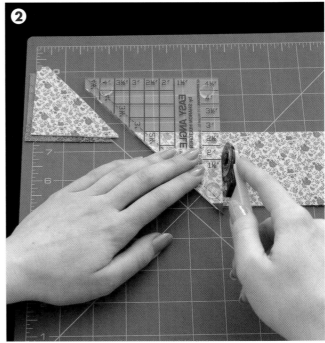

1. (With Easy Angle cutting tools) Align easy Angle cutting tool with 2½" (6.5 cm) fabric strip at the marking for 2½" (6.5 cm) right triangle; cut along diagonal edge of tool.

2. Flip tool over, keeping diagonal edge of tool along diagonal cut of fabric. Align cutting tool with edge of fabric strip at the marking for 2½" (6.5 cm) right triangle; cut along straight edge of tool. Continue to cut necessary number of triangles (page 269).

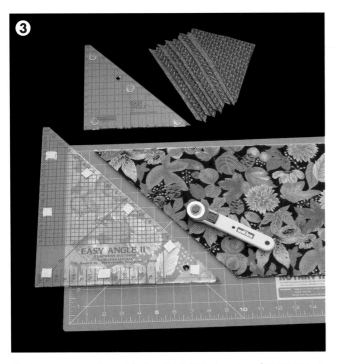

3. Repeat steps 1 and 2 for 4½" (11.5 cm) and 8½" (21.8 cm) strips, using Easy Angle II cutting tool for 8½" (21.8 cm) strips, and cutting the necessary number of triangles (page 269).

(Without Easy Angle cutting tools) Layer four 2⅞" (7.2 cm) squares, matching raw edges; cut through squares diagonally. Repeat with remaining 2⅞" (7.2 cm) squares, the 4⅞" (12.2 cm) squares, and 8⅞" (22.8 cm) squares.

How to Sew a Woven Stars Wall Hanging

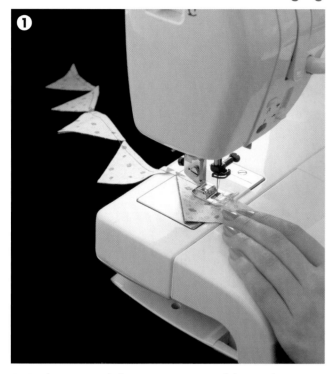

1. Stitch one triangle from inner star point fabric and one triangle from inner background fabric together, along the long edge, in ¼" (6 mm) seam. Continue piecing triangles until eight triangle-squares have been completed, using chainstitching as shown.

2. Repeat step 1 for middle and outer star fabric triangles. Clip units apart; press seam allowances toward darker fabric. Trim off points.

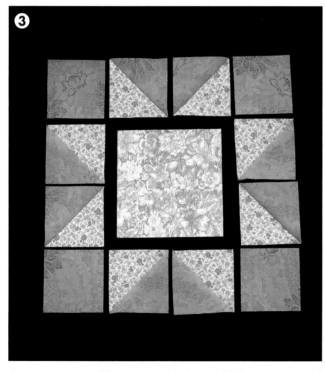

3. Arrange center fabric square, background fabric squares, and triangle-squares for inner star into quilt block design as shown.

4. Assemble block; finger-press seam allowances toward center square. Press block. (continued)

5. Use inner star block as center square for middle star, and assemble middle star block as on page 271, steps 3 and 4. Repeat for the outer star block, using middle star block as center square, to complete the quilt top.

6. Measure horizontally through middle of quilt top, and cut two border strips to that length for upper and lower borders.

7. Pin upper border strip to upper edge of quilt top at center and ends, right sides together; pin along length, easing in any fullness. Stitch. Repeat at the lower edge. Press seam allowances toward borders.

8. Measure vertically through middle of quilt top, including border strips; cut two border strips for sides equal to this length. Pin and stitch strips to sides of quilt top as in step 7.

9. Cut backing fabric 4" (10 cm) wider and longer than quilt top, piecing as necessary. Layer and baste quilt top, batting, and backing as on pages 92 to 97. Quilt, using stitch-in-the-ditch method (page 103), in seamlines of stars and borders.

10. Pin strips of lace, ribbon, and braid trim in random diagonals across quilt top. Quilt along strips, stitching close to edges of wide trims and stitching down center of narrow trims.

11. Attach fabric sleeve to wall hanging (page 171), and apply binding as on pages 111 to 116.

12. Embellish the quilt with buttons or charms as desired.

Zigzag Wall Hanging

Create this zigzag design in this wall hanging using a bundle of six hand-dyed fabrics. Choose a packet of fabrics that graduate in color value from light to dark, or select six different colors for a rainbow effect. For contrast, choose a printed fabric that coordinates with the hand-dyed packet to use along the upper and lower edges of the zigzag pattern.

The pieced portion of the quilt top inside the borders can be created either by using the templates on page 279 or by a set of triangle quilting tools for cutting triangles within squares. The set of quilter's tools comes with a tool for cutting a wide triangle and a tool for cutting a narrow triangle. Stitching two narrow triangles to a wide triangle makes a triangles-within-a-square unit. The triangle pieces are stitched together in the order shown in the diagram on page 279 to produce the zigzag effect. The wall hanging is quilted with decorative thread and is embellished along the quilting lines with coordinating beads.

The finished quilt measures about 42" x 44" (107 x 112 cm).

How to Cut Triangles

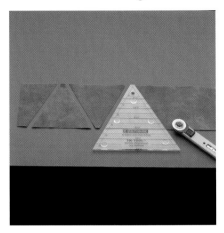

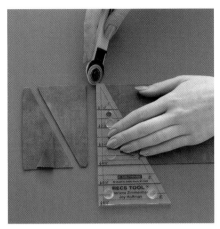

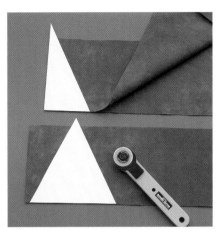

Quilter's tool (wide triangles). Align 4½" (11.5 cm) solid line on TRI TOOL with one long edge of 4½" (11.5 cm) fabric strip; cut along angled edges of tool. Rotate tool and align with opposite raw edge to cut second triangle. Repeat to cut additional triangles.

Quilter's tool (narrow triangles). Fold 4½" (11.5 cm) fabric strip in half crosswise, with the right sides together, matching raw edges. Align 4½" (11.5 cm) solid line on RECS TOOL with one long edge of fabric strip. Cut along sides of tool to make both a right and left triangle; trim along angle at top. Rotate tool and align with opposite raw edge to cut a second set of triangles. Repeat to cut additional triangles.

Templates (wide and narrow triangles). Make templates (page 279) from cardboard or template material. Cut the triangles as for quilter's tools, aligning short edges of templates with long edges of fabric; omit reference to angle at top of tool for narrow triangle. Points of triangles extend slightly beyond edges of pieced strips as shown.

YOU WILL NEED

- ¼ yd. (0.25 m) bundle of six hand-dyed fabrics in graduated colors.
- ⅔ yd. (0.63 m) printed fabric.
- ⅞ yd. (0.8 m) solid-colored fabric, for borders and binding.
- 1⅓ yd. (1.27 m) backing fabric.
- Batting, about 46" x 48" (117 x 122 cm).
- Set of triangle quilting tools, such as TRI-RECS by Quilt House, for cutting triangles within squares.
- Decorative thread.
- Beads.

CUTTING DIRECTIONS ✂

- From each hand-dyed fabric, cut three 4½" (11.5 cm) strips; cut the strips to make nine wide triangles and eighteen narrow triangles, using the quilting tools or templates as shown below.

- From the printed fabric, cut three 4½" (11.5 cm) strips; cut the strips to make thirty-four wide triangles and four narrow triangles, using the quilting tools or templates as shown below.

- From the printed fabric, also cut one 6½" (16.3 cm) strip for the upper border. From the solid-colored fabric, cut three 4½" (11.5 cm) strips for the lower border and side borders and five 2½" (6.5 cm) strips for the binding.

How to Sew a Zigzag Wall Hanging

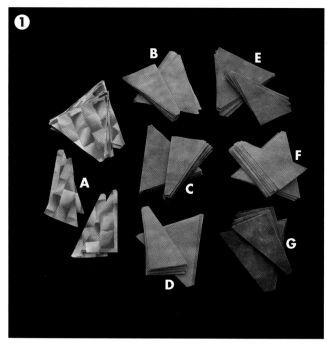

1. Label the triangles of hand-dyed fabrics from B to G, in the desired order (page 279). Label printed fabric Fabric A.

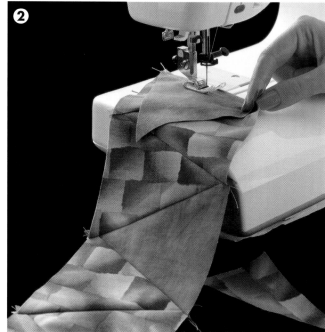

2. Stitch triangles for row one together in order shown in diagram on page 279.

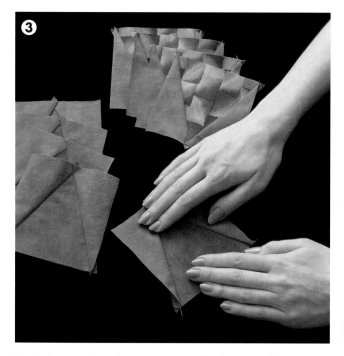

3. Make triangle-within-a-square unit for first unit of row two by stitching a narrow triangle to each side of wide triangle as shown in the diagram on page 279. Continue to make a total of nine triangles-within-a-square units as shown in diagram on page 279. Press seam allowances away from wide triangles.

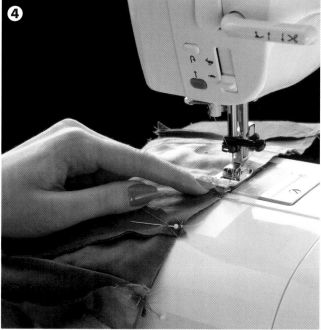

4. Stitch triangles-within-a-square units for row two together as shown in diagram on page 279. Stitch row two to row one, right sides together.

5. Following the diagram on page 279, continue as in steps 3 and 4 to complete and stitch together rows three to seven.

6. Stitch triangles for row eight together in the order shown in the diagram on page 279. Stitch row eight to row seven. Press quilt top.

7. Measure horizontally through the middle of quilt top and cut a 6½" (16.3 cm) strip from Fabric A equal to that measurement, for the upper border.

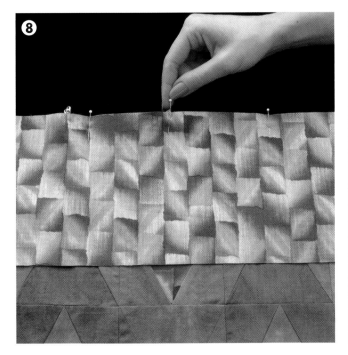

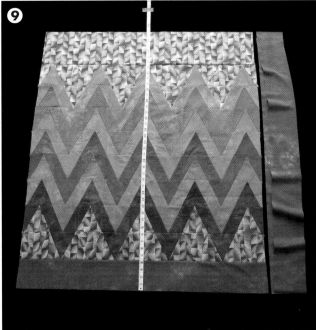

8. Pin upper border strip to upper edge of quilt top at center and ends, right sides together; pin along length. Easing in any fullness. Stitch. Repeat for lower border. Press seam allowances toward borders.

9. Measure vertically through middle of quilt top, including border strips; cut two 4½" (11.5 cm) strips from solid-colored fabric equal to that measurement. Pin and stitch to sides of quilt top as in step 8. Press seam allowances toward borders. Cut backing fabric 4" (10 cm) wider and longer than quilt top, piecing as necessary. (continued)

10. Mark quilting design lines on side borders of quilt, using chalk or pencil, by extending lines from seamlines of zigzag pattern to the edges of borders. Continue to mark additional quilting lines at top and bottom of side borders 1¾" (4.5 cm) apart; at top, extend markings into upper border.

11. Mark quilting lines in upper border by extending lines from seamlines of pieced triangles in row one. Repeat for lower border by extending seamlines from row eight into lower border. Layer and baste the quilt as on pages 92 to 97.

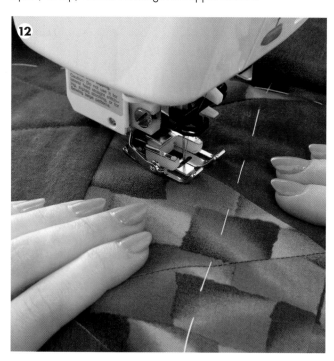

12. Quilt by stitching on the marked lines on side borders and continuing to stitch in the ditch (page 103) along zigzag pattern in piecing. Stitch on marked lines on upper border, continuing to stitch in the ditch along triangles in row one. Stitch on marked lines on lower border, continuing to stitch in the ditch along the triangles in row eight.

13. Attach fabric sleeve as on page 171, and apply binding as on pages 111 to 116. Stitch beads as desired along quilting lines.

Diagram of the Piecing of the Zigzag Wall Hanging

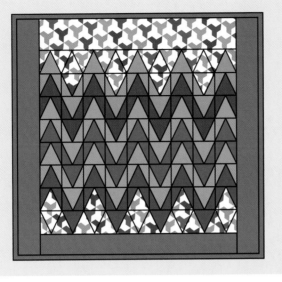

Row 1
Row 2
Row 3
Row 4
Row 5
Row 6
Row 7
Row 8

Color-coded Identification Chart for the Diagram of the Zigzag Piecing

Fabric A	
Fabric B	
Fabric C	
Fabric D	
Fabric E	
Fabric F	
Fabric G	
Border and Binding	

Templates for Wide and Narrow Triangles

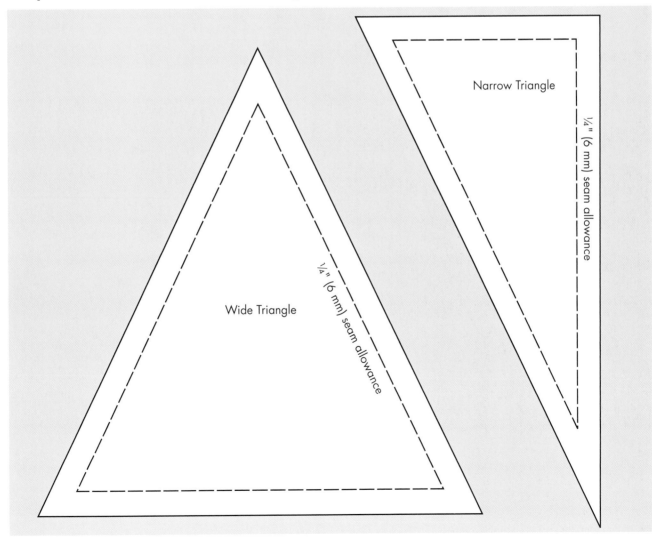

Narrow Triangle

¼" (6 mm) seam allowance

Wide Triangle

¼" (6 mm) seam allowance

Trip Around the World Wall Hanging

Create a simple wall hanging with a diamond design in which colors travel diagonally "around the world." The quilt below uses hand-dyed fabrics in graduated colors for a bright, bold impression; printed fabrics are combined for a softer look opposite.

For greater ease in cutting and piecing the small squares that make up this design, eight different strip sets were created. Strip sets are made by stitching strips of fabrics together in

a sequence. The sets are then cut to make strips containing squares of each color fabric.

The border of this quilt is embellished and quilted with seed beads. The beads are placed randomly around the border and are spaced a needle's length apart until the entire border is evenly covered. The finished quilt measures about 30½" (77.3 cm) square.

Cutting Diagram for Hand-dyed Fabrics

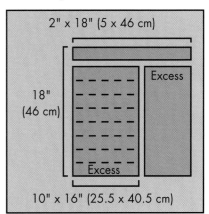

2" x 18" (5 x 46 cm)

Excess

18" (46 cm)

Excess

10" x 16" (25.5 x 40.5 cm)

Trip Around the World wall hanging can be made for either a traditional or contemporary look. Above, a quilt is made from printed fabrics and features silk ribbon embroidery embellishments. The quilt shown opposite is made of hand-dyed fabrics for a graphic look.

CUTTING DIRECTIONS

YOU WILL NEED

- ¼ yd. (0.25 m) bundle of eight hand-dyed fabrics or eight printed fabrics in a light-to-dark gradation.

- ⅜ yd. (0.35 m) fabric, for border.

- 1 yd. (0.95 m) fabric, for backing.

- Batting, about 32" (81.5 cm) square.

- Metallic thread.

- Seed beads.

- Cut one 2" (5 cm) strip across the width of each piece of hand-dyed fabric as shown in the diagram (above).

- Cut one 10" x 16" (25.5 x 40.5 cm) block from each remaining piece of hand-dyed fabric. From the 10" x 16" (25.5 x 40.5 cm) blocks, cut seven 2" x 10" (5 x 25.5 cm) strips across the width of each block as shown in the diagram above.

- Cut one 2" (5 cm) square from the excess fabric of color G.

- Cut four 3" (7.5 cm) strips across the width of the border fabric.

- Cut one 33" (84 cm) square from backing fabric.

How to Sew Strip Sets for a Trip Around the World Wall Hanging

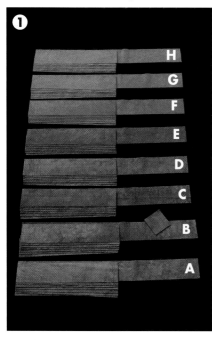

1. Label strips of hand-dyed fabric from A to H as shown.

2. Stitch 18" (46 cm) strips of Fabrics A and B, right sides together, along one long edge. Continue stitching strips of Fabrics C, D, E, F, G, and H to pieced unit in sequence. Label wrong side of strip set with the numeral 1, using a marking pencil or chalk.

3. Stitch 10" (25.5 cm) strips of Fabric B and C, right sides together, along one long edge. Continue stitching strips of Fabrics D, E, F, G, H, and A to pieced units in sequence. Label wrong side of strip set with the numeral 2, using a marking pencil or chalk.

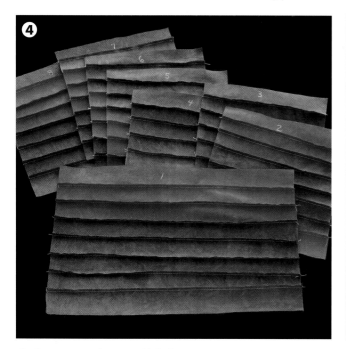

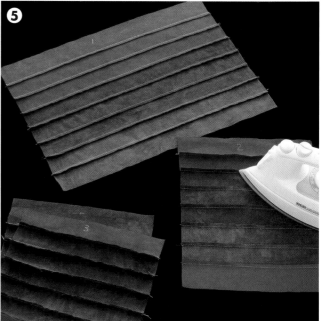

4. Continue stitching and labeling strip sets as in step 2, beginning with the next fabric in the sequence and starting again at the top of the sequence until eight strips are used. Stitch a total of eight strip sets.

5. Press seam allowances away from the top strip on odd-numbered strip sets. Press the seam allowances toward top strip on even-numbered strip sets.

How to Sew a Trip Around the World Wall Hanging

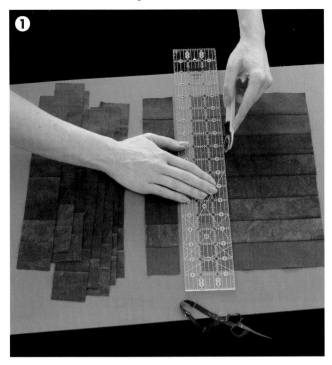

1. Trim one long edge of each strip set at 90° angle. Cut eight 2" (5 cm) strips across Strip Set 1 as shown. Cut four 2" (5 cm) strips across each remaining strip set; keep strips from each strip set together with colors in proper sequence.

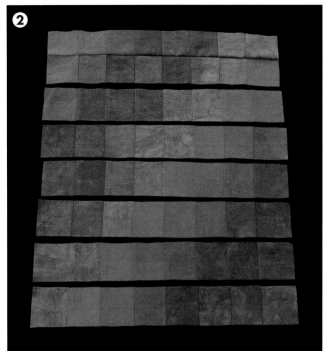

2. Stitch strips from Strip Sets 1 and 2, right sides together, along one long edge. Continue stitching strips from Strip Sets 3, 4, 5, 6, 7, and 8 to pieced unit in sequence.

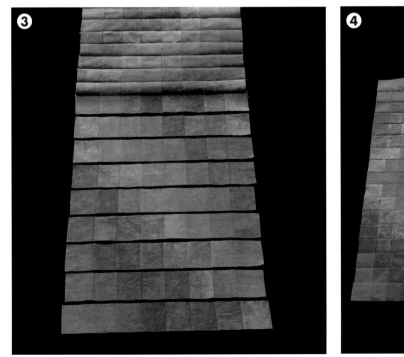

3. Stitch strip from Strip Set 1 along bottom of pieced unit. Continue stitching strips from Strip Sets 8, 7, 6, 5, 4, 3, 2, and 1 to pieced unit in that order. Press seam allowances away from middle strip.

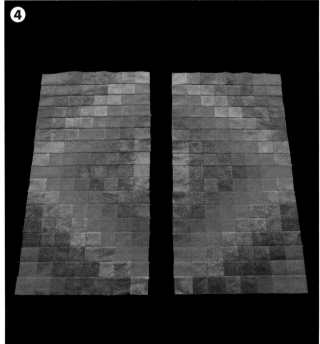

4. Repeat steps 2 and 3 to make a matching pieced unit. Arrange units next to each other so pattern resembles diamonds.

(continued)

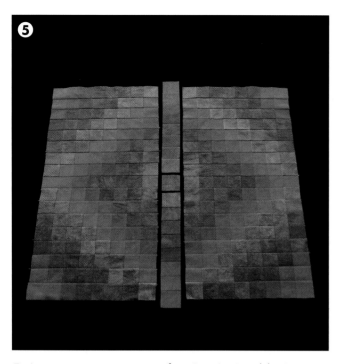

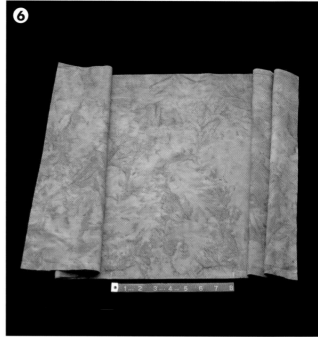

5. Arrange remaining two strips from Strip Set 1 and the 2" (5 cm) square from Fabric G between pieced units as shown. Stitch end of each strip from Strip Set 1 to 2" (5 cm) square to make final pieced strip. Stitch the pieced strip to each side of pieced units to complete pattern. Press seam allowances to one side.

6. Follow page 272, steps 6 to 8, to cut and apply the border strips. Fold backing fabric in half; cut in half along the fold of the fabric. Stitch halves, right sides together, along long edge; leave 8" (20.5 cm) opening in the middle for turning. Press seam allowances open. Cut backing to size of quilt top.

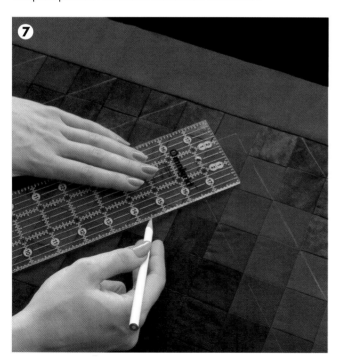

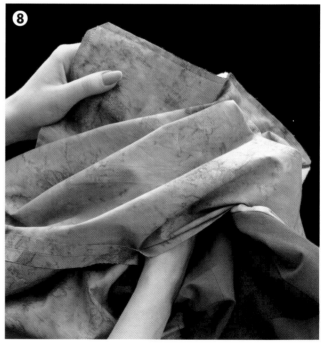

7. Mark quilting lines on each side of the diamond pattern through corners of squares for every other color of diamonds; begin and end lines at centers of squares at diamond points.

8. Place backing and quilt top right sides together. Place fabrics on batting, with backing piece on top; pin or baste layers together. Stitch around quilt top, ¼" (6 mm) from the raw edges. Trim batting to ⅛" (3 mm); trim corners. Turn quilt right side out; press. Slipstitch opening closed.

9. Baste quilt as on page 96. Quilt, using stitch-in-the-ditch method (page 103), in seamlines of borders. Quilt diamond design by stitching on the marked lines; pivot stitching at centers of squares at points of diamonds.

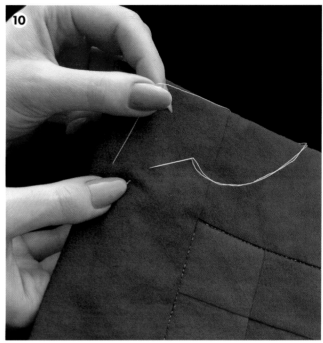

10. Quilt border, using seed beads. Conceal the knot of a single thread in batting by piecing the needle through quilt top ½" (1.3 cm) from location of first bead. Bring thread back through quilt top at desired location; pull thread snug, and rub knot with fingernail until it buries itself in quilt.

11. Place bead on needle, and slide to surface of quilt. Stitch through to back of quilt, and make a small stitch; then travel through batting a needle length away from first bead. Continue adding beads in this manner until border is completely quilted.

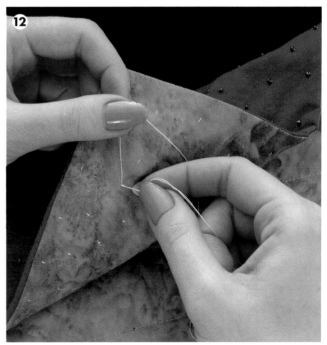

12. Knot end of thread on the back by winding the thread around the needle, as for a French knot. Reenter the back fabric through the same hole the thread came out of; travel through the batting ½" (1.3 cm) away from hole. Pull thread snug, and rub knot with fingernail until it buries itself in quilt. Attach fabric sleeve to wall hanging (page 171).

YOU WILL NEED

- ½ yd. (0.5 m) bundle of eight hand-dyed fabrics in a light to dark gradation; or ¼ yd. (0.25 m) each of eight fabrics for Lone Star design and inner border.

- ⅓ yd. (0.32 m) black or other dark fabric that contrasts with hand-dyed fabrics, for insert fabric.

- 1 yd. (0.95 m) fabric, for background and binding.

- ⅝ yd. (0.6 m) fabric, for outer border.

- 1½ yd. (1.4 m) fabric, for flower appliqués.

- ¼ yd. (0.25 m) fabric, for leaf appliqués.

- 1 package narrow double-fold bias tape, for vine.

- 6" x 24" (15 x 61 cm) plexiglass ruler, for cutting at 45 degree angle.

- Tear-away stabilizer.

CUTTING DIRECTIONS ✀

- Cut strips from hand-dyed fabrics and insert fabric for the Lone Star design as in steps 1 and 2.

- Cut four 11" (28 cm) squares from background fabric. Also cut one 16⅛" (40.8 cm) square from background fabric. Cut the square diagonally through opposite corners in both directions to make four triangles.

- Cut four 1½" (3.8 cm) strips from Fabric H, for the inner border. Cut five 3½" (9 cm) strips from the fabric for the outer border. Cut five 2" (5 cm) strips from the fabric for the binding.

- Cut ten leaves, using the leaf pattern (page 293), with fabric right sides together as on page 292, step 21. Cut ten circles, using patterns for yo-yo flowers as on page 293, step 24.

How to Sew a lone Star Wall Hanging with Flower Appliqués

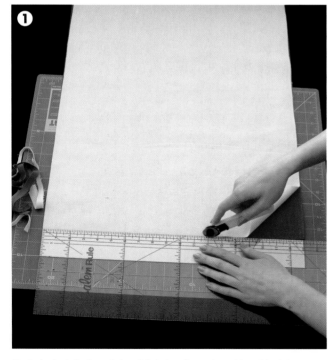

1. Label eight hand-dyed fabrics from A to H, with A being the lightest fabric and H being the darkest. Place Fabric A and Fabric H together, matching raw edges; fold in half. Cut 2" (5 cm) strip across fabrics. Repeat with Fabrics B and G, cutting two strips from each fabric.

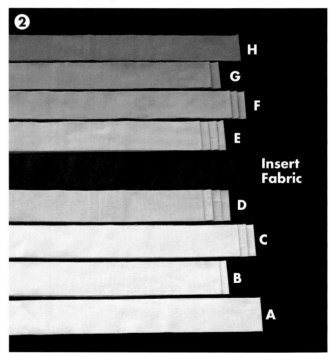

2. Cut three 2" (5 cm) strips from Fabrics C and F. Cut four 2" (5 cm) strips from Fabrics D and E. Cut five 2" (5 cm) strips from insert fabric. Arrange the fabric strips in order from A to H, placing the insert fabric between Fabrics D and E.

(continued)

Lone Star Wall Hanging with Flower Appliqués

Brighten a wall with this dramatic wall hanging that combines the Lone Star design with dimensional appliqués. The Lone Star design is made from eight hand-dyed fabrics the graduate from light to dark, from the center of the star out to the points. A contrasting fabric is also used to create a circle of interest within the star.

The center of the quilt is embellished with dimensional leaves and yo-yo flowers, attached to a vine made from double-fold bias tape. Select fabrics for the leaves and yo-yo flowers that repeat the colors found in the background fabric. The finished wall hanging measures about 43½" (110.5 cm) square.

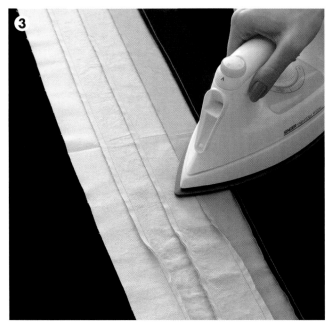

3. Stitch one strip of Fabric A to one strip of Fabric B, right sides together, along one long edge. Stitch one strip of Fabric C to long edge of Fabric B of pieced unit. Continue to stitch strips from Fabric D and insert fabric to unit in order to make a strip set. Press seam allowances toward lightest fabrics.

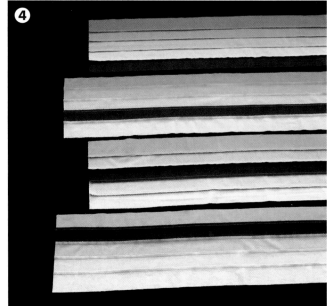

4. Stitch strips of Fabrics B, C, D, insert, and E together as in step 3 to make a strip set. Press seam allowances toward darkest fabrics. Stitch strips of Fabrics C, D, insert, E, and F together to make third strip set; press seam allowances toward lightest fabrics. Stitch strips of Fabrics D, insert, E, F, and G together to make fourth strip set; press seam allowances toward darkest fabrics. Stitch strips of insert fabric, Fabrics E, F, G, and H together; press seam allowances toward lightest fabrics.

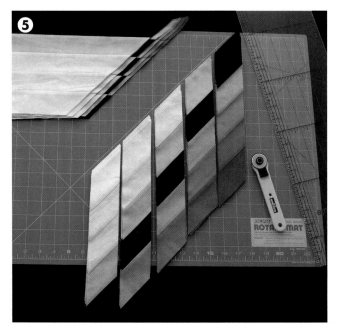

5. Cut ends of strip sets at 45° angles, using plexiglass ruler, keeping strips in order stitched in steps 3 and 4. Cut eight 2" (5 cm) diagonal strips from each strip set as shown. After every few strips, check 45° angle and recut edge, if necessary. Take care not to stretch bias edges. Stack strips together and arrange in order as shown.

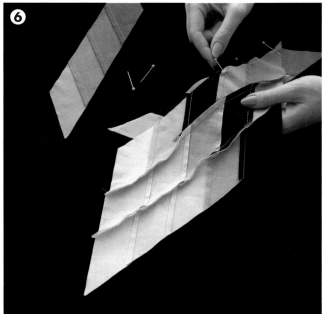

6. Stitch strip from each stack together in order shown in step 5, pinning strips together at seam intersections; do not press seam allowances open. Repeat to make a total of eight pieced diamonds.

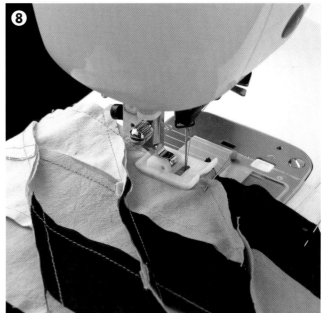

7. Mark wrong side of diamonds where ¼" (6 mm) seams will intersect, placing dots at the wide-angle corners. Mark the wrong sides of background pieces where ¼" (6 mm) seams will intersect, placing dots at right-angle corner of triangles and at one corner of each square.

8. Stitch two diamonds, right sides together, along one side, from the inner point of Fabric A to dot, pinning the strips together at seam intersections and finger-pressing seam allowances in opposite directions; backstitch at dot. Repeat for remaining diamonds.

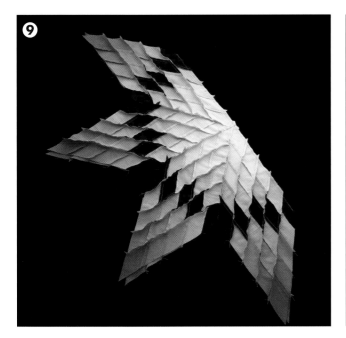

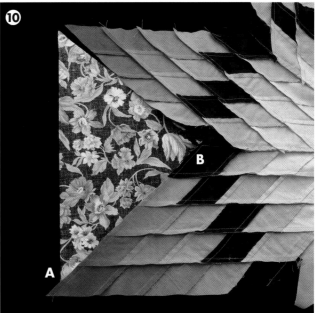

9. Stitch two 2-diamond units right sides together, as in step 8, finger-pressing seam allowances in opposite directions. Repeat with remaining units to make two 4-diamond units. Stitch units together along the long edge, between the dots, pinning at seam intersections; backstitch at dots. Press star carefully, taking care not to stretch fabric.

10. Align short side of triangle to a diamond, right sides together, matching edges at outer point (A) and dots at inner point (B). Stitch from the outer edge exactly to dot, with diamond side up; backstitch.

(continued)

11. Align remaining side of triangle to adjoining diamond, and stitch as in step 10, with triangle side up. Repeat for the remaining triangles, stitching them between every other set of points on the star.

12. Align squares to the sides of diamonds between remaining points of star, matching edges at outer point (A) and dots at inner point (B); stitch with diamond side up, as in step 10. Align remaining sides of squares and diamonds; stitch with square side up.

13. Release stitching within seam allowances at center of star, so seam allowances will lie flat. Press from wrong side, working from center out. Cut and apply inner border as for outer border of Woven Stars wall hanging on page 272, steps 6 to 8.

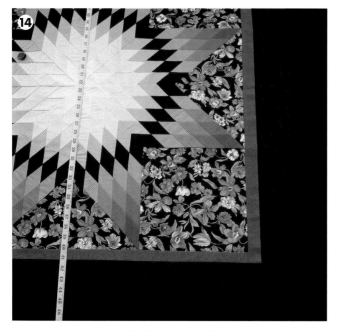

14. Measure horizontally through middle of quilt top and cut two outer border strips to that length for the upper and lower outer borders; stitch to quilt top as for inner border. Piece remaining outer border strips together as on page 114, step 2. Measure vertically through middle of quilt top, including outer border strips, and cut two outer border strips for sides equal to this length; stitch to quilt as for inner border.

15. Cut 40" (102 cm) length of bias tape; trim off one fold of tape on narrower side to reduce bulk. Pin tape to center of star, making a wavy circle as shown; butt the ends together. Position tear-away stabilizer, cut larger than design, on wrong side of the fabric.

16. Set machine for short blindstitch, with the stitch width about ⅛" (3 mm); use monofilament nylon thread in the needle. (Contrasting thread was used to show detail.) Blindstitch around bias tape, catching the edge with widest swing of the stitch; remove tear-away stabilizer.

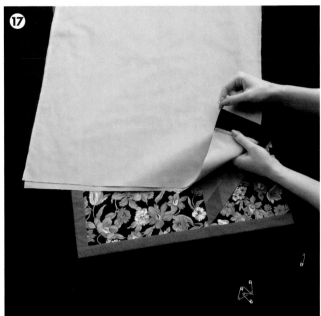

17. Cut backing fabric 2" to 4" (5 to 10 cm) wider and longer than quilt top, piecing with outer border fabric, if desired. Mark center of each side of quilt top and backing fabric with safety pins.

18. Mark quilting design lines on the background squares and borders by extending seamlines of star out to edges of quilt top. Mark quilting lines on the background triangles 1½" (3.8 cm) from the sides of triangle, extending lines into borders. Continue to mark additional lines on triangles 1½" (3.8 cm) from previous markings as shown.

19. Layer and baste the quilt as on page 96. Stitch in the ditch (page 103) in the seamlines of the star, from the bias tape out; extend stitching into the borders, following marked lines. Quilt background triangles by stitching on marked lines; begin and end stitching at the raw edge of the border.

(continued)

20. Stipple-quilt (page 102) the center of quilt inside circle of bias tape. Attach fabric sleeve as on page 171. Apply binding as on pages 111 to 116.

21. Trace pattern for leaf (opposite) onto tracing paper. Fold fabric for leaves right sides together; cut ten sets of leaves, using leaf pattern. Trim some leaves narrower or shorter.

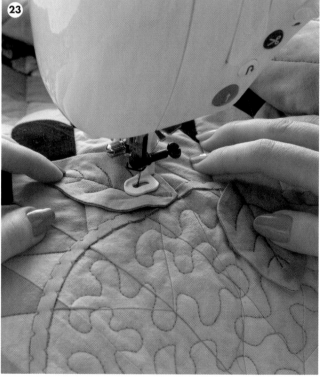

22. Stitch leaves, right sides together, ⅛" (3 mm) from raw edges, crossing over the beginning of stitching at end. Cut a slit in one layer, and turn leaf right side out, using a point tool to smooth outer edges from inside. Repeat for remaining leaves. Press leaves. Transfer markings for veins onto leaves.

23. Pin leaves to bias tape vine, covering the ends of bias tape with one leaf. Stitch leaves to quilt along the vein lines, using free-motion stitching (page 102).

24. Trace partial pattern for each size of circle onto tracing paper, placing dotted line on fold of paper. Cut on solid lines; open full-size circle patterns for yo-yo flowers. From each yo-yo pattern, cut five circles from fabric for flowers.

25. Turn ¼" (6 mm) of circle to wrong side, and stitch hand running stitches a scant ⅛" (3 mm) from folded edge. Pull up thread to gather circle, and tie off threads on the inside. Repeat with remaining circles. Pin yo-yo flowers to vine; position button in center, and hand-stitch in place.

Yo-Yo Flowers and Leaf Appliqués

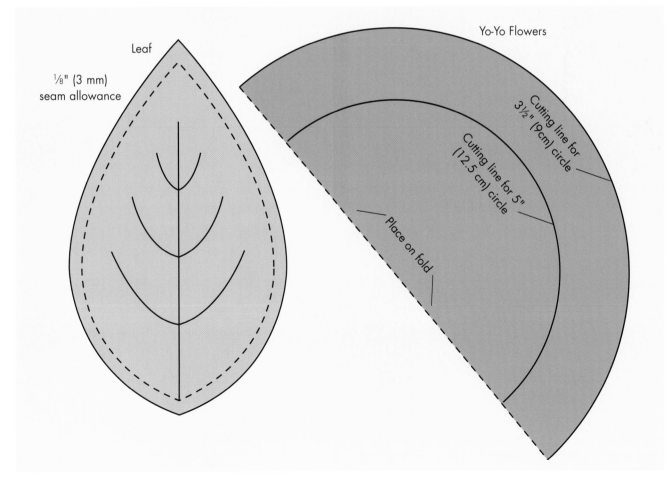

Leaf

⅛" (3 mm)
seam allowance

Yo-Yo Flowers

Cutting line for
3½" (9cm) circle

Cutting line for 5"
(12.5 cm) circle

Place on fold

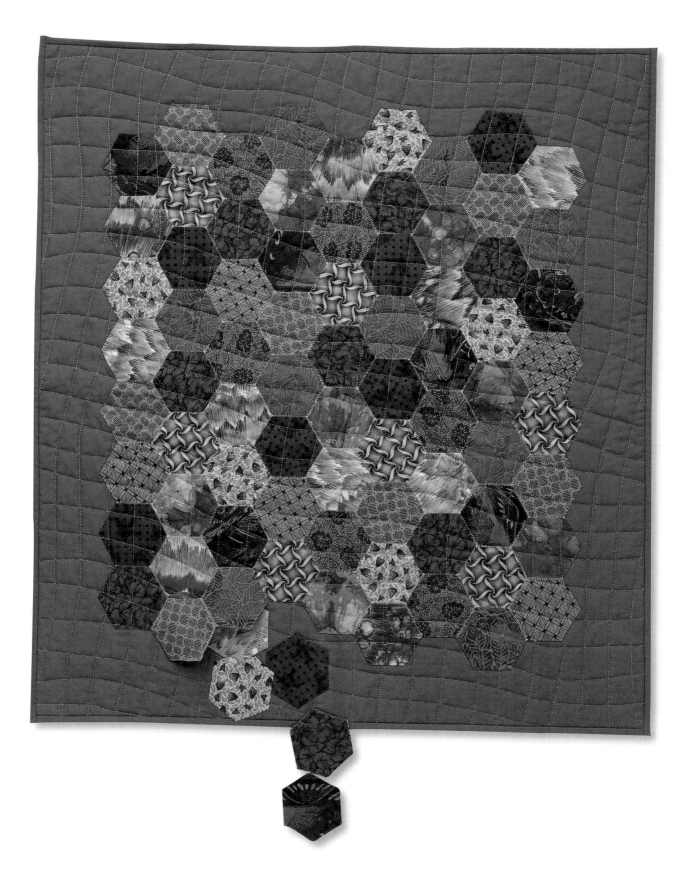

Tumbling Hexagon Wall Hanging

British patchworkers have long used paper piecing for all their designs. Today, it is used for quilt patterns that do not lend themselves well to machine sewing, such as those with no long rows to sew and pieces that need to fit together exactly. Paper piecing is used in combination with machine stitching to produce an accurate, extremely flat quilt top in the least amount of time.

For the Tumbling Hexagon wall hanging, fabric hexagons are first hand-basted to paper cutouts. The hexagons are arranged in any pattern or color combination, then are machine-stitched together, one by one, using a zigzag stitch, which is visible from the front of the pieced unit. The hexagons are steamed before removing the paper pieces in order to keep the hexagons flat and straight.

The hexagons in this wall hanging are arranged in nine rows. Some hexagons are blindstitched to the quilt top as if they are falling away from the rows. Additional hexagons are double-faced and hung loosely on the quilt for a three-dimensional embellishment. The finished wall hanging measures about 26½" x 28¼" (67.3 x 71.7 cm).

YOU WILL NEED

- ⅛ yd. (0.15 m) each of ten or more different fabrics, for hexagons.
- 1 yd. (0.95 m) fabric, for border and binding.
- ⅞ yd. (0.8 m) fabric, for backing.
- Batting, about 31" x 33" (78.5 x 84 cm).
- Monofilament nylon thread.
- Tear-away stabilizer.
- Decorative thread.
- Mediumweight fusible interfacing.

CUTTING DIRECTIONS ✂

- Make ten photocopies of the hexagon pattern on page 299. Cut the individual hexagons apart.
- Cut the desired number of hexagons from each hexagon fabric for a total of 84 hexagons; cut the hexagons ¼" (6 mm) larger than the paper on all sides.
- Cut one 27" x 29" (68.5 x 73.5 cm) rectangle from the border fabric.
- Cut four 2" (5 cm) strips from the binding fabric.

How to Sew a Tumbling Hexagon Wall Hanging

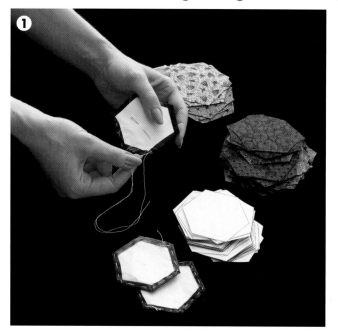

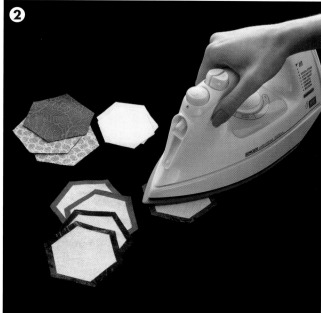

1. Pin paper hexagon to the back of fabric hexagon. Finger-press seam allowances to back of paper; hand-baste the hexagon to paper along seam allowances. Repeat for 75 additional hexagons.

2. Trace paper hexagon onto interfacing eight times; cut out hexagons. Follow step 1 to make eight more hexagons, substituting interfacing hexagons for the paper and fusing interfacing hexagons to the fabric, following manufacturer's instructions. Set aside these eight hexagons until step 11.

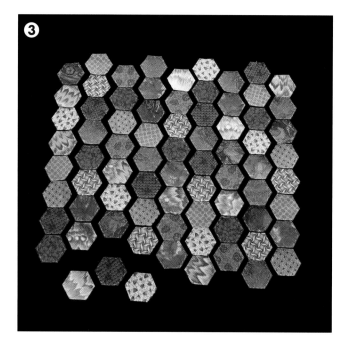

3. Arrange 76 hexagons on work surface in nine columns, alternating eight and nine hexagons in each column, in desired color sequence. Allow a few hexagons in last row to fall away from organized rows, as shown.

4. Stitch first two hexagons of first column, right sides together, using a zigzag stitch with a 1/16" (1.5 mm) stitch length and 1/16" (1.5 mm) stitch width, barely catching the fabric; backstitch at each end. If seam does not lie flat, loosen top thread tension. Repeat to stitch remaining hexagons together in column one. Repeat for remaining columns; set aside individual hexagons for tumbling from last row.

5. Stitch first two columns of hexagons together, one hexagon at a time, as in step 4. Continue to add columns until pieced unit is complete.

6. Steam pieced unit with paper hexagons still intact. Remove the basting stitches; steam a second time to remove basting marks. Remove the paper hexagons. Repeat with the individual hexagons reserved for tumbling from last row.

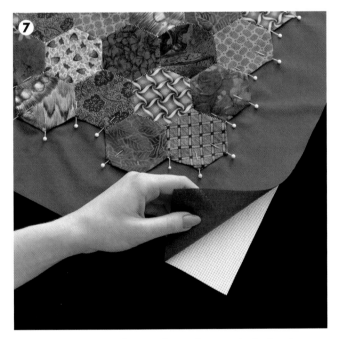

7. Pin or baste pieced unit to front of rectangle for border fabric. Position tear-away stabilizer; cut to size of border fabric, on wrong side of border fabric.

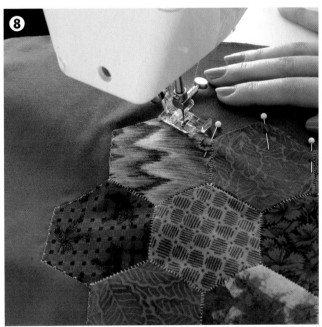

8. Set machine for short blindstitch, with the stitch width about 1/16" (1.5 mm); use monofilament nylon thread in the needle. Blindstitch around pieced unit, catching edge with widest swing of stitch. Remove tear-away stabilizer, taking care not to distort stitches.

(continued)

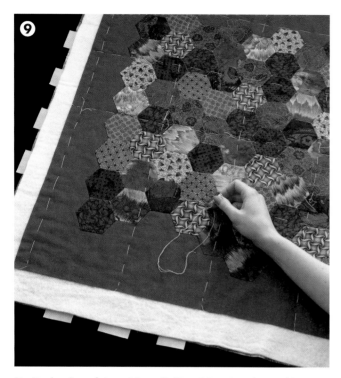

9. Cut backing fabric 2" to 4" (5 to 10 cm) wider and longer than quilt top. Layer and baste the quilt top, batting, and backing as on pages 92 to 97.

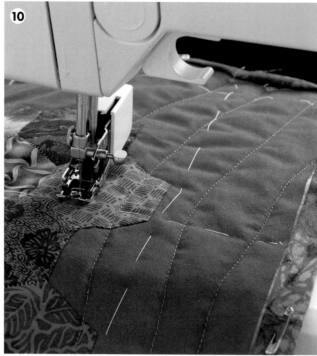

10. Quilt in long, flowing lines across quilt top in two directions, using walking foot. Attach fabric sleeve to wall hanging (page 171), and apply the binding as on pages 111 to 116.

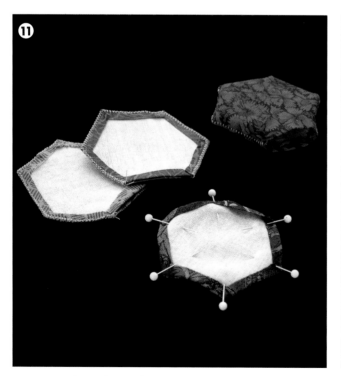

11. Steam the eight interfacing hexagons. Remove the basting stitches; steam a second time to remove basting marks. Pin two hexagons right sides together; zigzag around five sides as on page 296, step 4. Turn right side out; press. Whipstitch along remaining side. Repeat with remaining hexagons.

12. Hand-stitch individual hexagons to border to appear to be falling away from pieced unit; hand-stitch faced hexagons to pieced unit and to lower edge of quilt.

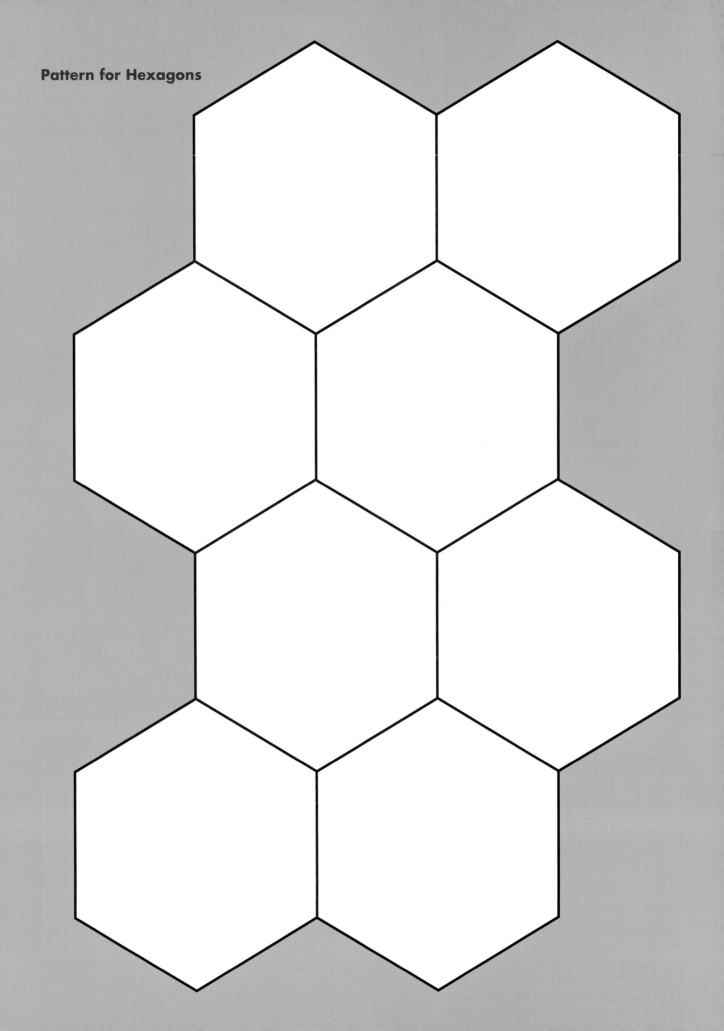

Pattern for Hexagons

QUILTED LANDSCAPE WALL HANGING

The quilt blocks in this wall hanging use a number of different techniques to create three-dimensional embellishments. All the blocks combined make a unique scenic wall hanging.

Landscape quilt blocks are assembled separately, then are joined by spacer strips. Quilt blocks and spacer strips are stitched together to make three columns, which are stitched together to make the quilt top. Each block is quilted in a

unique way, using a variety of decorative threads.

The finished quilt measures about 36½" x 48" (91.8 x 122 cm). The blocks for the Pine Tree, Desert, and Stream measure 12" (30.5 cm) square. The Winter Plains and Autumn Hills blocks measure 9" (23 cm) square. The Seascape block measures 9" x 12" (23 x 30.5 cm). Blocks of the same size are interchangeable in the wall hanging.

YOU WILL NEED

For the Landscape Wall Hanging:

- 1½ yd. (1.4 m) fabric, for spacers, border, and binding.

- 1½ yd. (1.4 m) fabric, for backing.

- Batting, about 41" x 53" (104 x 134.5 cm).

- Tear-away stabilizer.

- Water-soluble stabilizer, such as Solvy.

- Fine-point permanent-ink marker.

- Glue Stick.

- Monofilament nylon thread.

- Tracing paper.

- Transfer paper.

- Paper-backed fusible web.

For the Seascape Quilt Block:

- ⅓ yd. (0.32 m) fabric, for water.

- Scraps of fabric, for rock or sand floor, rock wall, and seaweed.

- Scrap of fish print fabric, for fish appliqués.

- Pearlescent beads.

For the Winter Plains Quilt Block:

- Scraps of three fabrics, for sky, snow, and snowdrift.

- Scraps of shimmery white organza, for snow overlay.

- White and silver metallic thread.

- Black and white rayon thread.

- 9" (23 cm) embroidery hoop.

CUTTING DIRECTIONS ✂

(for the Landscape Wall Hanging)

- Cut two 3½" (9 cm) strips across the width of the fabric for the spacers; cut two 12½" (31.8 cm) lengths and one 27½" (69.8 cm) length from the strips. Cut one 6½" (16.3 cm) strip across the width of the fabric for the spacers; cut two 9½" (24.3 cm) lengths and one 15½" (39.3 cm) length from the strip. Cut four or five 5" (12.5 cm) strips across the width of the border fabric. Cut five 2½" (6.5 cm) strips across the width of the binding fabric.

(for the Seascape Quilt Block)

- Cut one 10" x 13" (25.5 x 33 cm) rectangle from the water fabric. Cut one 4" x 13" (10 x 33 cm) rectangle from the rock wall fabric. Cut one 5" x 8" (12.5 x 20.5 cm) rectangle from the rock or sand floor fabric. Cut three 1½" x 12" (3.8 x 30.5 cm) strips from the seaweed fabric. Cut the desired number of fish appliqués from the fish print fabric, leaving a scant ⅛" (3 mm) of background around the fish.

(for the Winter Plains Quilt Block)

- Cut two 11" (28 cm) squares from water-soluble stabilizer. Cut one 5" x 10" (12.5 x 25.5 cm) rectangle from the fabric for the sky. Cut one 6" x 10" (15 x 25.5 cm) rectangle from the fabric for the snow and from white organza. Cut one 6" x 10" (15 x 25.5 cm) rectangle from snowdrift fabric.

(for the Desert Quilt Block)

- Cut one 1¾" x 22" (4.5 x 56 cm) strip from seven desert fabrics. Cut one 5" x 13" (12.5 x 33 cm) rectangle for the sky. Cut cactus designs from the cactus fabric, using the patterns on page 312.

(for the Stream Quilt Block)

- Cut one 9" (23 cm) square of water-soluble stabilizer. Cut one 5½" x 13" (14 x 33 cm) rectangle from the fabric for the sky. Cut one 5" x 13" (12.5 x 33 cm) rectangle from the fabric for the background hill. Cut one 7" x 13" (18 x 33 cm) rectangle each, from the fabric for the stream and from the lace. Cut one 3½" x 7" (9 x 18 cm) rectangle for the foreground. Cut one 1½" x 8" (3.8 x 20.5 cm) and one 1" x 13" (2.5 x 33

cm) rectangle from the fabric for the grass. Cut the desired number of fish for the steam. Cut one 16" (40.5 cm) square of tear-away stabilizer. Cut one 10" (25.5 cm) square of water-soluble stabilizer.

(for the Autumn Hills Quilt Block)

- Cut two 9" (23 cm) squares of water-soluble stabilizer. Cut one 10" (25.5 cm) square from the sky fabric. Cut one 6" x 10" (15 x 25.5 cm) rectangle from the main hill fabric. Cut one 4" x 10" (10 x 25.5 cm) rectangle and one 3" x 6" (7.5 x 15 cm) rectangle from the secondary hill fabrics. Cut one 2" (5 cm) strip from the tulle, for the wind. Cut slivers and small pieces from the leaf fabric, using a rotary cutter.

(for the Pine Tree Quilt Block)

- Cut one 13" (33 cm) square from the sky fabric. Cut one 6" x 13" (15 x 33 cm) rectangle from the fabric with the pine tree print. Cut two 7" (18 cm) squares from the mountain fabric. Cut one 9" (23 cm) square from the pine tree branch fabric. Cut the moon and trunk appliqués as on page for the tree branches as on page 310, step 4.

For the Desert Quilt Block:

- Scraps of seven coordinating fabrics, for desert background.
- Scrap of fabric, for sky.
- Scraps of three fabrics, for cactus.
- 4 mm bright pink silk ribbon and 4 mm and 2 mm yellow silk ribbon, for cactus flowers; chenille needle 20.

For the Stream Quilt Block:

- Scraps of fabric, for sky, hills, grass,

stream, and foreground.

- Scrap of lace, for stream.
- Scrap of fish print fabric.
- 7 mm green silk ribbon.

For the Autumn Hills Quilt Block:

- Scrap of fabric, for sky.
- Scraps of three fabrics, for hills.
- Scrap of tulle, for wind.
- Scrap of fabric, for leaves.

- Decorative thread, as desired.

For the Pine Tree Quilt Block:

- Scrap of fabric, for sky.
- Scrap of fabric with pine tree print.
- Scrap of dark green fabric, for pine tree branches.
- Scraps of two green print fabrics, for mountains.
- Scrap of fabric, for tree trunk.
- Gold metallic fabric scrap, for moon.
- Gold metallic thread

How to Sew the Seascape Quilt Block

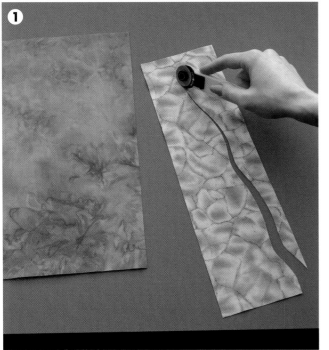

1. Trim the fabric for rock wall along long side of rectangle in a wavy pattern as shown; discard excess.

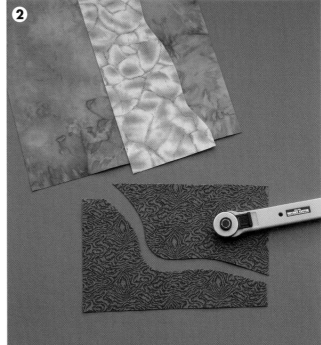

2. Trim the fabric rectangle for rock or sand floor diagonally in a wavy pattern as shown; discard the upper half.

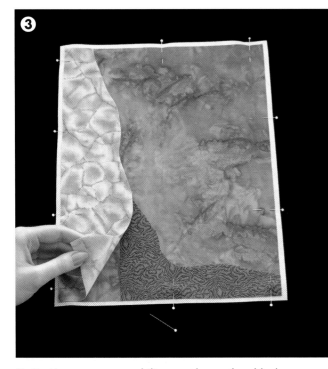

3. Position tear-away stabilizer, cut larger than block, on wrong side of water fabric. Pin rock wall to the left edge of rectangle for water, matching long edges. Pin rock or sand floor piece to block, tucking left edge under rock wall fabric.

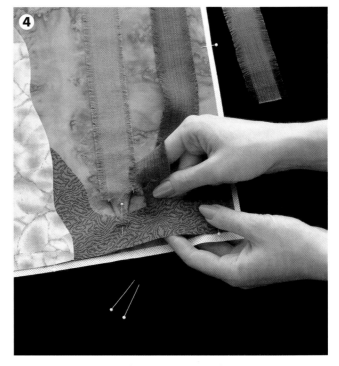

4. Pull several threads from long edges of seaweed strips to fray. Gather and pin one short end of each strip under upper edge of sand or rock floor piece.

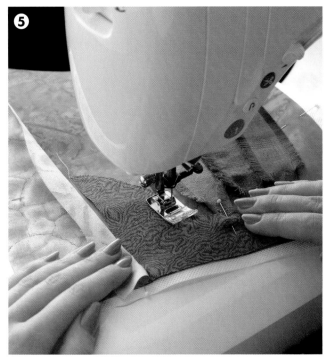

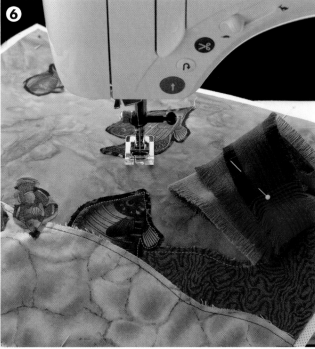

5. Twist seaweed strips; pin to water fabric. Stitch floor piece ⅛" (3 mm) from upper edge; do not stitch over rock wall piece. After quilting block in step 4 on page 311, stitch short ends of seaweed strips to water fabric.

6. Glue-baste fish appliqué pieces, as desired, on quilt block; tuck tail of one fish behind rock wall. Stitch around rock wall and fish ⅛" (3 mm) from raw edges of fabric. Trim quilt block to 9½" x 12½" (24.3 x 31.8 cm).

How to Sew the Winter Plains Quilt Block

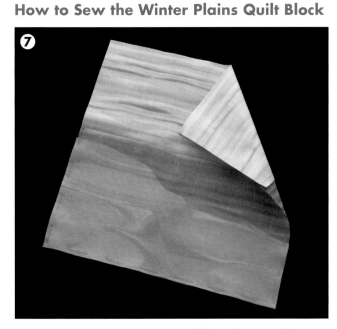

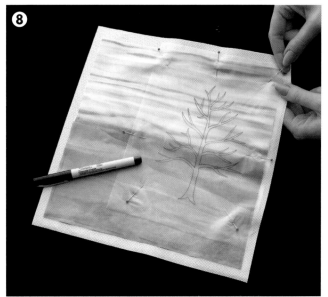

1. Cut curved line on upper edge of fabric for snow-drifts; layer over rectangle of snow as shown. Baste rectangle of organza over these fabrics a scant ¼" (6 mm) from raw edges. Stitch the basted rectangle for snow to the rectangle for sky, right sides together, in ¼" (6 mm) seam. Press seam allowances toward rectangle for snow.

2. Mark trunk and tree branches on piece of water-soluble stabilizer, using a fine-point permanent-ink marker. Pin stabilizer over pieced block, positioning trunk as desired; position tear-away stabilizer, cut larger than block, under block.

(continued)

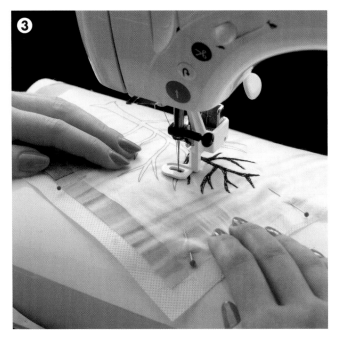

3. Attach darning foot to machine, and cover feed dogs with cover plate or lower them. With desired thread for trunk in machine, begin free-motion stitching as on page 104 at the tips of tree branches with a forward-backward motion. Continue stitching all branches and down trunk of tree.

4. Tear away the excess water-soluble stabilizer, and remove tear-away stabilizer on back side of block. Spray the tree with water to dissolve any remaining stabilizer. Blot block with paper towel; press from wrong side of block.

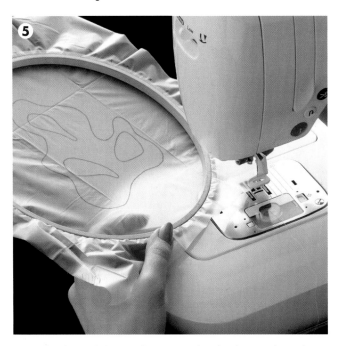

5. Draw desired shape of snow overlay for the tree branches on water-soluble stabilizer. Position square of water-soluble stabilizer over the outer embroidery hoop; push inner hoop into outer one, and tighten. Thread white metallic thread through machine, and wind white rayon thread on bobbin. Position the embroidery hoop under needle of sewing machine, with stabilizer against throat plate and with darning foot in position as in step 3, above.

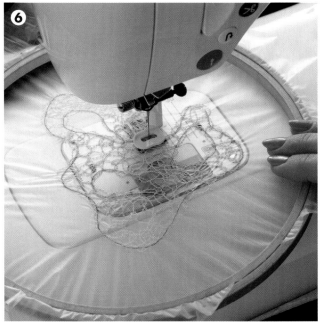

6. Draw up bobbin thread; holding threads, stitch in place a few times to secure stitches. Clip off thread tails. Using free-motion stitching (page 104), make loops or lines of stitching to represent outline of tree branches. Go over stitching several times, making a dense circular cover of stitches. Change thread in machine to silver metallic, and stitch over stitched design again.

7. Remove stabilizer from hoop, and trim off excess. Place stitched treetop design in water until stabilizer dissolves; set aside to dry.

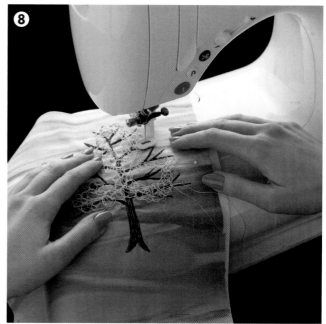

8. Position stitched treetop design over branches of tree; position tear-away stabilizer under block. With white metallic thread in machine, stitch treetop to trunk, using free-motion stitching. Remove stabilizer. Trim block to 9½" (24.3 cm) square.

How to Sew the Desert Quilt Block

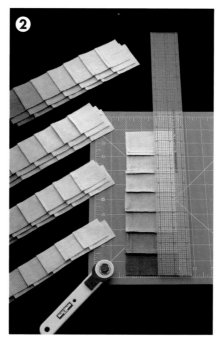

1. Stitch the seven desert fabrics together lengthwise, using ¼" (6 mm) seams. Press the seam allowances in one direction.

2. Cut 1¼" 1½", 1¾", and 2" (3.2, 3.8, 4.5, and 5 cm) strips across the pieced strip.

3. Stitch the strips together in ¼" (6 mm) seams, staggering strips and alternating widths to make a zigzag pattern about 13" (33 cm) long. Trim off upper and lower edges to make pieced strip 11¼" (28.7 cm) wide. (continued)

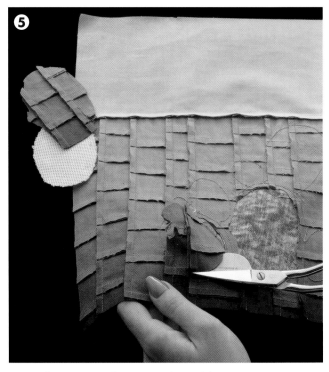

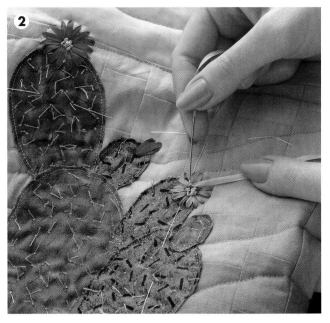

4. Stitch rectangle for sky to pieced unit along 13" (33 cm) edge, in ¼" (6 mm) seam. Press the seam allowances toward desert. Apply glue stick to edges of cactus design, and position over block as desired. Position tear-away stabilizer, cut larger than block, under block.

5. Stitch ⅛" (3 mm) from raw edges of the cactus pieces. Remove stabilizer. Trim away the excess fabric from behind the cactus designs. Trim block to 12½" (31.8 cm) square. After quilting block on page 312, step 8, embroider flowers on cactus, using silk ribbon as in steps 1 and 2, below.

How to Silk-ribbon-Embroider Cactus Flowers

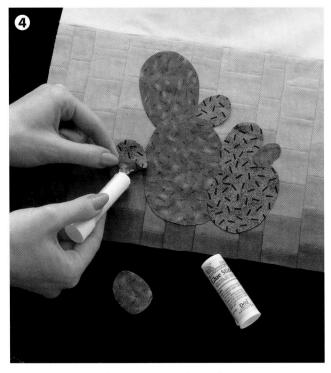

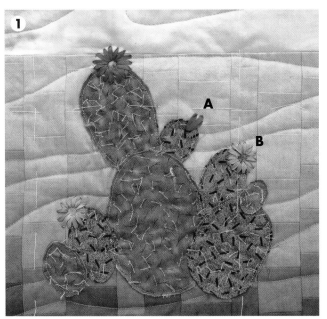

1. Stitch cactus flower bud (A) by making three closely spaced Japanese ribbon stitches, using 4 mm pink silk ribbon. Stitch open cactus flower (B) by stitching 14 to 16 petals in a Japanese ribbon stitch; leave scant ¼" (6 mm) circle of space at center of petals.

2. Make a three-twist French knot in center of the petals, using 2 mm yellow silk ribbon. Make about five two-twist French knots around center knot, using same ribbon.

How to Sew the Stream Quilt Block

1. Cut a curving line along one long edge of the rectangles for hills. Layer lace over stream fabric and cut curve through both fabrics as shown. Cut ½" (1.3 cm) clips close together along one long edge of 1" x 13" (2.5 x 33 cm) rectangle of fabric for grass. Cut 1" (2.5 cm) clips on wider grass strip. Curl longer grass by pulling with fingers as shown.

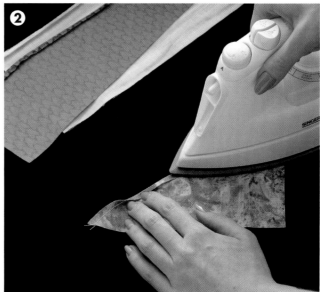

2. Layer stream fabrics. Stitch scant ¼" (6 mm) from curved edge of stream and hill fabrics. Press ¼" (6 mm) to wrong side along curved edge so stitching is on back side.

3. Glue-baste fish to stream fabric under the lace. Arrange the stream and hills to form a 13" (33 cm) square, and pin to the tear-away stabilizer. Insert the grass as shown. Glue-baste along the edges to hold pieces in place.

4. Set machine for narrow blind-hem stitch. Using monofilament nylon thread in machine, blindstitch along the curved edges of the hills and stream.

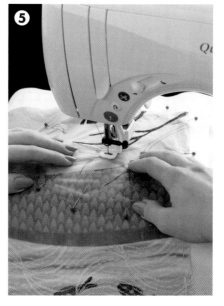

5. Draw tree branch design on piece of water-soluble stabilizer, using a fine-point permanent-ink marker. Position in upper right corner; pin. Follow page 304, steps 3 and 4, to stitch branch design. Trim block to 12½" (31.8 cm) square. After quilting the block on page 311, step 5, embroider leaves on branch, using Japanese ribbon stitch.

How to Sew the Autumn Hills Quilt Block

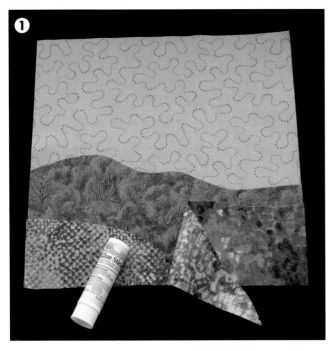

1. Cut curved lines on upper edges of all hill fabrics as shown. Layer background hill fabric over sky fabric. Glue-baste in place. Repeat for additional hill fabrics.

2. Draw shape for tree trunk and branches on water-soluble stabilizer as on page 303, step 2, and mark the position of trunk on hill seamlines. Place tear-away stabilizer under block. Satin-stitch along upper edges of all hill fabrics on each side of position for the tree trunk. Follow page 304, steps 3 and 4, to make the tree trunk and branches.

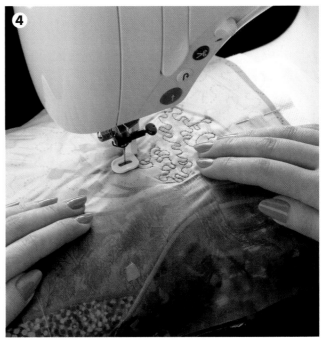

3. Position slivers of leaf fabric over tree branches, allowing parts of branches to show. Position some leaves on the sky and grass fabrics, as though they are blowing from the tree.

4. Cover leaf fabric slivers with piece of water-soluble stabilizer to hold slivers in position; pin. Stitch slivers to tree and background, using free-motion stitching (page 104), catching all slivers with stitches.

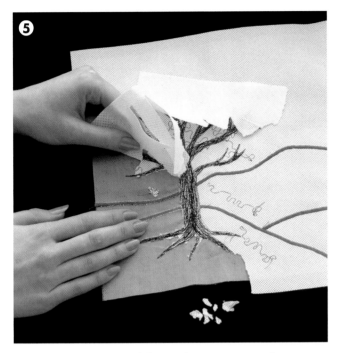

5. Remove tear-away stabilizer, taking care not to distort stitches. Remove water-soluble stabilizer, and press as on page 304, step 4. Trim the block to 9½" (24.3 cm) square.

6. Twist wind tulle strip and position across sky fabric as shown. Hand-baste tulle through center to secure. Remove pins.

How to Sew the Pine Tree Quilt Block

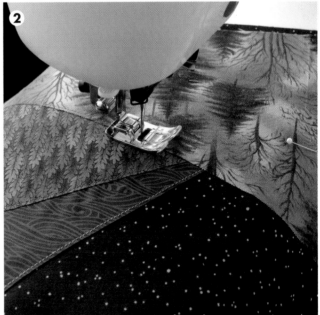

1. Cut curves along the upper edges of rectangles for background hill and mountains. Arrange hill, mountain, and sky fabrics as shown; pin. Glue-baste upper edges of curved pieces.

2. Stitch ⅛" (3 mm) from upper edges of hill and mountain fabrics.

(continued)

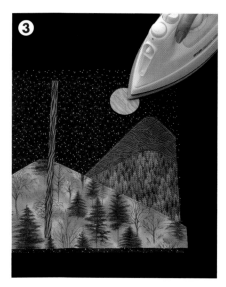

3. Apply paper-backed fusible web to wrong sides of fabric scraps for trunk and moon, following manufacturer's directions. Cut 11" x ⅜" (28 x 1 cm) strip from trunk fabric. Cut 2" (5 cm) circle from moon fabric. Fuse trunk and moon appliqués to block as shown. Stitch ⅛" (3 mm) from raw edges of moon.

4. Transfer six pine tree branch pattern pieces (page 313) onto tracing paper; transfer designs to tree-branch fabric, using transfer paper. Cut pieces from fabric, cutting just inside marked lines. Glue-baste top edges of tree branches to trunk as shown.

5. Stitch tree branches ⅛" (3 mm) from top edges. Clip the bottom edges of branches to create fringe as shown. Trim the block to 12½" (31.8 cm) square.

How to Sew a Quilted Landscape Wall Hanging

1. Stitch 6½" x 9½" (16.3 x 24.3 cm) spacer between Seascape and Winter Plains block as shown to make first column. Stitch 3½" x 12½" (9 x 31.8 cm) spacer between Desert block and Pine Tree block as shown to make middle column. Place 3½" x 27½" (9 x 69.8 cm) spacer strip between first and second column; stitch.

2. Stitch 6½" x 9½" (16.3 x 24.3 cm) spacer on left side of Autumn Hills block. Stitch 3½" x 12½" (9 x 31.8 cm) spacer on left side of Stream block. Stitch 6½" x 15½" (16.3 x 39.3 cm) spacer between the Autumn Hills and Stream blocks to make third column. Stitch third column to right edge of middle column.

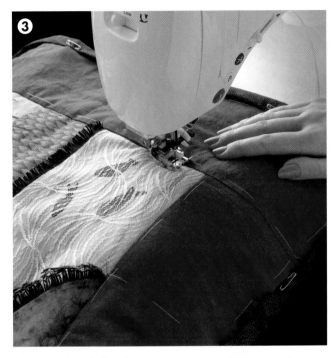

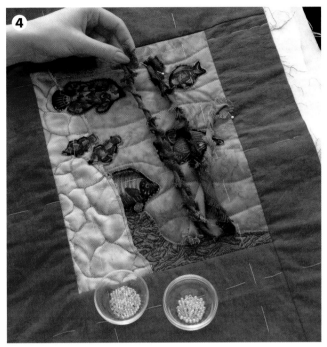

3. Cut and apply border strips as on page 272, steps 6 to 8. Cut backing fabric 2" to 4" (5 to 10 cm) wider and longer than quilt top. Layer and baste quilt top, batting, and backing as on pages 92 to 97. Stitch in the ditch (page 103) between quilt blocks and spacers and around borders.

4. Quilt design lines on rock wall, rock or sand floor, and water for Seascape block. Stitch beads to block. Stitch upper edges of seaweed strips in place. Brush seaweed to fray edges.

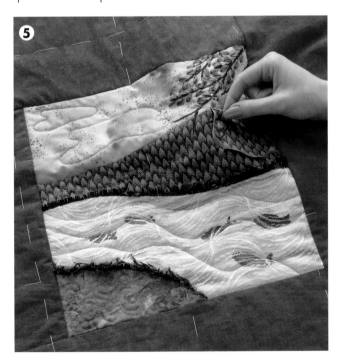

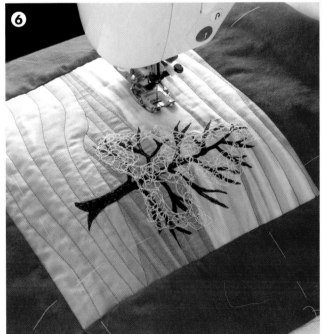

5. Quilt Stream block by stitching wavy lines for water and cloud lines in the sky as shown; follow any design lines in fabric, if desired. Stipple-quilt (page 104) foreground. Embroider leaves on the tree, using Japanese ribbon stitch.

6. Quilt (pages 100 and 105) Winter Plains block by stitching curving lines in sky and snow as shown.

(continued)

7. Quilt along rolling hills, close to satin stitching. Quilt around roots of tree. Stipple-quilt sky, catching tulle in place.

8. Quilt wavy lines across sand dune background and sky. Quilt cactus needles for Desert block by stitching with a narrow zigzag stitch; set stitch length to zero. Position cactus needles ⅜" to ½" (1 to 1.3 cm) apart; trim threads about ⅜" (1 cm) long. Embroider flowers of cactus as on page 306.

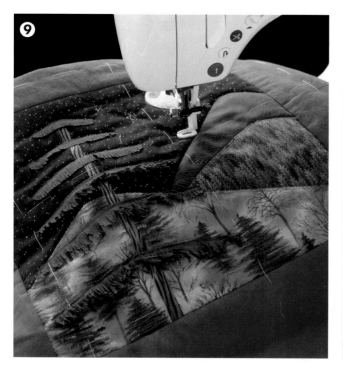

9. Motif-quilt, using machine-guided or free-motion stitching (page 104), upper edges of hill, mountains, and tree branches of the Pine Tree block. Quilt in a zigzag pattern over pine trees on lower hill. Outline moon, and quilt stars randomly in the sky. Quilt mountains as desired.

10. Quilt in desired method (pages 104 and 105) on spacers and borders. Attach fabric sleeve to the wall hanging (page 171), and apply binding as on pages 111 to 116.

Patterns for the Desert Cactus and Pine Tree Branches

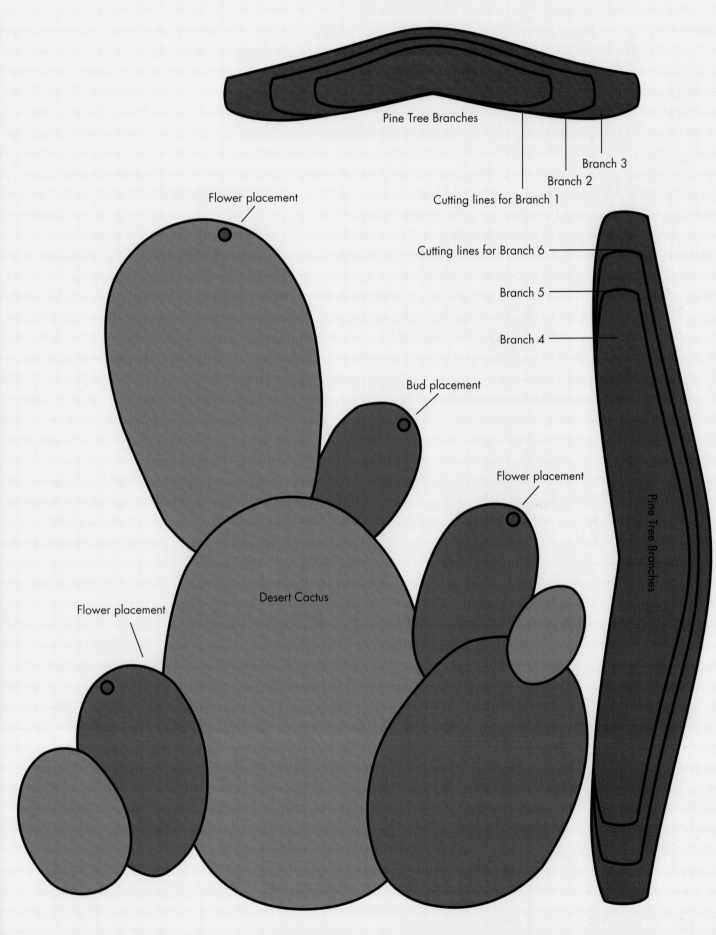

Pine Tree Branches

Branch 3

Branch 2

Cutting lines for Branch 1

Flower placement

Cutting lines for Branch 6

Branch 5

Branch 4

Bud placement

Flower placement

Pine Tree Branches

Desert Cactus

Flower placement

Maple Leaf Table Runner

Raw-edge appliqués in the shape of maple leaves add dimension and a unique, falling-leaf appearance to a maple leaf table runner. The edges of the leaves can be frayed with a stiff brush, or a more natural frayed look can be achieved after laundering. This more contemporary look gives texture to an embellished quilt. For minimal fraying, use a tightly woven fabric for the appliqués.

Fabric spacers are used on both sides of single quilt blocks to complete every other row in the table runner. Alternating rows are composed of two quilt blocks and no spacers. The spacers are of varying width and add to the unstructured feel of the quilt.

The finished size of the table runner shown is approximately 12" x 42" (30.5 x 107 cm). The table runner can be lengthened by adding additional rows of quilt blocks and spacers. For a wider table runner, increase the width of the spacers and add spacers to rows with two quilt blocks.

YOU WILL NEED

- ¼ yd. (0.25 m) each of ten fabrics, for pieced leaves.

- ¼ yd. (0.25 m) each of six to ten fabrics, for background of leaf blocks and for spacer strips.

- Scraps of fabric, for appliquéd leaves.

- ⅛ yd. (0.15 m) fabric, for leaf stems.

- ½ yd. (0.5 m) fabric, for backing.

- Batting, about 16" x 46" (40.5 x 117 cm).

- ¼ yd. (0.25 m) fabric, for binding.

- Glue stick.

CUTTING DIRECTIONS ✂

- For the Maple Leaf quilt blocks, cut three 2½" (6.5 cm) squares from each of ten leaf fabrics. Cut two 2⅞" (7.2 cm) squares from each of ten leaf fabrics; then cut the squares into triangles as on page 51, cutting without Easy Angle cutting tools. Cut 2½" (6.5 cm) squares from background fabrics for a total of ten squares. Cut three 2⅞" (7.2 cm) squares from each of six background fabrics and six 2⅞" (7.2 cm) squares from two background fabrics; then cut the squares into triangles as on page 51.

- Cut ten 1" x 3¼" (2.5 x 8.2 cm) strips from the stem fabric.

- Cut eight strips from the fabrics for the spacers as follows: one 1½" x 6½" (3.8 x 16.3 cm) piece, two 2½" x 6½" (6.5 x 16.3 cm) pieces, two 3½" x 6½" (9 x 16.3 cm) pieces, two 4½" x 6½" (11.5 x 16.3 cm) pieces, and one 5½" x 6½" (14 x 16.3 cm) piece.

- Cut seven leaves for the appliqués from leaf fabrics, using pattern (page 317); do not add seam allowances.

- Cut four 2" (5 cm) strips from the binding fabric.

How to Sew a Maple Leaf Table Runner

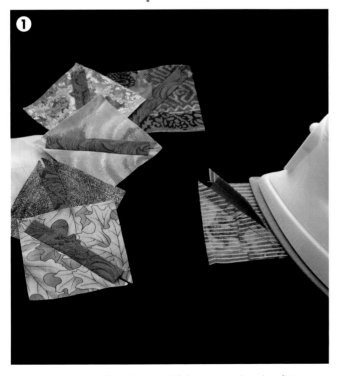

1. Stitch triangle of background fabric to each side of 1" (2.5 cm) stem strip, right sides together. Repeat for remaining triangles of background fabric and nine stem strips. Press seam allowances toward stem strips.

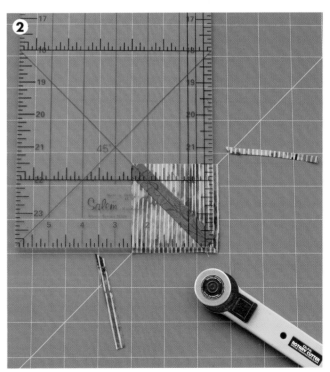

2. Cut 2½" (6.5 cm) squares from each pieced unit, taking care that stem goes through opposite corners of squares.

(continued)

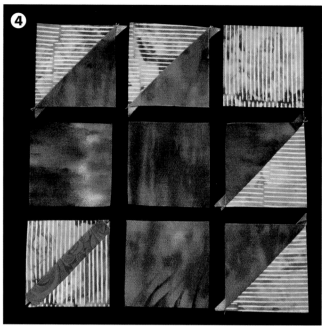

3. Stitch one triangle from one leaf fabric and one triangle from one background fabric together, along long edge, in ¼" (6 mm) seam. Continue piecing triangles until four matching triangle-squares have been completed for each quilt block, using chainstitching as shown. Clip units apart; press seam allowances toward leaf fabric.

4. Arrange one stem square, one background fabric square, three leaf fabric squares, and four triangle-squares into quilt block design as shown. Assemble block, using chainstitching (page 10); finger-press seam allowances toward center square. Press block. Repeat to make a total of ten leaf quilt blocks.

5. Assemble the quilt blocks and spacer fabrics as shown in the diagram opposite. Stitch the blocks into rows; stitch the rows together, finger-pressing seam allowances in opposite directions. Press quilt top.

6. Glue-baste leaf appliqué pieces randomly on quilt top. Cut backing fabric 2" to 4" (5 to 10 cm) wider and longer than quilt top. Layer and baste quilt top, batting, and backing as on pages 92 to 97.

7. Quilt parallel lines about ½" (1.3 cm) apart across the width of the table runner, catching leaf appliqués in the stitching. Curve lines slightly and switch stitching directions with each line to prevent distorting the quilt. Apply binding as on pages 111 to 116.

Pattern for the Maple Leaf Appliqué

Diagram of Block and Spacer Arrangement

2½" x 6½"
(6.5 cm x 16.3 cm)

5½" x 6½"
(14 cm x 16.3 cm)

3½" x 6½"
(9 cm x 16.3 cm)

2½" x 6½"
(6.5 cm x 16.3 cm)

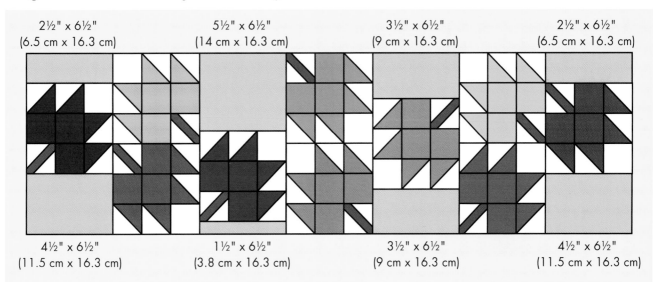

4½" x 6½"
(11.5 cm x 16.3 cm)

1½" x 6½"
(3.8 cm x 16.3 cm)

3½" x 6½"
(9 cm x 16.3 cm)

4½" x 6½"
(11.5 cm x 16.3 cm)

Index